The Art of Retreat

The Art of Retreat

How Sensitive Minds Can Reset, Restore, and Rise After Social Overload

Miriam Everhart

Mindful Pages

Published in 2025

ISBN: 9789371772112 (PB)
ISBN: 9789371772938 (eBook)

Published by

Mindful Pages
Imprint of Alpha Editions LLC
312 W. 2nd St #1834
Casper, WY 82601, USA

This book was developed using advanced writing tools to support the drafting and ideation process. All content has been thoughtfully curated, refined, and reviewed to ensure quality and relevance.

Content

Introduction
The Unspoken Cost of Connection

There is a paradox quietly unfolding at the centre of modern life. We are more connected than ever—pinging, scrolling, replying, absorbing—yet an increasing number of people, particularly those with sensitive nervous systems, are finding themselves drained, disoriented, and disheartened by the very relationships and interactions that once offered meaning and belonging. For some, the world has become too loud. Not in decibels, but in demands. It is not the shout of conflict that fatigues them, but the hum of constant engagement—the relentless thrum of social expectations, digital exposure, and the subtle yet ceaseless responsibility of emotional attunement.

This book is written for them.

For the thinkers who feel before they speak. For the listeners who absorb not just words but the pauses between them. For the professionals who can intuit a colleague's stress before it's verbalised, and the parents who sense their child's emotional undercurrents even when smiles are fixed in place. It is for those who cannot help but *notice*, and for whom noticing comes at a cost.

In the culture's race toward hyperconnectivity, one group is quietly losing ground. Sensitive individuals—those whose perceptual systems are more finely tuned, whose empathy is not a skill but a default setting—are often misunderstood, pathologised, or simply ignored in broader conversations about wellbeing and productivity. But their experiences are not marginal. They are the canaries in the coal mine of human overstimulation. And what they are showing us is not weakness, but warning.

The Myth of Limitless Connection

In contemporary life, we operate under a pervasive and largely unexamined assumption: that more connection is inherently better. We equate sociability with success, availability with relevance, and constant responsiveness with moral character. The unspoken ethic of our times is one of limitless accessibility. We are to be reachable, affable, cooperative—across time zones, platforms, and personal boundaries. This ethic is reinforced by both technology and temperament. We carry digital portals in our pockets, receive notifications as if they were vital signs, and silently measure our worth by how quickly we can attend to others' needs.

But every nervous system has a threshold. And sensitive ones reach theirs sooner, not because they are deficient, but because they are absorbing more. Just as a high-definition lens captures more light and detail, so too do sensitive minds absorb more sensory, emotional, and relational data. Their internal processing is not slower; it is deeper. Yet this depth of engagement is rarely acknowledged as labour—especially when that labour takes the form of feeling.

This book begins by naming a truth that has long been obscured: social engagement carries energetic consequences. Even positive interactions—those that are warm, meaningful, or professionally fulfilling—can leave the sensitive system fatigued. This is not social anxiety. This is not introversion, though the two may overlap. This is the cost of being biologically and psychologically attuned to others in a world that neither values nor supports periodic withdrawal.

We are sold the idea that connection should be constant, that solitude is suspicious, and that the ability to keep showing up—without visible wear—is the hallmark of strength. But this cultural script is written in ignorance of biological reality. Human beings, especially sensitive ones, are not designed for unending social exposure. They require cycles of contact and retreat, engagement and restoration, stimulation and integration. Without the latter, the former becomes corrosive.

Sensitivity as Perceptual Mastery

To be sensitive is not, as the dominant culture often implies, to be weak, fragile, or emotionally unstable. Rather, it is to possess a kind of perceptual mastery—a heightened responsiveness to internal and external stimuli, coupled with a deep capacity for pattern recognition and relational nuance. Sensitive people often excel in professions that demand emotional intelligence, creative problem-solving, and intuitive insight. They are the therapists who sense what's left unsaid, the artists who give form to subtle feeling, the leaders who perceive team dynamics before conflict erupts.

But this mastery comes with requirements. It demands periods of disconnection—not as indulgence, but as necessity. Like any high-performance instrument, the sensitive nervous system needs to be recalibrated regularly. Without intentional recovery, it begins to fray at the edges: sleep becomes shallow, focus evaporates, emotions grow volatile, and physical symptoms surface. These are not signs of personal failure; they are signals of physiological overload.

And yet, we rarely grant permission for retreat. In workplaces, rest is treated as a reward for endurance, not as a prerequisite for effectiveness. In families, those who seek solitude are gently, or not so gently, nudged back into social roles. Even in wellness spaces, recovery is often framed in terms of optimisation—another thing to hack, track, or schedule. The result is a population of deeply perceptive individuals who are perpetually overextended, silently suffering, and unsure why traditional self-care advice leaves them unchanged.

The Promise of Ritualised Renewal

This book offers an alternative. Not a list of quick fixes or vague encouragements, but a comprehensive, science-grounded system for recognising, respecting, and restoring the sensitive nervous system. It introduces the concept of *ritualised retreat*—a structured approach to renewal that draws on neuroscience, somatic practices, bioenergetics, and ancient traditions of sacred withdrawal.

Unlike a weekend getaway or temporary digital detox, ritualised retreat is not escapism. It is a practice of self-regulation, woven into the rhythms of daily, weekly, and seasonal life. It is both deeply personal and neurologically precise. It involves the creation of micro-sanctuaries, the use of sensory cues to signal safety, the cultivation of somatic awareness, and the intentional modulation of social exposure. Most importantly, it reframes withdrawal not as avoidance, but as skill.

The sensitive mind does not need fixing. It needs fortification. And that fortification cannot occur in the same environments that cause the depletion. True recovery requires a shift not only in behaviour but in paradigm—from viewing retreat as a sign of dysfunction to seeing it as a pathway to mastery.

Why This Book Is Different

Much of what is published in the realm of wellbeing fails to speak directly to sensitive individuals. At best, it offers tips for managing symptoms: breathe deeply, say no, take a bath. At worst, it suggests that sensitivity itself is the problem. The result is often frustration—tools that skim the surface of overwhelm without touching its root.

This book goes deeper. It integrates the latest findings from neuroscience, including the emerging field of polyvagal theory, which explains how the autonomic nervous system shapes our responses to safety, danger, and social engagement. It draws on bioenergetic models that account for how emotion becomes lodged in the body, and how movement, breath, and stillness can restore flow. It weaves in somatic psychology, showing how the body speaks its truths in sensation and posture, not just in words. And it honours ancient wisdom traditions that have long recognised the value of cyclical withdrawal as a source of power and clarity.

Throughout, real-world stories provide grounding and relatability. You will meet a therapist who lost herself in the emotional gravity of her clients, a nurse who discovered micro-retreats in the margins of her hospital shifts, an artist who unlocked a creative renaissance in structured solitude, and a CEO who found moral clarity in a silent retreat. These are not cautionary tales; they are demonstrations of what becomes possible when retreat is embraced as a form of strength rather than failure.

What distinguishes this book is its central claim: that sensitivity, when paired with intentional restoration, is not merely manageable—it is masterful. It can lead to deeper relationships, greater creativity, sharper intuition, and a profound sense of self-trust. But only when its needs are met.

A Call to the Sensitive

If you have ever found yourself inexplicably fatigued after a seemingly ordinary day of social interaction, this book is for you. If you have ever been told you're "too much" or "too quiet," "too intense" or "too soft," you will find resonance here—not only in language but in lived experience. And if you have sensed, somewhere beneath the surface of cultural noise, a call to reclaim your energy, your insight, and your sovereignty, this book will help you answer it.

The Art of Retreat is not a retreat from life. It is a movement toward a different way of living—one in which sensitivity is not simply tolerated, but cultivated; not endured, but refined. It is an invitation to those who feel everything to stop apologising and start restoring. Not in isolation, but in rhythm. Not in silence, but in sanctuary.

The time has come to stop treating sensitivity as a liability and to begin treating it as a leadership quality. But leadership of a different kind—one that leads not by noise or dominance, but by presence, depth, and discernment. To lead in this way, the sensitive mind must be nourished, protected, and rhythmically renewed.

This is the art we are here to reclaim.

Chapter 1
The Architecture of Overwhelm: Inside the Sensitive Nervous System

We are all wired for survival, but the circuitry is far from uniform. For those who live with high sensitivity, the nervous system is not a neutral receiver of life's signals. It is, rather, a finely tuned, sometimes volatile interface—one that translates every flicker of the outer world into a corresponding stir within. These individuals register subtleties others skim past: the faint shift in tone that betrays disappointment in a colleague's voice, the crease of unease across a friend's brow just before they insist they're "fine," the strange dissonance in a meeting where the language is cooperative but the atmosphere anything but. This depth of perception—emotional, sensory, relational—is not a quirk of personality. It is biological fact. And as with all such facts, it bestows both privilege and burden.

The privilege is undeniable. Heightened sensitivity often comes with unusual empathy, a talent for creative synthesis, and a capacity for systems-level insight. Sensitive people spot patterns early, sense group dynamics before they surface, and approach both people and ideas not at arm's length but with full immersion. Yet immersion implies exposure. And exposure, untempered by recovery, tilts into overwhelm. That overwhelm is not only mental; it is written into the physiology of the sensitive nervous system—operating on a lower threshold for stimulation, and a higher gear of inner processing.

To live in the state of constant engagement demanded by modern life is to edge towards a slow collapse. Not the spectacular kind that results in breakdown or resignation, but something more insidious: a steady erosion of vitality, of mental clarity, of emotional coherence. The sensitive mind does not tire because it is frail, but because it is perpetually active—absorbing, parsing, adjusting, attuning to currents invisible to most. That hidden labour extracts its toll.

The story begins in the brain.

Sensitivity is too often described in behavioural shorthand, when in truth its roots are neurological. Functional MRI scans reveal that highly sensitive individuals show heightened activity in brain regions linked to empathy, awareness, and sensory integration—the insula, the anterior cingulate cortex, the mirror neuron systems. Presented with emotionally charged images or social tasks, their brains do not simply flare more brightly—they light up across wider networks, engaging areas that parse meaning, context, consequence. The sensitive brain doesn't merely react; it reflects. It runs simulations. It wonders what this event implies, not just what it is.

This explains the gifts of sensitivity: the deep connection, the intuition that feels more like knowledge than conjecture, the creativity born of synthesis rather than novelty. But the same wiring also explains vulnerability to overload. If your mind is designed to run full-scale models on every social cue, even the simplest exchange becomes metabolically costly. It is not the quantity of incoming data that undoes you, but the extent of the processing.

And the flow of data never stops. In overstimulating environments—open-plan offices, ceaseless messaging apps, social platforms engineered for emotional provocation—the sensitive brain is granted no reprieve. Every cue is another input demanding analysis. For most, a crowded room is mildly draining. For the highly sensitive, it is a neurological trial. The lights are harsher, the sounds sharper, conversations not only overlap in volume but in emotional tone. Each thread demands weaving, until the nervous system is tangled in a tapestry too dense to sustain.

More taxing still is social input. Here the cost multiplies. Emotional labour—once a term of sociology—is now the lived backdrop of entire professions: carers, educators, leaders, frontline staff. For the sensitive individual, emotional labour is not an occasional duty. It is their resting state. Their systems are continually monitoring, modulating, mirroring others' moods—often without conscious choice.

This is the mirror neuron system at work: those cells that fire not only when we act, but when we see others act. They allow for empathy, for resonance. In sensitive people, they fire with greater intensity, granting them extraordinary capacity for collaboration, for healing, for art. Yet this very strength leaves them prone to empathic saturation. They do not merely witness another's state—they embody it. They carry it. And they rarely switch it off.

Over time, the consequence is relational fatigue. Not fatigue from conflict, nor from toxicity, but from sheer volume—too much emotional signal, all absorbed, sorted, metabolised. Even joy contributes: a party, a tender exchange, a shared vulnerability. Beautiful as these are, they still flood the system. Stimulation, whether painful or pleasant, has to be processed.

What compounds the difficulty is that this cost often goes unrecognised, even by the sensitive themselves. We equate fatigue with overexertion, burnout with personal failure, withdrawal with avoidance. Thus, when the sensitive person finds themselves dulled, irritable, oddly numb, they assume fault. They tell themselves they lack resilience, that they are not tough enough for the world's demands. What they overlook is that their exhaustion is not a malfunction. It is the system doing what it is designed to do—only under unworkable conditions.

Take Mara, a psychotherapist in her forties, esteemed by clients for her uncanny intuition. Many described her as someone who could "see straight through" to what they were feeling. And she could. But the gift cost her dearly. After sessions she would find herself rattled, unable to sleep, replaying clients' stories in an endless loop. Her weekends offered no real recovery: either edgy reactivity or total collapse. The difficulty wasn't her clients' trauma—it was the resonance. She had no filter. Every emotion she encountered entered her system wholesale.

When she first encountered the idea of ritualised retreat, she scoffed. A silent morning? Structured decompression? Surely too indulgent. But desperation nudged her to experiment. She started small: a walk each day without a phone, the scent of lavender oil as a deliberate boundary between work and home, an hour each week without input of any kind—no voices, no music, no screens. The changes were gradual but unmistakable. Her sleep deepened. Her emotional range returned. She began to discern the line between her own states and the residual echoes of others. In time, her capacity did not shrink but expanded—because now it followed rhythm. It had boundaries. It had recovery baked in.

Mara's story is hardly unusual. It is, in fact, representative. It illustrates a wider truth: that for sensitive individuals, sustainability is impossible without intentional restoration. And restoration is not luxury. It is necessity—part of the design itself. Retreat is not abdication of life but the creation of conditions in which life can be engaged fully, without losing oneself in the process.

This chapter seeks to unpick the architecture of sensitive overwhelm. We will trace its neurological roots, showing how depth of processing both empowers and exposes. We will explore the true cost of emotional labour, not merely as sociological theory but as neurobiological reality. We will look at mirror neurons and the double-edged gift of their relentless empathy. And we will trace the subtle, often invisible slide from high-functioning engagement to quiet depletion—and, importantly, the way back.

This is not a lament. It is not an ode to fragility. It is a structural analysis of a nervous system type, offered so that those who live inside it may stop berating themselves for what is, in fact, brilliance operating without its safeguards. The purpose is clarity—not only intellectual but visceral. The kind that makes a reader pause and think: *So that's it. That's what's happening. That's why I feel this way. And here's what I can do differently.*

The pages that follow are meant as foundation. To craft a resilient life as a sensitive person, one must first understand the terrain. This—this is the architecture of overwhelm. Real, tangible, not imagined. And once mapped, it can be rebuilt.

The Brain Wired for Depth

Walk into a crowded café, and most people will notice the obvious: the barista calling out names, the whirr of an espresso machine, someone tapping at a laptop in the corner. But a certain subset of individuals will absorb much more. They will register the fleeting tension between two patrons at the counter, detect the subtle flatness in the server's usual cheer, notice how the playlist is slightly faster-paced than last week—and feel internally altered by all of it. This is not distraction. It is deep processing. And for the highly sensitive brain, it is the default mode of operation.

The term *high sensitivity* has long suffered from cultural misinterpretation—conflated with emotional fragility, introversion, or overreactivity. But growing research in affective neuroscience and sensory processing paints a more precise picture. High sensitivity is not a flaw or personality style. It is a biological disposition marked by heightened responsivity in brain regions associated with attention, empathy, and environmental scanning. The highly sensitive person (HSP) is neurologically wired to process information more thoroughly than the average individual, which results in a qualitatively different experience of daily life—one that is both uniquely rich and acutely taxing.

At the centre of this trait lies a neurological feature: depth of processing. Functional imaging studies have repeatedly shown that HSPs exhibit more activity in the insula, which integrates emotional and sensory data; the prefrontal cortex, involved in planning and reflection; and the mirror neuron system, which facilitates empathic attunement. These regions do not merely react—they contextualise. The highly sensitive brain does not skim stimuli; it analyses them through layers of implication, memory, emotional resonance, and future consequence. A comment from a colleague is not just heard—it's deconstructed, stored, and mentally replayed with potential subtexts.

What's often misunderstood is that this form of processing is not optional. It's not a matter of overthinking or rumination in the casual sense. It's structural. The sensitive brain is more reactive to subtle cues—facial micro-expressions, tonal inflections, background noise, and visual clutter—and it recruits more neural circuitry to evaluate these inputs. What most people experience as white noise, the HSP experiences as signal. In low-stimulation settings, this can be a gift: they spot patterns others miss, anticipate outcomes with eerie accuracy, and bring nuance to conversations that otherwise remain superficial. In high-stimulation environments, however, the system becomes inundated.

Take, for instance, sensory integration. Where a neurotypical brain might filter irrelevant sensory information—background chatter, peripheral movement, a faint perfume—the sensitive brain tends to register these stimuli with equal weight. This makes multitasking, open-plan offices, crowded events, and fast-paced digital interfaces disproportionately exhausting. It's not that HSPs lack resilience; it's that their systems are processing more data per unit of time. Imagine running multiple tabs on a computer, each one high resolution, each one interactive—and none allowed to close.

The cognitive labour involved in this kind of depth is often invisible, which leads to a pervasive misjudgement: that the sensitive person is simply more easily overwhelmed. But this interpretation misses a crucial point. Sensory and emotional exhaustion is not a reflection of weakness; it's a consequence of throughput. The system isn't shutting down because it's under-functioning—it's protecting itself from overfunctioning. This is a key insight for reframing the HSP not as delicate but as highly capable under the right conditions.

In social contexts, the costs of this depth can be even more profound. Because of their attunement to non-verbal cues and their highly active mirror neuron systems, sensitive individuals often engage in what might be called *relational vigilance*. They are constantly scanning for changes in emotional tone, interpersonal micro-shifts, and unspoken needs. This allows them to connect deeply and genuinely—traits revered in therapy, teaching, caregiving, and leadership. But it also exposes them to a unique form of depletion: empathic saturation.

Mirror neurons, which fire both when an individual acts and when they observe the same action in others, form the neurological basis of empathy. In sensitive individuals, these neurons appear to be more active or more responsive, enabling them to internalise others' emotions as if they were their own. While this facilitates profound understanding and relational depth, it also creates a porous boundary between self and other. Over time, repeated exposure to the emotional states of others—whether patients, clients, family members, or strangers—can lead to a subtle but chronic erosion of internal equilibrium.

This phenomenon is especially prevalent in roles that demand emotional labour—those in which one must manage their own emotional expression while simultaneously absorbing and responding to the feelings of others. Consider healthcare, education, or high-touch corporate leadership. For the highly sensitive person in such roles, the demand is not simply to perform, but to *feel for*, *feel with*, and *feel through* others—while maintaining outward composure. Over time, the cumulative load of such labour can result in emotional exhaustion, even if the work is meaningful or fulfilling. Importantly, the emotional exhaustion often goes unnoticed until it breaches the surface as irritability, disorientation, or uncharacteristic detachment.

The irony, of course, is that this very depth—of empathy, creativity, insight—is often the source of an HSP's most celebrated contributions. Sensitive people routinely lead innovation in fields that require lateral thinking, emotional nuance, or complex systems awareness. Their minds generate layered, original insights because they integrate more variables. But the act of integrating—of taking in not just content but *context*—is metabolically costly. Creativity, for them, is rarely casual. It draws upon the full nervous system. It requires a kind of permeability, which, if unbuffered by rest and containment, leads to burnout disguised as "just needing to push through."

Take the example of Daniel, an acclaimed film editor known for his uncanny ability to shape scenes that feel emotionally true without being overwrought. His colleagues admired his work ethic and collaborative sensitivity. But Daniel found himself increasingly unable to "switch off" after hours. Watching other people's footage left him feeling emotionally used, even when the content was fictional. He began to dread meetings, avoided even light-hearted social events, and lost the capacity to enjoy films—his lifelong passion. What he didn't initially understand was that his brain's perceptual depth, which allowed him to extract nuanced emotional truths from subtle acting and camera work, was not turning off at the end of the workday. It remained engaged, parsing, extrapolating, anticipating. When he introduced structured retreats—silent walks, digital-free evenings, and tactile creative projects with no professional objective—his sense of vitality slowly returned. Not because he stopped caring, but because he began *pacing* his caring.

This pacing is crucial. Depth of processing is a gift, but one that requires calibration. Without regular intervals of low stimulation and reflective space, the very systems that enable empathy and insight begin to work against themselves. Sleep becomes disturbed, cognition fragmented, and emotions less reliable. In extreme cases, the person may begin to withdraw entirely—not as a lifestyle choice, but as a form of self-protection.

To support this sensitive architecture, retreat is not a luxury—it is a requirement. The nervous system, when operating at high fidelity, must downregulate periodically or it will start to short-circuit. Crucially, these downregulations must be intentional and embodied, not merely distractions or escapism. Scrolling on a phone, consuming digital content, or numbing with low-level background noise may provide a temporary reprieve, but they do not offer true restoration. The highly sensitive brain does not just need less stimulation; it needs integration time. Time to reflect, consolidate, and reset its thresholds.

This biological rhythm of engagement and retreat has been recognised for centuries in contemplative traditions. Monastic life, structured solitude, artistic sabbaticals—these are not merely spiritual choices, but adaptive strategies for high-sensitivity temperaments. Our modern challenge is to integrate these ancient rhythms into daily life, without romanticising them or rendering them impractical. This requires more than good intentions. It requires systems. Ritualised decompression. Environmental curation. Psychological permission to step back.

For professionals operating in high-demand environments, understanding the biology of depth can be transformative. Rather than aspiring to "keep up" with less sensitive colleagues by overriding their systems, HSPs can begin designing workflows, communication practices, and social rhythms that *support* rather than suppress their natural processing. They can learn to recognise the early signs of saturation—mental static, reduced affective range, strained concentration—and act before collapse occurs. They can, quite literally, build a life around their sensitivity, not in spite of it.

The sensitive brain is not a broken machine in need of repair. It is a precision instrument in need of the right operating environment. Depth of processing should not be pathologised or glamorised—it should be understood. The aim is not to blunt the system, but to care for it well enough that it can continue to offer its remarkable insights, empathy, and originality without self-erasure.

Sensitivity, when supported, becomes mastery. Not a mastery of other people, or even of circumstances, but of *signal*. Of knowing when to engage, when to step back, when to listen more deeply, and when to stop listening altogether. The sensitive person, when properly resourced, is not overwhelmed by life's complexity—they become a guide through it. But first, they must learn the architecture of their own mind. And respect it.

The Energy Cost of Social Absorption

Not all exhaustion comes from effort. Some of it comes from *exposure*. This distinction—between what we *do* and what we *absorb*—is particularly relevant for highly sensitive individuals, whose emotional and relational landscape is shaped not only by what they give but by what they *receive*, consciously or not. Much of modern life, particularly professional life, hinges on an unspoken expectation: that we will not only perform tasks and meet deadlines, but that we will manage emotions—our own and others'—as part of the social contract. For sensitive people, this requirement is not only demanding but metabolically expensive. Even the most affirming social interactions can leave them drained, not due to interpersonal conflict or negativity, but because of the invisible labour involved in continuously processing emotional nuance.

This is the undercurrent of emotional labour—a term that has been widely referenced, often misunderstood, and rarely applied with nuance to the experience of sensitivity. Originally coined by sociologist Arlie Hochschild in her seminal 1983 work *The Managed*

Heart, emotional labour referred to the requirement in certain professions to regulate one's emotional expression in service of organisational goals. Flight attendants smiling through turbulence, nurses absorbing distress without visible recoil, teachers modulating tone to manage classroom energy—these are classic examples. What Hochschild began to uncover, and what neuroscience has since affirmed, is that managing emotional tone is not merely a surface-level task. It engages the nervous system in subtle and cumulative ways.

For highly sensitive individuals, the scope of emotional labour expands well beyond professional obligation. It becomes a near-constant background process. Their heightened perceptual systems detect and internalise emotional cues at a granular level—facial micro-expressions, subtle shifts in voice, body posture, pacing, tension—and unconsciously attempt to modulate their own responses to maintain interpersonal harmony. This is not strategic politeness; it is an automatic, often compulsive, neurobiological response. When one lives in a state of emotional vigilance—subtly adjusting to the moods of others, reading between the lines, tracking emotional safety in every interaction—social life becomes energetically taxing, no matter how outwardly pleasant.

Crucially, this depletion is not always traceable to "difficult" people or conversations. It occurs even in supportive relationships, even in conversations that feel nourishing. Why? Because the *act* of emotional tracking is demanding. It requires attention, empathy, inhibition of self-expression at times, and the continuous toggling between self and other. For sensitive people, this toggling is so fluid, so habitual, that they may not recognise it as effort. But biologically, it is just that. The brain is evaluating social dynamics in real-time, comparing them to past experiences, and calculating potential outcomes—all while trying to stay attuned, kind, helpful, responsive. This is not neuroticism; it is social intelligence operating in overdrive.

Consider the example of Lara, a communications officer at a mid-sized NGO. Her job involves coordinating between departments, managing emotionally nuanced conversations with donors, and facilitating group discussions in cross-cultural teams. She is highly regarded for her warmth, insight, and ability to "read a room." But by the end of each day, Lara feels flattened. Not upset, not demoralised—just blank. Even after weekends with friends she adores, she often feels a strange blend of mental static and emotional depletion. It wasn't until she began tracking her energy—not her mood—that the pattern became clear. It wasn't negativity that was exhausting her. It was *relational effort*, the cost of sustaining coherence across countless micro-interactions.

This kind of fatigue doesn't show up in blood tests. It doesn't always qualify as burnout in traditional frameworks. But its signs are unmistakable to those who live with it: a sense of being permanently behind on internal processing, a delayed emotional crash after social events, difficulty transitioning from group settings to solitude without friction, and a chronic low-grade fog that lifts only with extended withdrawal. These symptoms are not signs of social inadequacy; they are reflections of an energy system that is overly tasked by continuous emotional attunement.

From a neuroscientific standpoint, this depletion can be partially explained by the involvement of the prefrontal cortex and anterior cingulate cortex—regions responsible for social cognition, empathy, and self-regulation. For sensitive individuals, these regions tend to be more active during social tasks, especially those involving ambiguity or potential relational risk. While this heightened activity enhances relational insight and responsiveness, it also leads to greater cognitive load. When that load is sustained over hours or days without restorative intervals, the system begins to dysregulate. Sleep becomes compromised. Decision-making slows. Irritability surfaces. Importantly, these are not personal failings; they are biological feedback.

There is a paradox here that deserves attention: *positive* social experiences can still be energetically expensive. This runs counter to much of mainstream psychology, which tends to frame social interaction as universally restorative. Indeed, for many people, a dinner with close friends or a day of collaborative work might be invigorating. But for sensitive individuals, restoration depends less on *emotional valence* and more on *stimulus volume and processing intensity*. Even enjoyable interactions can be dense with emotional and sensory data. The nervous system, in trying to take it all in, consumes resources regardless of the emotional tone.

This misunderstanding often leads to well-intentioned but misguided advice. "You just need to get out more." "You're too isolated." "Surround yourself with positive people." While these suggestions may be valid for someone experiencing social withdrawal from depression or anxiety, they are counterproductive for someone whose exhaustion stems from *over-engagement*, not under-connection. Sensitive people often know they are not lonely in the conventional sense; they are saturated. The solution is not always more connection, but more containment.

Containment is not avoidance. It is a strategic form of boundary-setting that acknowledges the energy cost of emotional absorption. It includes practices such as pausing before responding to emotional cues, deliberately lowering eye contact during overstimulating conversations, scheduling decompression time after meetings or social events, and limiting unnecessary emotional multitasking. Crucially, containment does not mean emotional shutdown—it means discerning where one's energy is most responsibly directed. It means knowing the difference between availability and attunement.

The ethical implications here are also worth unpacking. Sensitive individuals are often drawn to roles of service—education, healthcare, mental health, social justice—not despite their sensitivity, but because of it. They can hold emotional complexity, tolerate ambiguity, and offer profound presence. Yet these roles disproportionately rely on the unpaid and often unrecognised labour of emotional absorption. When institutions fail to account for this labour, they risk extracting the very qualities they most value until the individual becomes too depleted to continue. Retention issues in healthcare and social work are often discussed in terms of workload and policy, but less often in terms of *energetic design*. If the relational expectations of a role exceed the nervous system's ability to recover, no amount of passion or purpose can compensate.

There is, however, a powerful countercurrent: the intentional structuring of relational life around energy awareness rather than social obligation. This is not a call to retreat from connection, but to engage with it more consciously. Sensitive individuals who learn to monitor their energy levels with the same attentiveness they offer others' emotions can begin to make subtle, meaningful adjustments. They can distinguish between interactions that are merely habitual and those that are truly reciprocal. They can design their days not around availability but around resonance. They can build in rituals of closure—simple practices like naming the end of a conversation, engaging in grounding touch, or using symbolic transitions—that signal to the nervous system that attunement is complete.

There is a dignity in this kind of relational sovereignty. It allows the sensitive person to continue offering their depth without forfeiting their vitality. It reframes emotional labour not as a silent tax, but as a resource to be managed wisely. And it opens the door to a kind of social engagement that is not only sustainable, but generative.

The modern world is not designed for this kind of discernment. It rewards speed, charisma, and constant responsiveness. But those very traits, if unexamined, lead to shallow connection and chronic fatigue. The sensitive person, by necessity, must play a different game. One in which energy, not just emotion, is the currency of connection. And where choosing when *not* to absorb becomes an act of self-respect, not selfishness.

Mirror Neurons and Empathic Saturation

Empathy, widely celebrated as a cornerstone of moral intelligence and social cohesion, is not an inexhaustible resource. It has a cost—neurologically, energetically, and psychologically—especially for individuals with heightened sensitivity to emotional cues. While cultural narratives often elevate empathy as an unequivocal good, they rarely acknowledge its biological underpinnings or its limitations. To understand why highly sensitive people often struggle with unexplained fatigue after interpersonal engagement, we must turn to the mechanics of the brain itself, beginning with a system that quietly governs our capacity to feel with others: mirror neurons.

Discovered in the early 1990s through research conducted on macaque monkeys in Parma, Italy, mirror neurons are a class of brain cells that activate both when an individual performs an action and when they observe someone else performing that same action. The implications for human behaviour were immediate and profound. These neurons are not just about movement—they are about meaning. When we witness another person's emotional or physical experience, our brains simulate it. This neurological mirroring is thought to form the basis of empathy, imitation, and even cultural learning.

In humans, mirror neuron systems are believed to reside primarily in the premotor cortex and inferior parietal lobule, with connections to the limbic system—the brain's emotional processing centre. This means that observing someone in distress can trigger not only cognitive recognition but also an *embodied response*. We don't just *know* that someone is sad; we *feel* it, often before we've consciously registered the expression on their face. For most, this process is modulated, buffered by context and internal filters. But for highly sensitive individuals, this buffer appears to be thinner. They absorb more emotional information, more quickly, and with greater intensity. The mirror system runs hot, and unless consciously managed, it doesn't cool down easily.

This heightened neural mirroring can manifest in various forms—emotional contagion, anticipatory empathy, vicarious trauma, or even physical symptoms that appear to reflect others' states. It creates a kind of internal resonance chamber in which another person's suffering reverberates. And when exposure to these emotional states is prolonged, especially in the absence of resolution, the system begins to strain. What starts as compassion can quietly tip into exhaustion—a state known as empathic saturation.

Empathic saturation is not the same as compassion fatigue, though they are often conflated. Compassion fatigue implies a numbness, a withdrawal of feeling, often observed in frontline workers exposed to chronic suffering. Empathic saturation, by contrast, is a form of overwhelm *before* numbness sets in. It is marked by emotional flooding, porous boundaries, difficulty distinguishing between self and other, and a sense of being emotionally hijacked by others' experiences. For highly sensitive individuals, this state can occur even in relatively benign contexts—offices, family gatherings, classrooms—where unspoken emotional dynamics are dense and unmanaged.

Consider Rachel, a senior HR executive in a high-stakes corporate environment. Her role demands emotional agility: mediating conflicts, handling redundancies, supporting employee wellbeing, and advising leadership—all while maintaining professional neutrality. She is excellent at it. Her colleagues describe her as intuitive and steady. But privately, Rachel often feels emotionally overrun. A tense one-on-one with a distressed employee leaves her depleted for hours. Casual hallway conversations linger in her mind well into the night. After group meetings, she needs physical solitude—not to reflect, but simply to recover. Her mirror system is constantly engaged, not by dramatic confrontations, but by the quiet emotional undercurrents that many around her don't even perceive.

Rachel's experience is not unusual. In fact, it reveals a critical insight: *attunement itself is metabolically expensive*. Whether or not an interaction is emotionally intense, the *act of tracking* others' emotional states activates complex neural pathways, often engaging both the default mode network and salience network—systems implicated in self-referential thought and the detection of emotionally relevant stimuli. For sensitive individuals, these systems are primed. They pick up shifts in voice tone, eye contact, pacing, hesitation. The data is constant, and the simulation engine of the brain doesn't easily shut off once it's been activated.

What makes this even more taxing is the difficulty in discerning where another person's emotional energy ends and one's own begins. This is the hallmark of empathic saturation—the gradual erosion of emotional boundaries. It's not that the sensitive person lacks a sense of self, but that their perceptual filters are so fine-tuned that others' affective states slip through as if they were their own. Over time, this produces internal confusion, mental clutter, and emotional noise. It becomes harder to make decisions, harder to rest, harder to know one's true emotional baseline. The system is no longer responding—it is *reacting*, reflexively and continuously.

Yet empathy is still heralded as an unqualified virtue. In many professional and social contexts, to be empathic is to be trustworthy, emotionally intelligent, and socially skilled. This ideal, while laudable, often leaves sensitive individuals vulnerable to exploitation—social, emotional, and energetic. Because they are able to sense and respond to others' needs, they are often asked to do so, implicitly or explicitly, without regard for the cost. The mirror neuron system has no off switch, only modulation. And unless the sensitive person learns how to regulate exposure, set energetic boundaries, and prioritise recovery, they are at risk of depletion not through trauma, but through *too much empathy*.

One might ask: is the answer to be *less* empathic? To dull the mirror system? Neuroscience offers a more elegant solution—*differentiated empathy*, the capacity to maintain attunement while preserving a strong sense of internal distinction. This involves cultivating interoceptive awareness (the ability to perceive internal bodily states), engaging in practices that ground the nervous system, and developing cognitive frames that allow one to witness without absorbing. In essence, it is the shift from reflexive mirroring to intentional resonance.

This is not easy work. It requires a willingness to question deeply ingrained beliefs about responsibility, care, and relational loyalty. It often involves grief—the recognition that not all feelings are meant to be held, and not all needs can be met. But for the sensitive person, this is a critical threshold. Without such boundaries, empathy becomes entrapment. With them, it becomes power.

The ethical dimension here cannot be overlooked. In a world increasingly reliant on emotional labour—especially in sectors such as healthcare, education, social work, and diversity initiatives—there is a structural expectation that those who *can* feel deeply *should* feel continuously. But just because someone has the capacity for deep attunement does not mean it should be accessed indiscriminately. Institutions that benefit from empathic labour must begin to consider the neurological realities of empathic saturation and invest in systemic safeguards: structured debriefing, protected rest periods, sensory-friendly environments, and permission for emotional containment without stigma.

There is also a social cost to neglecting these insights. A culture that overvalues continuous emotional availability breeds performative empathy and shallow connection. It teaches people to express concern without integration, to "feel for" without understanding how to feel *through* and then let go. Sensitive individuals, by contrast, often carry the emotional residue of interactions long after the moment has passed. Unless they learn to metabolise this residue, they will eventually begin to withdraw—not out of apathy, but out of self-preservation. And when sensitive people withdraw, institutions lose some of their most perceptive, creative, and stabilising forces.

But the sensitive brain, when properly supported, does not need to choose between connection and self-protection. It can engage with discernment. It can learn to attune without absorbing. It can hold presence without erasure. This is not about emotional detachment, nor is it about spiritual bypassing. It is about acknowledging the reality that *feeling is work*, and work must be resourced.

Empathy, at its best, is a dialogue—not a download. The mirror neuron system can be a source of profound human connection, but only when paired with boundaries, containment, and deliberate recovery. For sensitive individuals, understanding this is not just useful—it is essential. Because the alternative is not endless giving; it is quiet collapse. And sensitivity, when preserved, is not only sustainable—it is transformative.

Real-World Case: The Therapist Who Couldn't Switch Off

Dr Anna Clarke was not the kind of therapist who merely listened—she *absorbed.* Her colleagues described her as preternaturally attuned, a clinician who could sit with someone's pain and make it feel bearable simply by her presence. Her patients trusted her instantly, often disclosing experiences they hadn't shared with anyone, not even themselves. She had the rare ability to hold silence without awkwardness, to name what others circled around, and to reflect emotional truths with clarity and compassion. Her practice was full, her referrals constant, and her reputation quietly exceptional. But behind this clinical excellence was a nervous system under siege.

Anna's days were densely packed with emotionally charged sessions—trauma survivors, couples on the brink of separation, individuals navigating grief or identity collapse. She was adept at holding complexity, rarely flinching, never rushing to soothe or fix. What no one saw was what happened after hours. She didn't sleep well. Her dreams were often replays of client material, not literal, but emotionally coded. She found herself compulsively thinking about certain clients at odd hours, wondering if they were safe, if they would return, if she had missed something crucial. Her body grew subtly tighter—shoulders hunched, jaw clenched, digestion erratic. She was not spiralling. She was eroding.

Initially, Anna attributed the strain to workload, a manageable if uncomfortable occupational hazard. Like many in the helping professions, she had been conditioned to expect some level of depletion. But the tiredness didn't lift with weekends or holidays. It was not the kind of fatigue that could be slept off. It was subterranean, the result of cumulative absorption. She wasn't just witnessing pain—she was *carrying* it.

What Anna was experiencing was not classic burnout in the sense of disengagement or reduced efficacy. She was still competent, still connected. Her clients were thriving. But internally, she was beginning to fragment. The boundary between her professional empathic presence and her personal psychic life had become porous. Even moments of joy or neutrality in her own life were tinged with a kind of emotional ghosting—the residue of others' unprocessed pain. Her mirror neuron system, intensely active during sessions, had become over-engaged. She wasn't switching off because her system had lost the ability to distinguish signal from noise. Everyone's suffering was implicitly her responsibility. Every emotional nuance demanded a response.

What made this more complicated was that Anna's sensitivity had always been her gift. Long before she trained as a psychotherapist, she had been the child who noticed everything—the tension between adults, the friend who was secretly struggling, the unspoken needs of teachers, siblings, strangers. Her capacity to intuit and attune had been her way of navigating the world, and later, her clinical superpower. But it had also become her vulnerability. What she didn't yet understand was that *attunement without boundaries is not compassion—it's enmeshment.*

Anna tried various strategies—cutting back hours, taking occasional Fridays off, more yoga. These helped at the margins but failed to address the deeper pattern. The problem wasn't quantity of work; it was quality of absorption. She needed to develop a fundamentally different relationship to her own nervous system—one that recognised the biological mechanisms underlying her empathy, and the energetic cost of unregulated emotional resonance.

Her turning point was not dramatic. It came quietly, during a professional development seminar on polyvagal theory. As she listened to the presenter explain the physiological markers of ventral vagal activation—calm, social engagement, grounded presence—followed by the states of sympathetic arousal (anxiety, vigilance) and dorsal shutdown (numbness, fatigue), something clicked. She realised her baseline had shifted. What she had come to accept as normal—a slight jitteriness, low-grade hypervigilance, emotional leakage—was, in fact, a chronic state of *sympathetic dominance.* Her body had not been grounded for years. She was living in a state of quiet emergency, even while appearing calm.

Anna began to study the nervous system in earnest—not to accumulate knowledge, but to map her own. She started tracking her arousal states before and after sessions, paying attention to subtle cues: breath rate, muscle tone, internal dialogue. She noticed that after particularly intense sessions, her system remained activated for hours, sometimes until the following morning. She had no rituals of closure. No energetic boundaries. No structured decompression. She was, effectively, emotionally open all the time.

What changed everything was the introduction of *ritualised retreat.* This was not a spa day or vacation, but a set of repeatable, sensory-informed practices designed to cue her nervous system into safety and signal the end of empathic engagement. She started small. Between sessions, she began using tactile objects—smooth stones, textured fabric—as transitional anchors. She introduced a scent that was used *only* at the end of her clinical day—vetiver oil, grounding and earthy. She designated a corner of her flat as a post-work decompression zone—no screens, no stimulation, just a dim light, a heavy blanket, and a sound bowl whose resonance marked her shift from clinician to individual.

These practices weren't symbolic; they were somatic. They created a physiological threshold, a neural marker that allowed her to re-enter her own emotional field without the residues of others'. Over time, she added brief restorative practices—five minutes of shaking to discharge activation, restorative yoga poses to reset vagal tone, humming to stimulate the parasympathetic branch. These were not hobbies or distractions. They were neurobiological hygiene.

Within three months, Anna noticed a measurable shift. She was no longer dreaming about clients. Her sleep deepened. Her digestion stabilised. But more importantly, she began to *feel like herself* again—someone whose own emotions, desires, and thoughts were no longer background noise. She became more effective in her sessions, not less. Her boundaries didn't diminish her empathy; they sharpened it. Because she was no longer flooded, she could attune with precision, then release. Her clients noticed too. They described her as clearer, more energised, more direct. She had not withdrawn. She had reconstituted.

Anna's experience offers an important counter-narrative to the glorification of endless empathy. The ability to feel deeply is not inherently healing. It is healing only when paired with regulation, discernment, and cyclical withdrawal. For therapists, caregivers, educators, and anyone engaged in relational work, the lesson is not to give less, but to *recover better*. The nervous system cannot remain perpetually available without consequences. It must complete the cycle—engagement, resonance, then recalibration.

Empathic saturation is not a moral failure or professional weakness. It is a biological inevitability when exposure exceeds recovery. What Anna demonstrates is that sensitivity, once properly resourced, does not diminish—it matures. It becomes less reactive, more intentional. The key is not to dampen sensitivity, but to design a life around it that includes deliberate, embodied boundaries.

This includes reimagining what we consider professionalism. In a culture that rewards stoicism and continuous output, retreat can appear indulgent. But as Anna discovered, retreat is not a retreat from clients, vocation, or service—it is a return to coherence. And coherence is what makes true empathy possible. Not the empathy of merging or rescuing, but the empathy of presence, precision, and humility.

Anna continues to practise as a psychotherapist, but now with a structurally embedded retreat rhythm. Her week includes scheduled sensory decompression periods. Her calendar is not only organised by clients and commitments, but by *energetic recovery zones*. She doesn't strive for balance as an abstract ideal; she engineers it as a biological necessity.

Her story is not prescriptive. Not everyone needs vetiver oil, a sound bowl, or yoga. But *everyone* working with emotion needs a way to complete the arc—emotionally, physiologically, energetically. The absence of such rituals is not benign. Over time, it leads to internal erosion, even in the most seasoned professionals. And yet, when restoration is given equal weight to engagement, the result is not only personal wellbeing, but deeper, more sustainable care for others.

Sensitivity, when left uncontained, consumes itself. But when structured through ritual, it becomes a rare form of clarity—one that can feel *everything*, but no longer carry it all.

Chapter 2
The Polyvagal Dance: Safety, Danger, and Social Engagement

Most people enter social spaces with little thought, moving through handshakes, small talk, or the rhythm of meetings almost as if on autopilot. But for the highly sensitive, these moments often strike with disproportionate weight, as though every interaction carried a hidden weather system. A clipped tone, a pause too long, an ambiguous glance—such cues are not dismissed as irrelevant background noise. They lodge in the body, in the pulse, in the tautness of muscle, in the quiet commentary of the mind. What drives this difference is not simply temperament or childhood conditioning, but the wiring of the nervous system itself. Beneath the surface, the autonomic system is continually orchestrating a primal inquiry: Am I safe here?

To grasp why sensitive people experience such piercing emotional texture in ordinary encounters, one must look at the nervous system not as a rigid machine but as a living, responsive hierarchy. It is exquisitely tuned to assess risk and signal safety, and here polyvagal theory—pioneered by neuroscientist Dr Stephen Porges—offers a profound shift in understanding. Rather than the tidy binary of sympathetic (fight/flight) versus parasympathetic (rest/digest), Porges described a third pathway, the ventral vagal complex. This more recent evolutionary system governs social engagement: the cadence of the voice, the softness of facial expression, the ability to reach out without fear. It is not an optional refinement; it is central to human connection. And in sensitive individuals, it often works at full stretch.

The sensitive system does not simply absorb more data—it makes more meaning. Each flicker of tone or movement is run through an elaborate hierarchy of interpretations, with safety always the paramount concern. Long before the conscious mind has formed a story, the body has already made a call. Is that smile genuine? Is that silence charged? Are those footsteps hurried or calm? Porges named this subterranean scanning *neuroception*—a pre-conscious mechanism of threat detection. For most people, it ticks quietly in the background. For the sensitive, it often takes centre stage.

The result is a style of social navigation that feels paradoxical: poised and perceptive outwardly, but inwardly buffeted by shifts in state from moment to moment. What others call a "productive" meeting might leave them exhausted. A cheerful dinner party can spark days of subtle unease. The mismatch between internal turbulence and external expectation breeds not only fatigue but a hidden labour—keeping the social surface smooth while metabolising reams of unspoken data underneath.

Part of the difficulty is that in modern life, signals of safety are surprisingly scarce. Not the existential kind—few of us are running from predators—but the subtler relational cues. Crowded commutes, clipped emails, fractured attention, shallow exchanges: all contribute to a background hum of minor threat. For sensitive people, this hum is not easily filtered out. Their neuroceptive system keeps scanning, not because they are paranoid, but because their physiology has been shaped—by temperament, by history, sometimes by trauma—to expect disruptions.

Inevitably, this vigilance has a cost. It produces what might be called social fatigue: not loneliness, but depletion from prolonged immersion in unsupportive relational climates. Polyvagal theory again helps to clarify. When the ventral vagal system receives steady signals of safety—gentle eye contact, warmth in tone—it stays dominant, enabling ease and connection. But let danger creep in—a flat expression, a voice raised, a missed cue—and the system shifts. Sometimes into sympathetic arousal: urgency, anxiety, a readiness to act. Other times into dorsal collapse: numbness, withdrawal, the impulse to disappear. Sensitive individuals may cycle through these states many times in a single day, leaving them feeling unsteady without knowing why.

This looping, known clinically as autonomic cycling, becomes so familiar that it often masquerades as personality. People describe themselves as mercurial, inconsistent, or prone to burnout, unaware that what they are wrestling with is not "who they are" but a dysregulated nervous system. Without tools to notice and modulate these shifts, they remain trapped in repetition: drawn to connection, drained by its intensity, then forced into retreat—only to repeat the cycle with diminishing reserves.

To see how this plays out in real life, consider Thomas, a management consultant whose career seemed effortless from the outside. In the boardroom, he could read the dynamics in minutes—sensing hesitation before it surfaced, diffusing tensions before they flared. Yet this brilliance carried a hidden cost. After each high-stakes meeting, he would collapse into exhaustion, describing it as "being hit by a truck once the adrenaline wore off." His body began to show strain: broken sleep, creeping inflammation, anhedonia where once there was pleasure. Outwardly, his success was intact. Inwardly, he was unravelling.

When he eventually sought support, he discovered that his nervous system was caught in a pattern of sympathetic overdrive punctuated by dorsal shutdown. His attunement, so prized professionally, was fuelled by a hyperactive neuroceptive system that no longer knew how to step down. The very skill that made him indispensable was slowly hollowing him out.

His recovery began not with abandoning his sensitivity but with learning to harness it differently. Through polyvagal-informed practices, he mapped his states somatically—tracking shifts in breath, posture, and thought as cues of regulation or dysregulation. He reorganised his schedule, not just by tasks but by nervous system needs: building in rituals of recovery, surrounding himself with safe co-regulators, embedding sensory anchors that signalled safety. In time, his system stabilised. He could still read a room, but he was no longer consumed by it. The locus of his identity returned to his own body, rather than floating untethered in the signals of others.

Thomas's journey illustrates a larger principle: sensitivity is not sustainable without self-regulation. The very qualities that make the sensitive person invaluable—attunement, empathy, nuance—will otherwise pull them into depletion, detachment, and collapse. Polyvagal theory does more than offer a conceptual framework; it provides a practical route back to coherence.

This chapter aims to show how the architecture of the nervous system underpins every social encounter—and why, for the sensitive, overlooking this truth leads to misdiagnosed distress and unnecessary suffering. We will trace the neural circuits that assess safety and threat, their entanglement with memory and trauma, and the mismatch between these ancient systems and the modern environments we now inhabit. We will explore concrete ways to recognise signs of dysregulation, and interventions—grounded in both science and lived testimony—that help restore balance.

Above all, this is a manual for decoding the body's social intelligence. It is a call to move from reflex to response, from endless scanning to deliberate signalling, from survival mode to agency. For the sensitive, the aim is not to avoid danger entirely—that would be impossible—but to train the nervous system to meet it, recover from it, and remain whole. And that training begins with recognising the intricate dance already underway.

The Nervous System's Social Hierarchy

If we were to design a truly accurate model of human intelligence, it would not begin with cognition—it would begin with safety. Before the brain interprets meaning, solves problems, or chooses action, it performs a primal, unspoken scan: *Am I safe right now?* This assessment is not conscious, and it does not rely on logic. It is enacted through the autonomic nervous system, which operates beneath our awareness yet governs how we engage, withdraw, listen, speak, and connect. For highly sensitive individuals, this scanning process is not just more frequent—it is more refined, more reactive, and often more consequential. The experience of interacting with others is not simply psychological; it is somatic. It begins in the body, with a neurobiological algorithm that prioritises survival before expression.

Polyvagal theory offers a compelling framework for understanding this system. Developed by neuroscientist Dr Stephen Porges, it proposes that the autonomic nervous system is not a binary switch between arousal and relaxation, but a hierarchical network with multiple branches that evolved over time. Each branch governs a different mode of response—social engagement, mobilisation, or shutdown—and each is activated in response to perceived safety or threat. The innovation of polyvagal theory is its explanation of how social behaviour and physiological state are inextricably linked. The way we smile, speak, move, or make eye contact is governed not by habit or etiquette alone, but by ancient neural circuits that are constantly shifting in response to context.

At the top of this hierarchy is the *ventral vagal complex*, a component of the parasympathetic nervous system responsible for social engagement. When we feel safe, this system enables us to connect—our facial muscles relax, our voice becomes melodic, our eyes become expressive, and we become capable of reciprocal, emotionally intelligent interaction. This system is unique to mammals and especially vital in humans, who depend on social cooperation for survival and psychological wellbeing. The ventral vagal state is not passive; it is *interactive*. It allows us to co-regulate, meaning that our nervous systems can synchronise with others in ways that facilitate trust, empathy, and mutual understanding. For highly sensitive individuals, this capacity is typically enhanced—they are more likely to pick up on subtle cues, more attuned to relational shifts, and more able to modulate their own state in response to others'.

However, this heightened sensitivity comes with trade-offs. Because the nervous system is constantly scanning for signs of threat or safety—what Porges termed *neuroception*—sensitive individuals are more likely to detect cues that others overlook. A momentary hesitation in someone's tone, a flicker of disapproval in a glance, an unusually long pause in a text reply—these are not dismissed. They are registered. And in the absence of reassurance, they may be interpreted as danger. This does not mean that sensitive people are paranoid or irrational. It means that their neuroceptive systems are finely calibrated, designed to protect against rupture in relational environments.

When a cue of danger is detected—whether physical, emotional, or energetic—the system moves down the hierarchy to the *sympathetic branch* of the nervous system. This is the domain of mobilisation: fight or flight. Heart rate increases, breath becomes shallow, muscles tense, and the mind prepares for action. In social contexts, this might manifest as anxiety, defensiveness, urgency, or conflict avoidance. For a sensitive person, sympathetic activation can be triggered by something as minor as being interrupted during a conversation, sensing exclusion in a group dynamic, or encountering unpredictability in someone's behaviour. The nervous system perceives these not just as inconveniences, but as potential threats to relational safety—and responds accordingly.

If mobilisation does not resolve the threat—or if the environment is perceived as overwhelming and inescapable—the system may shift again, this time into *dorsal vagal shutdown*. This is the most primitive response, associated with freeze, disconnection, and collapse. It is the body's last resort, a strategy for conserving energy when neither fight nor flight are viable. In social terms, this might look like emotional numbness, dissociation, withdrawal, or chronic fatigue. For sensitive individuals, dorsal states are often misunderstood. They may be labelled as introverted, depressive, or disengaged, when in fact they are in a state of *nervous system conservation*, protecting against overstimulation or prolonged exposure to subtle but unrelenting stress.

What makes polyvagal theory especially useful for understanding sensitive people is that it offers a biological explanation for their social experiences—one that transcends personality theory or simplistic diagnoses. Sensitivity is not merely a trait; it is an orientation of the nervous system that prioritises relational safety through hyper-attunement. This attunement can foster deep empathy and meaningful connection when the environment supports it. But it also renders the individual vulnerable to dysregulation in environments that are emotionally inconsistent, non-verbal, or energetically chaotic.

Modern life rarely offers a stable stream of safety cues. Digital communication, social media, open-plan offices, and hyper-efficient workplaces often deliver ambiguous or contradictory signals. A compliment delivered with a distracted tone, a supportive message sandwiched between critical feedback, a silent room filled with latent tension—these are common occurrences, but for the sensitive nervous system, they are destabilising. The ventral vagal system cannot operate optimally without cues of safety: eye contact, prosodic vocal tones, predictable rhythms, and authentic relational presence. When these cues are absent or contradictory, the system shifts. Over time, this shifting becomes chronic, leading to what many sensitive people describe as "social fatigue," "emotional burnout," or the inability to be "on" all the time.

Importantly, this is not a failure of resilience. It is a biological signal. The nervous system is doing what it evolved to do—protect the organism from potential harm. The problem arises when the signals of modern social environments are misaligned with the needs of sensitive physiology. And without an understanding of polyvagal dynamics, sensitive individuals often blame themselves. They may interpret their social exhaustion as weakness, their need for withdrawal as dysfunction, and their emotional reactivity as over-sensitivity, rather than recognising these as valid nervous system responses to perceived inconsistency or threat.

The implications for self-regulation are profound. Polyvagal-informed awareness allows sensitive individuals to *work with* their nervous systems rather than against them. Recognising which branch is active—ventral, sympathetic, or dorsal—can help reframe internal states as adaptive rather than pathological. From there, the task becomes learning how to up-regulate or down-regulate appropriately: how to re-access ventral vagal safety through breath, movement, vocalisation, or co-regulation with trusted others. This is not a matter of "calming down," but of restoring access to the biological platform where connection, creativity, and resilience become possible.

It also calls for a shift in how we conceptualise emotional intelligence. Traditional models often emphasise control—managing impulses, expressing feelings constructively, demonstrating social finesse. But from a polyvagal perspective, true emotional intelligence begins with *state awareness*. A person who can recognise that they are in sympathetic mobilisation is more likely to avoid reactive behaviour. A person who senses dorsal vagal collapse can prioritise rest or re-engagement rather than forcing performance. For sensitive individuals, this kind of intelligence is not a luxury—it is survival.

In therapeutic, educational, and organisational contexts, the relevance of polyvagal theory is increasingly recognised. Trauma-informed practices, somatic therapies, and nervous system regulation techniques are making their way into professional development and clinical settings. Yet the sensitive population remains under-supported, in part because their responses often don't fit the conventional markers of distress. They are functional, articulate, and outwardly composed, even as their systems are working double-time to maintain equilibrium. What they need is not just validation but infrastructure—environments that cue safety, systems that honour recovery, and language that respects the biology beneath behaviour.

The nervous system's social hierarchy is not a metaphor. It is a living system, operating in every conversation, meeting, and interaction. For sensitive people, understanding this hierarchy is not just intellectually satisfying—it is a practical necessity. It allows them to decode their own responses, stop pathologising their needs, and begin designing lives that are not just manageable but optimised for depth, presence, and relational authenticity. Because when safety is reliably cued, the sensitive nervous system does not retreat. It expands. It connects. It leads.

When Safety Becomes Scarcity

Ask most people if they feel safe on a typical day, and the response is often affirmative. No immediate threat, no physical harm, no visible crisis. But the body tells a different story. Muscles held tight for hours without awareness. Shoulders inching upward. Breath shallow. A heart that beats just a little faster when someone raises their voice or when a message is left on 'read' too long. These aren't signs of dramatic threat—they're signals of subtle but consistent exposure to micro-stressors that the nervous system interprets as cues of danger. And for highly sensitive individuals, whose perceptual filters are tuned more acutely to social and sensory nuance, these micro-signals are not just irritations. They're *data.* Data that accumulates, compounds, and if unacknowledged, leads to chronic dysregulation.

To understand how safety becomes scarce, we need to begin with the biological truth that the human nervous system is not built for neutrality—it is constantly scanning. As polyvagal theory describes, the autonomic nervous system evaluates every environment and interaction to determine safety or threat through a mechanism known as *neuroception.* This process operates below conscious awareness and does not rely on logical reasoning. It scans tone of voice, body posture, eye contact, spatial arrangement, background noise, and more, making a near-instantaneous judgement: *Is it safe to connect here, or should I mobilise or withdraw?*

For most people, this system filters out the non-essential. But for sensitive individuals, the filter is thin. The nervous system doesn't just receive the dominant cues—it registers *everything.* A colleague's sigh in a meeting, a partner's distracted reply, the way someone avoids eye contact during a discussion—none of it is dismissed as background. Each cue enters the body like a question: *Is something wrong? Did I miss something? Should I adjust?* This hyper-attunement isn't a cognitive habit; it is a physiological reflex. The ventral vagal system, which governs social engagement, is constantly on standby, ready to shift into sympathetic arousal (fight or flight) or dorsal withdrawal (shutdown) depending on the smallest shift in relational tone.

In an ideal world, social cues would be mostly consistent. Trustworthy. Regulated. But the reality of modern life is that most environments are riddled with mixed signals. Consider the open-plan office, where faces are visible but emotional states are hidden behind polite professionalism. Or the Zoom meeting, where delayed reactions, muted microphones, and fixed facial expressions make reading social feedback ambiguous and often misaligned. The nervous system, deprived of reliable cues, interprets this ambiguity as threat—not because it wants to, but because *safety is biologically expensive and cannot be presumed.* For the sensitive person, what might be described as a "neutral" environment is often experienced as unpredictably charged.

This is where the danger lies—not in one acute incident, but in the *cumulative weight* of subtle disruptions. Micro-expressions, sudden tone shifts, indirect communication, dissonance between words and body language—all these are interpreted as potential breaches in social safety. Each one may seem negligible on its own. But for a nervous system wired to detect pattern rather than isolate events, the accumulation is significant. Over time, the body begins to stay prepared. The sympathetic system remains slightly activated, even during rest. Muscles don't fully relax. Sleep becomes lighter. The person begins to feel "on edge," even when there's no clear reason why.

The result is a form of low-grade chronic stress that is largely invisible. It doesn't typically trigger panic attacks or emotional outbursts. Instead, it shows up as fatigue that's resistant to sleep, emotional blunting, forgetfulness, increased sensitivity to noise or criticism, and a growing reluctance to engage socially. These are not failures of resilience. They are symptoms of a system that has been *over-exposed to minor, ambiguous, unresolved cues of danger.* And when no time or space is allowed for physiological down-regulation, the ventral vagal system—which allows for presence, connection, and receptivity—begins to recede. The person may appear fine but is operating at a deficit, drawing from internal reserves that are never adequately replenished.

Take the case of Nadine, a clinical psychologist working in a large hospital. On paper, she was thriving: respected by her peers, requested by patients, known for her empathic presence. But internally, she felt increasingly brittle. Small things started to get to her—people arriving late, meetings running over time, casual jokes that felt a shade too sharp. She began dreading her commute, not for the travel itself but for the unpredictability of morning interactions. What she didn't initially realise was that her nervous system had shifted into chronic vigilance. Years of subtle exposure—to grief, suppressed rage, institutional ambivalence, and the microtensions of medical hierarchies—had pushed her system out of a sustained state of safety. She wasn't clinically burnt out. She was *relationally depleted.*

What's essential to grasp here is that safety is not defined solely by the absence of threat. *It is created through the presence of coherent, consistent signals of attunement and predictability.* A facial expression that matches tone. A spoken boundary that is honoured. A response that arrives when expected. These cues are the currency of social safety, and they allow the nervous system to relax. When they are absent—or worse, when they are present intermittently—the system adapts by becoming vigilant. For sensitive people, this vigilance becomes the water they swim in. Over time, they may forget what actual safety feels like in the body. Their baseline becomes a state of slight activation—functional, high-performing, even affable—but never quite grounded.

This baseline matters, because the cost of living in subtle dysregulation is not immediately catastrophic—it is gradually eroding. The sensitive person might continue to function, but creativity flattens, relational joy dulls, and their tolerance for ambiguity shrinks. The world begins to feel more brittle. Interactions feel like obligations. Social spaces, once energising, begin to deplete. And because no single event can be identified as *the cause*, the person often assumes it's a personal failure—lack of stamina, poor mindset, emotional instability—rather than recognising the slow drip of unmet safety needs over months or years.

The ethical implications of this dynamic are worth naming. In high-stakes, emotionally demanding professions—therapy, education, healthcare, activism—sensitive individuals are often celebrated for their attunement. They're the ones who "notice what others miss," who intuit unspoken needs, who track subtle power dynamics in the room. But rarely are they resourced to manage the cost of this hyper-attunement. Institutions reward output, not nervous system recovery. Colleagues may praise insight but overlook the toll of perpetual vigilance. Over time, this gap between expectation and energetic support leads to withdrawal—not out of apathy, but necessity.

The solution is not to desensitise. It is to *rebalance.* To understand that safety is not just a mood or a mindset—it is a neurophysiological state, one that must be cultivated, protected, and regularly restored. This means paying attention not just to moments of acute stress, but to *patterns of subtle misattunement.* It means learning to recognise the early signs of scarcity—emotional contraction, decision fatigue, aversion to social engagement—and treating them not as personal quirks, but as signals that the system needs down-regulation.

Creating safety for sensitive nervous systems doesn't require dramatic lifestyle changes. It requires consistency. Predictable transitions. Honest communication. Sensory environments that don't overload. Relationships where emotional coherence is not the exception, but the baseline. When these elements are present, the sensitive person's capacity doesn't diminish—it expands. Their creativity sharpens. Their presence deepens. Their reactivity decreases. Not because they've toughened up, but because their nervous systems are no longer under siege.

Safety, then, is not a luxury for sensitive people—it is the prerequisite for sustainable functioning. When it is abundant, attunement becomes a strength. When it is scarce, even empathy becomes extractive. And when we recognise the micro-signals that shape our internal landscape, we reclaim the ability to choose—not just our responses, but our environments, our rhythms, and ultimately, our well-being.

Shutdown and Hyperarousal: Two Sides of Social Fatigue

There is a particular kind of exhaustion that doesn't announce itself with yawns or drooping eyelids. It emerges as a paradox: a state where the mind races while the body feels hollow; where social settings spark simultaneous urgency and withdrawal; where the nervous system oscillates between high alert and total disengagement. For highly sensitive individuals, this experience is often mislabelled as burnout, introversion, or even mood instability. But beneath the surface lies a more accurate, physiological explanation: *the cycling between hyperarousal and shutdown*, two distinct yet intimately linked autonomic states driven by unresolved social overload.

This pattern is not a personal flaw. It is a predictable response of a finely tuned nervous system attempting to adapt to persistent signals of social danger or uncertainty. Polyvagal theory, developed by Dr Stephen Porges, offers a framework to understand this cycling. It explains that our autonomic nervous system does not function as a simple on-off switch, but rather operates along a *hierarchical continuum*. At one end lies the *ventral vagal system*, which supports calm connection and social engagement. When this system is dominant, we feel open, grounded, and capable of relating to others with ease. But when perceived threats arise—often subtle ones for sensitive individuals—the nervous system quickly mobilises a defensive response. It first activates the *sympathetic branch*, which prepares the body to fight or flee. If that state becomes unsustainable, the system may then collapse into the *dorsal vagal state*—a form of physiological shutdown marked by emotional numbing, dissociation, or withdrawal.

The paradox lies in the speed and frequency with which sensitive individuals can move between these states. In one moment, they may feel overwhelmed by a conversation, heart racing, mind scanning for exits. Minutes later, they may find themselves unable to feel anything at all—emotionally flat, cognitively foggy, physically disconnected. This oscillation isn't dramatic or theatrical. More often, it's subtle and internal. To the outside world, the person may appear present, even composed. But internally, their nervous system is doing the impossible task of trying to stay relational while managing mounting dysregulation.

Consider the case of Mateo, a highly empathic software engineer working in a collaborative team environment. Meetings were a regular source of tension—not due to overt conflict, but because of the subtle, often unspoken hierarchies at play. A missed cue from a manager, a moment of awkward silence, or a dismissive glance would trigger a sympathetic response in his body. He would feel a spike of anxiety, a need to prove himself, a drive to clarify or over-explain. But when these signals accumulated without repair—when the social feedback remained ambiguous or invalidating—his system would abruptly shift. He would go quiet. Not out of strategy, but because his nervous system had gone into conservation mode. What felt to him like self-preservation often read to others as disengagement or disinterest.

What's critical to understand is that neither of these states—hyperarousal or shutdown—is pathological on its own. They are adaptive mechanisms designed to protect the organism. The sympathetic response helps us mobilise to face threat; the dorsal response allows us to conserve energy when escape or resolution feels impossible. The problem arises when these states are triggered chronically in response to subtle, unresolved social stressors, with little access to ventral vagal regulation. For sensitive people, whose systems are more easily triggered and slower to return to baseline, this cycling becomes a way of life. And over time, it takes a profound toll on energy, mood, relationships, and identity.

This cycle can be particularly disorienting because the shifts often occur without conscious awareness. A sensitive person may wake feeling relatively stable, only to be sent into sympathetic arousal by a difficult email, a disapproving glance from a colleague, or the anticipatory stress of a full day of social obligations. By mid-afternoon, they may feel flattened—not because the stress has resolved, but because the system has become overwhelmed. In this collapsed state, even basic tasks feel Herculean. Motivation disappears. Words feel distant. The social world becomes too much. But rather than recognising this as a physiological shutdown, the individual often self-criticises: *Why can't I focus? Why am I being lazy? What's wrong with me?*

The cost is not only internal. Relationships suffer too. Friends may experience the sensitive person as unpredictable—sometimes expressive and energetic, other times distant and unresponsive. Partners may misinterpret shutdown as emotional withdrawal or lack of interest. Colleagues may view sympathetic activation as overreaction. Without a shared language of nervous system dynamics, these patterns get pathologised as personality issues rather than seen for what they are: *biological adaptations to invisible overwhelm.*

It is important to recognise the role of context in these states. Highly sensitive individuals are often navigating social environments that are emotionally incongruent or overstimulating. Open-plan offices, video meetings, constant notifications, ambient noise, and unspoken power dynamics all contribute to a state of perpetual vigilance. These are not minor inconveniences for a sensitive system—they are unresolved signals that require continuous processing. When the system does not have sufficient time or space to discharge this activation, it defaults into shutdown—not as a choice, but as a circuit-breaker.

This is compounded by the cultural narrative that equates productivity with worth, sociability with health, and performance with stability. Sensitive individuals often internalise these values, pushing themselves to remain externally functional even as their systems are crying out for retreat. Hyperarousal is often masked as drive; shutdown is hidden behind the excuse of needing time to "think." But the cost of suppressing these states is cumulative. Without deliberate practices that support nervous system regulation—such as breathwork, movement, restorative solitude, or co-regulation with trusted others—the system begins to break down. What was once a cycle becomes a trap.

Recovery begins with recognition. Sensitive individuals must be taught—not just encouraged—to identify the signs of shifting state early. Hyperarousal may present as racing thoughts, irritability, a sense of being "on edge," or a compulsion to fix social problems that don't yet exist. Shutdown may appear as zoning out, procrastination, anhedonia, or even physical disconnection from the body. Neither state is wrong, but both are information: cues that the system needs something different. What's required is not more control, but more *containment*—spaces, practices, and relationships that allow for decompression without judgment.

One of the most damaging myths is that emotional regulation is simply a matter of mindset or discipline. But no amount of willpower can override a nervous system that feels unsafe. Regulation begins not in the mind, but in the body. A few minutes of diaphragmatic breathing can signal the ventral vagal system to re-engage. A slow walk in a familiar environment can reduce sympathetic charge. Gentle eye contact with a calm, supportive person can serve as a co-regulatory cue. These are not fringe wellness practices—they are biological imperatives for sensitive nervous systems seeking equilibrium.

It is also vital to build rhythms that anticipate dysregulation rather than react to it. This means structuring social engagement in a way that honours the body's capacity for activation and recovery. Sensitive individuals often benefit from *buffering transitions*: brief windows between meetings, social events, or responsibilities where they can recalibrate. Sensory boundaries matter too—curating sound, light, and visual input can reduce ambient stress that keeps the system in low-level alert. And perhaps most importantly, relationships must be chosen for *nervous system compatibility*, not just intellectual or emotional connection. Being around others who do not demand constant performance or emotional clarity creates the conditions for genuine rest.

The paradox of shutdown and hyperarousal is not a contradiction. It is a cycle—an elegant, if exhausting, mechanism by which the body tries to stay safe in the absence of consistent cues of safety. For sensitive individuals, the path forward is not to suppress this cycle, but to understand it. To intervene early. To design life in ways that support nervous system rhythm rather than override it. When this happens, what was once perceived as fragility reveals itself as sensitivity with structure—depth with resilience, empathy with discernment. Not because the cycle disappears, but because the person learns to move through it with awareness, agency, and care.

Real-World Case: The Overachiever's Collapse

On paper, Daniel was enviably successful. A management consultant in a prestigious international firm, he was known for his strategic clarity, his ability to build client trust in record time, and his relentless delivery on high-stakes projects. His calendar was fully booked three months in advance. Executives sought his counsel not only for technical insights but for his uncanny ability to "read the room" and adjust communication to the psychological contours of each stakeholder. He was the person you brought in when negotiations were fragile, when morale was fraying, or when a boardroom needed both rigour and relational dexterity. But behind the façade of high-functioning expertise, Daniel was beginning to fray. And not from pressure in the conventional sense, but from the sustained *overuse of his nervous system's social faculties*—his empathy, his perceptiveness, his capacity for co-regulation.

What led to Daniel's eventual collapse wasn't a dramatic rupture. It was *cumulative adaptation.* His system had been living in a state of hyper-engagement for years, scanning for threat and nuance in every meeting, every email, every social cue. As a highly sensitive individual, Daniel didn't just process information—he *absorbed it,* especially in relational contexts. He could intuit misalignment between departments before anyone voiced concerns. He could feel when a CEO was subtly resisting an organisational change initiative, even if the data and words suggested compliance. These capacities made him an elite performer in environments that prized social finesse and systems-level thinking. But they also placed a hidden demand on his nervous system: *stay on, stay attuned, stay ahead*—without pause.

For a while, Daniel managed. He had the stamina of someone in their prime, and the reward system of high achievement buffered the toll. But the cracks began subtly. A mild sense of dread before Monday meetings. Increased difficulty falling asleep, even after mentally taxing days. A growing reliance on wine in the evenings—not for enjoyment, but to *switch off*. His partner noticed the change first: a distant gaze, a delay in emotional responsiveness, irritability during benign conversations. But Daniel dismissed it as normal fatigue. "Everyone's tired," he told himself. "This is what it means to be at the top of your game."

What Daniel didn't recognise—what most high performers don't—is that there's a difference between *effortful performance* and *autonomic overload*. His sympathetic nervous system, responsible for mobilisation, had been dominant for too long. It kept him alert, precise, persuasive—but increasingly at the cost of rest, digestion, emotional range, and internal coherence. He began to experience what he later described as "professional dissociation"—a condition where he could perform the expected roles flawlessly, but with a growing sense of inner detachment. He wasn't just tired; he was becoming unreachable, even to himself.

The turning point came during a leadership retreat in the Swiss Alps, ironically designed to foster renewal and connection. Midway through a roundtable discussion on vulnerability in leadership, Daniel suddenly felt dizzy. His heart began to race. A strange tightness wrapped around his chest. The room, though serene, felt airless. What followed was not a heart attack, but a full-blown sympathetic surge—his body entering a fight-flight state in response to what his rational mind could not name as danger. His neuroception, the nervous system's pre-conscious safety detection system, had interpreted the emotional exposure of the moment—and the years of unprocessed relational overload—as intolerable. He left the session, made it to his room, and collapsed into sleep for nearly twelve hours.

This episode was not isolated. It marked the beginning of what Daniel would later understand as *a forced reorganisation of his nervous system.* He could no longer maintain the pace, the attunement, or the output he had previously normalised. Attempting to do so led to shutdown—emotional flatness, memory lapses, social withdrawal. But this wasn't depression. It was dorsal vagal activation, the final state in the autonomic hierarchy when neither social engagement nor mobilisation feels safe or sustainable. His system had gone into conservation mode.

With the help of a trauma-informed coach and a polyvagal-trained therapist, Daniel began to reconstruct his relationship to work, to performance, and most crucially, to his own physiology. He learned to map his nervous system states—not through abstract journaling, but through interoceptive tracking: breath depth, vocal tone, posture, eye engagement. He could tell when he was moving into sympathetic activation—his thoughts would become narrow and future-focused, his emails terse, his shoulders elevated. He learned to detect the early signs of dorsal drift: a sense of futility, emotional muting, and desire to cancel social commitments. This awareness allowed him to *intervene before collapse*, a skill he had never been taught in either business school or corporate coaching.

Daniel also began experimenting with *micro-recovery rituals.* These were not performance hacks or productivity enhancers. They were neural recalibrations. Between client calls, he would take three minutes to stand barefoot on his balcony, orient to the horizon, and breathe rhythmically. After a strategy session, he would listen to slow, resonant cello music—not for entertainment, but to stimulate vagal tone and return his system to ventral regulation. On Fridays, he blocked two hours for undirected thinking—time without stimulus or output, allowing his brain to integrate rather than accumulate. These weren't wellness practices in the trendy sense. They were survival structures for someone who had spent a decade misusing his biological assets.

Perhaps the most transformative shift was in how Daniel viewed his own sensitivity. What he had once labelled as over-thinking or emotional exhaustibility, he now understood as *unbuffered empathic labour*. His nervous system had been working overtime not because he was inefficient, but because his strength—attunement—had been operating without scaffolding. He had no rituals for closure. No language for emotional boundaries. No practices for transitioning between high-stakes relational intensity and private restoration. Once these were in place, his capacity returned—not all at once, but gradually. His cognition sharpened. His energy stabilised. His relationships deepened—not because he was more available, but because he was *more regulated.*

Daniel eventually redesigned his consulting model. He reduced the number of clients, shifted to deeper engagements rather than wider reach, and incorporated somatic orientation sessions into his onboarding process. His new philosophy was simple but revolutionary in his field: *We can only think clearly when we feel safe.* He began to teach this to executive teams—not in abstract terms, but through the language of regulation, safety cues, and recovery rhythm. The impact was immediate. Clients who had previously sought him for strategy began to see him as a relational architect—someone who could help redesign not just operations, but the *human systems underneath them.*

The lesson from Daniel's collapse is not that high performance is incompatible with sensitivity. It's that *sustained engagement without restoration is a form of self-abandonment*, especially for those whose nervous systems are designed for relational depth. The sensitive consultant, therapist, educator, or leader does not need to toughen up or switch off. They need structures—both internal and external—that honour the physics of their nervous system. That recognise the cost of continual output. That legitimise the need for repair not as a reward, but as a precondition for coherence.

Daniel's story is emblematic of a wider pattern: high-functioning professionals whose collapses are not signs of failure, but *systemic feedback*. They are the nervous system's last-ditch attempt to rebalance after years of silent overextension. And when these individuals finally learn to listen—not just to content, but to state—

they don't become less ambitious. They become more *strategic*, more *relationally intelligent*, and crucially, more *sustainable.* They stop chasing resilience as an identity, and begin practising it as a rhythm. A rhythm that starts not with achievement, but with awareness. Not with doing more, but with *feeling more safely.* And for the sensitive nervous system, that shift is not cosmetic. It's everything.

Chapter 3
Cultural Sabotage: Myths That Exhaust Sensitive People

It is one of the cruellest paradoxes of contemporary life: the very traits that enable a person to perceive nuance, to connect deeply, and to read the emotional undercurrents of a room are often the same ones that leave them estranged from the cultures in which they live. Sensitivity—though an evolutionary refinement of perception and survival—is habitually misinterpreted through a societal lens that measures worth in productivity, visibility, and the suppression of personal need. For those whose nervous systems are wired to register subtleties, this dissonance is not simply inconvenient. It is systemic. Their biology is not merely overlooked in modern culture; it is recast as liability—misdiagnosed, corrected, and punished in ways that strike at the core of being.

The cultural forces that undermine sensitivity rarely announce themselves with hostility. Instead, they operate as invisible scripts, shaping classrooms, workplaces, family rituals, and even the frameworks of healthcare and religion. These scripts are internalised long before they are questioned, and once internalised, they do more than sculpt behaviour—they alter identity, sometimes even physiology. What begins as a natural gift becomes reframed as defect. Sensitivity ceases to be something worth safeguarding and is instead treated as an error requiring correction. This quiet sabotage is one of the most potent sources of nervous system strain in sensitive individuals, not for what it demands outright, but for what it withholds: permission to pause, to replenish, to simply exist without constant output.

Take, for instance, the myth most of us now swim in without noticing—the cult of productivity. Its sermons are not delivered in temples but in metrics, calendars, and performance reviews. In this creed, rest is only permissible if it can be rebranded as optimisation. Sleep is "recovery time," meditation a "performance tool," solitude a "creativity hack." The idea of rest for its own sake—rest that is unapologetic, purposeless, and non-transactional—has no foothold here. Sensitive nervous systems, which demand frequent recalibration, inevitably clash with this ethic. Needing to withdraw is read as weakness. Craving stillness is mistaken for disengagement. Even pleasures that are gentle, quiet, or slow are seen as somehow lacking legitimacy compared to ambition, excitement, or the ceaseless hustle.

This dissonance is nowhere more evident than in professional settings, where sensitivity often takes the form of invisible labour. It is the subtle smoothing of tensions, the unspoken regulation of group dynamics, the intuitive awareness of colleagues' emotional states. Such labour is not easily measured, and therefore it rarely counts. What does count are deliverables, outcomes, outputs. Sensitive professionals end up spending vast reserves of energy maintaining social climates that keep teams functional, only to find their contributions unrecognised. Over time, the bind becomes cruel: either continue this unpaid emotional labour at the cost of one's own health, or abandon the very qualities that make one most effective. Little wonder, then, that some of the most burnt-out individuals in high-achieving environments are also those most attuned to emotional nuance. Their invisible service is never praised, but their exhaustion cannot be hidden.

If the productivity myth erodes recovery, another ideology undermines rhythm: the cultural elevation of extroversion. From childhood, the message is plain—speak up, be visible, participate. Silence is pathologised as shyness. Preference for solitude is treated as aberration. Classrooms reward quick answers, not deep reflection. Workplaces prize networking and group visibility, often above solitary insight. Even the language of mental health carries extroverted bias: "social withdrawal" is a diagnostic red flag, while constant outward engagement is framed as neutral or even beneficial. For the sensitive person—whose nervous system requires intervals of solitude to reset—such assumptions become intrusive, even physiologically harmful.

To be clear, extroversion and productivity are not inherently detrimental. The danger lies in their cultural elevation into universal ideals. When a society insists that one mode of operating is the only valid one, the cost is borne by those whose biology does not fit. An open-plan office may energise one worker while draining another. Social platforms that reward immediacy may silence those whose insights ripen slowly. Over time, the sensitive person internalises this mismatch as personal defect—feeling guilty for needing rest, ashamed of preferring silence, confused by their exhaustion in environments others find enlivening. This is not frailty. It is a design built for depth colliding with a culture addicted to surface.

The most morally fraught myth, however, is the sanctification of self-sacrifice. Found most visibly in caregiving and service professions—nursing, teaching, therapy, social work—but also in family and spiritual life, this narrative equates depletion with virtue. The more one gives, the more worthy one becomes. To need nothing is framed as the highest good. For sensitive people, whose nervous systems are naturally geared toward responsiveness and care, this ethos becomes a trap. The nurse who skips meals to tend a patient is praised as dedicated. The therapist who sees clients without pause is admired for devotion. The teacher who carries their students' burdens home is considered noble. Exhaustion is rewarded, not questioned.

The consequence of such stories is severe. They bind self-worth to depletion. To stop giving feels selfish. To create boundaries feels like betrayal. Sensitive individuals, already wired to find meaning in connection and service, become ensnared in identities of overextension. Their empathy and intuition—genuine gifts—are co-opted by cultural myths that exploit rather than protect them. Eventually, the body begins to resist in ways culture will not name: chronic fatigue, anxiety, autoimmune shifts, a loss of joy. These are not pathologies of weakness but the nervous system's rebellion against an ethic it cannot sustain.

The aim here is not to condemn culture wholesale. Societies must value different traits at different times. But cultural narratives are never neutral. They teach us what to celebrate, what to tolerate, and what to shame. When sensitivity is consistently downgraded, the effects are not just psychological—they reverberate through the body. Nervous system health is not an individualised phenomenon; it is shaped by relationships, environments, and the narratives that scaffold them. To restore sensitive lives requires more than personal resilience. It requires cultural re-storying: the reclaiming of values that recognise rest, solitude, and selective giving as not indulgences but necessities.

The work ahead is both diagnostic and prescriptive. We will unpick the machinery of hustle culture and its quiet punishment of those who pause. We will dissect extroversion bias—not to diminish the outgoing, but to restore legitimacy to the reflective. We will name the subtle violence of moralised self-sacrifice and begin to imagine frameworks that allow sensitive givers to serve without erasing themselves. These are not luxuries of theory. They are survival tools. They are also cultural tools, for without them, the very sensitivities that make humans capable of empathy, depth, and care will continue to be squandered in service to myths that never had biology—or sustainability—on their side.

The Productivity Cult

Walk into almost any workplace, scroll through professional development content, or attend a leadership seminar and you will encounter the same unspoken creed: the busier you are, the more valuable you must be. Rest is tolerated, if not actively discouraged—allowed only when reframed as "optimisation," "recovery for performance," or "strategic pausing." The implicit message is clear: unless it feeds output, rest is laziness. In this paradigm, productivity is not just a metric—it is a moral posture, a form of virtue signalling. And for sensitive individuals whose biological rhythms include cycles of retreat, this cultural mandate isn't just inconvenient; it's physiologically hostile.

The modern productivity ethos is not merely a preference for action—it is a system of belief, reinforced by economics, media, and cultural storytelling. It is what anthropologists might call a *totalising narrative*: one that frames how success is defined, how identity is shaped, and how worth is distributed. From Silicon Valley hustle mantras to corporate "grindset" philosophies, the modern workplace venerates relentless availability. We valorise early risers, celebrate endurance, and prize those who remain responsive long after the workday ends. Holidays are a badge of flexibility if we continue to check emails; burnout is brushed off as an unfortunate side effect of ambition.

For the highly sensitive person—whose nervous system is calibrated for depth, subtlety, and extended recovery—this becomes an existential mismatch. It is not simply a question of preference; it is a question of survival. Sensitive individuals are biologically predisposed to process more information per stimulus. The act of responding to an email, facilitating a conversation, or navigating a team conflict often involves layers of cognitive and emotional integration that others may bypass. What is read as efficiency in one nervous system may be registered as overexertion in another. And yet, when this biological reality expresses itself through fatigue, the cultural response is rarely one of accommodation. Instead, it is suspicion—an insinuation that something must be wrong with the person, not the environment.

One reason this dynamic is so damaging is because it creates *invisible exhaustion*. Sensitive individuals often continue performing outwardly, even when their nervous system is fraying. Unlike physical exhaustion, which may be observable, *nervous system overload is often masked by professionalism*. They remain competent, articulate, composed. But beneath the surface, regulatory systems are under strain: heart rate variability drops, cortisol remains elevated, and the subtle capacity for attunement—so essential to their social and cognitive gifts—begins to erode. The tragedy is that their very adaptability becomes a liability. The better they are at hiding depletion, the more likely they are to be overused.

There is also a troubling psychological loop embedded within the productivity cult: the idea that one must *earn* rest. Recovery is granted as a reward, not as a biological imperative. This structure mirrors the extractive logic of industrial systems: run the machine until it shows signs of wear, then schedule maintenance. But humans are not machines. And sensitive nervous systems, in particular, do not perform best when pushed to breaking point. They function optimally when cycles of output and input, expression and integration, are respected. By treating rest as optional or indulgent, the culture structurally denies sensitive people the conditions under which their true capacities emerge.

Consider, for instance, the experience of Ava, a senior project manager in a multinational tech firm. Known for her meticulous execution and intuitive leadership, Ava consistently delivered high-quality work. But what her colleagues didn't see was the immense effort it took for her to sustain interpersonal harmony across departments. She would often replay conversations in her head, worry about unspoken tensions, and absorb the emotional tenor of team members without consciously intending to. To maintain her edge, she sacrificed lunch breaks, worked weekends, and masked her growing sense of depletion behind a façade of enthusiasm. When she finally requested a sabbatical, her manager was surprised: "But you've been doing so well." The assumption was that high performance precluded the need for recovery. No one had considered that her excellence came *at the cost of a strained nervous system operating without pause.*

This dissonance is intensified by how popular culture frames effort. Films, biographies, and social media influencers often glamorise sleep deprivation, sacrifice, and the relentless pursuit of goals. Success is not portrayed as the result of pacing, but of pushing—always pushing. Even wellness narratives have begun to co-opt this ethos: meditation is marketed as a tool to increase output, not presence. Breathwork is pitched as a productivity enhancer, rather than a way to access internal stillness. The message remains the same: rest must justify itself through productivity. It is never enough to rest *because one is tired.*

But biology is indifferent to cultural messaging. The autonomic nervous system does not adapt to ideology. It requires rhythm, balance, safety. When these are absent, no amount of mental determination will compensate. Sensitive individuals may temporarily override their exhaustion through stimulants, self-talk, or suppression. But this only compounds the eventual cost. Chronic sympathetic activation—staying in "go mode" for too long—leads to hormonal imbalance, sleep disruption, decreased immune function, and emotional numbing. At a certain threshold, the system can no longer sustain mobilisation and drops into dorsal collapse—a shutdown state marked by withdrawal, disconnection, and a flattened affect. From the outside, it may look like depression. Internally, it feels like existential depletion.

To dismantle the productivity cult, we must first expose its moral architecture. At its core is the false equivalence of activity with virtue. The hard worker is not only respected—they are admired, trusted, even romanticised. Conversely, those who pause, recalibrate, or withdraw are seen as suspect, selfish, or weak. This binary is not just inaccurate; it is harmful. It privileges a narrow bandwidth of nervous system functioning and pathologises any deviation. It treats restoration as a defect to be corrected, rather than a wisdom to be honoured. And for sensitive people, whose systems often signal the need for retreat earlier and more acutely, this can result in profound self-doubt. They learn to distrust their signals. To apologise for their needs. To perform resilience long after it has expired.

But there is another way. Reframing productivity as *relational coherence* rather than continuous output offers a radically different model. Sensitive individuals often bring depth, insight, and ethical clarity to their work. These are not the results of hustle. They emerge from well-regulated nervous systems with access to creativity, empathy, and foresight. When rest is legitimised—not as indulgence but as strategy—these gifts are amplified. The goal is not to do less, but to do differently. To design systems of work that honour cyclical rhythms, respect sensory thresholds, and reward discernment as much as drive.

This reframing is not just personal; it must also be structural. Organisations that wish to retain sensitive talent need to rethink how they define excellence. Metrics should account for *sustainability*, not just short-term gains. Leadership models should reward *coherence*, not just charisma. And cultural narratives must expand to include those whose contribution is felt not through volume, but through *presence*. The teacher who creates psychological safety in her classroom. The manager who senses team misalignment before conflict erupts. The nurse who communicates care in subtle micro-gestures. These are not soft skills. They are *somatic intelligences*—and they require protection through rest.

The productivity cult will not be dismantled overnight. But it can be resisted, one nervous system at a time. Each time a sensitive person honours their need for pause without apology, they are creating a counterculture. Each time a leader integrates cycles of retreat into team schedules, they are modelling a new ethic. And each time someone stops measuring their worth by their output, they reclaim not just their health, but their *humanity*. Rest is not the opposite of work. It is the soil from which sustainable contribution grows. And for sensitive minds, that soil is not optional. It is sacred.

The Extroversion Ideal

Spend an hour inside a modern boardroom, school auditorium, networking event, or even a dating app and you'll observe the same subtle performance standard at play: be outgoing, responsive, emotionally available, and socially fluid—or risk being perceived as cold, difficult, or disengaged. We don't merely live among extroverts; we have built institutions, educational systems, and cultural ideals around them. Sociability is prized, gregariousness rewarded, and silence viewed as awkward or antisocial. In such a climate, introversion is not neutral—it is countercultural. For sensitive individuals, whose perceptual gifts flourish in low-stimulation, reflective settings, the extroversion ideal is not merely alienating. It's neurologically taxing.

What often goes unexamined is just how entrenched this ideal has become—not just socially, but structurally. It is coded into hiring practices that privilege "culture fit" over cognitive diversity, school assessments that reward vocal participation over listening acuity, and team-building initiatives that treat group activities as universal good. More than a personal preference, extroversion has come to define what is considered emotionally healthy, professionally competent, and socially competent. But this norm is not neutral; it has consequences—particularly for those whose nervous systems are calibrated for depth rather than breadth, stillness rather than stimulation.

The bias begins early. From childhood, many sensitive individuals are told—implicitly or explicitly—that their quiet nature is something to overcome. The shy child is encouraged to "come out of their shell," the student who prefers solitary reading over group discussion is urged to "speak up more," and the adult who needs solitude to recharge is questioned for their perceived aloofness. This pattern of well-meaning correction creates an internalised sense that one's natural orientation toward reflection, subtlety, or restraint is not just different, but deficient. As a result, sensitive people often become skilled at masking. They learn the mannerisms of sociability—not because it suits their temperament, but because it buys social acceptance.

Yet masking comes at a cost. When a person must continuously perform against their neurobiological grain, the nervous system must compensate. This creates what might be termed *social dissonance fatigue*—a gradual erosion of vitality caused not by overt conflict but by subtle, chronic misalignment. Sensitive individuals are often exquisitely attuned to others' emotional states, facial micro-expressions, and tonal variations. This makes them gifted listeners, compassionate friends, and attentive colleagues. But it also means that sustained social engagement—especially in environments that reward performance over authenticity—can drain their resources rapidly. Unlike naturally extroverted individuals, who may gain energy from external stimulation, sensitive minds often process more per interaction. The volume of data—verbal, emotional, energetic—is higher. And so is the cost.

It is important to note that this is not about introversion in the narrow psychological sense. Rather, what is at stake here is *sensory processing sensitivity*—a biologically rooted trait associated with heightened awareness of subtle stimuli, depth of processing, and emotional responsiveness. While it frequently overlaps with introversion, it is not synonymous. Many sensitive people enjoy connection and are capable of deeply meaningful social interactions. But they require more space around them—both temporally and physically—to integrate these experiences. The extroversion ideal, with its emphasis on constant availability, public enthusiasm, and group immersion, ignores this need entirely.

Nowhere is this pressure more evident than in professional environments where visibility equates to advancement. Consider Nadia, a talented research analyst whose insights routinely saved her company significant costs in operations. Her brilliance lay in her capacity to spot patterns that others missed—not in boardroom presence or networking polish. Yet year after year, feedback centred on her "low profile" and "limited engagement" in cross-departmental settings. Despite outperforming her peers in output and innovation, she was passed over for promotions. It was not the quality of her thinking that was questioned, but the *mode* of her contribution. She was judged not for being ineffective, but for being insufficiently visible.

This bias also permeates healthcare, education, and leadership. The archetype of the charismatic doctor, the lively teacher, the outgoing manager—these roles are often imagined through an extroverted lens. Patients are assumed to trust warmth over stillness, students are rewarded for hands-in-the-air enthusiasm, and team leaders are expected to energise rooms. Yet some of the most impactful figures in these fields defy these stereotypes. The soft-spoken clinician who notices the overlooked symptom. The quiet professor whose lectures ripple with conceptual clarity. The reflective executive who says little but listens incisively. Their impact is *measured in depth, not volume*. But because this depth operates beneath the social frequency most people are tuned to, it often goes under-recognised.

At the root of this misalignment is a cultural conflation of sociability with emotional health. We are taught that the more you share, the more you trust. That openness means accessibility. That being expressive equates to being engaged. But these assumptions overlook the complexity of nervous system regulation. For many sensitive people, emotional safety is not produced by being "seen" constantly—it is produced by being *understood*, often in quieter, slower, more deliberate spaces. Their withdrawal is not avoidance; it is integration. Their silence is not lack of opinion; it is often the presence of discernment.

And yet, the pressure to adapt remains strong—especially in environments that pathologise solitude or stillness. It's not uncommon for sensitive individuals to be misread as cold, disinterested, or socially awkward, simply because they do not conform to extroverted behavioural norms. The irony, of course, is that many sensitive people are profoundly relational. They do not avoid connection—they *cherish* it. But they seek connection that is sincere, low-stimulation, and energetically balanced. What they recoil from is *performance-based relating*—the forced small talk, the groupthink rituals, the relentless visibility.

This is not an argument against extroversion. It is an argument against its monopoly. For cultures to be emotionally inclusive, they must learn to distinguish between visibility and value, between charisma and coherence, between noise and nuance. They must make room for nervous system diversity—not just in theory, but in infrastructure. Meetings that allow asynchronous input. Classrooms that balance verbal and written participation. Workplaces that reward substance over showmanship. And above all, a social ethic that honours presence in all its forms.

Shifting this paradigm will not be easy. The extroversion ideal is deeply woven into the fabric of Western society. It reflects broader themes—capitalist output, performative belonging, and the myth of the self-made individual. But it is neither universal nor inevitable. Indigenous cultures, contemplative traditions, and some Eastern societies have long valued inwardness, stillness, and subtlety. They remind us that wisdom does not shout. That some of the most trustworthy leaders speak rarely. That relational depth often requires quiet.

For the sensitive person navigating extroverted landscapes, the invitation is not to become louder, faster, or more outwardly expressive. The invitation is to *anchor in their own rhythm*—to reclaim their nervous system's truth as valid, needed, and worthy of protection. And for those shaping systems—educators, employers, clinicians, policymakers—the challenge is to ask: what brilliance might we be missing because it doesn't announce itself? What intelligence goes underutilised because it doesn't mirror our preferred frequency?

The future of collective resilience will not come from louder voices alone. It will come from more attuned systems—those that recognise that *social intelligence* includes the quiet, the slow, the deeply perceptive. Sensitivity is not a liability in these systems. It is a stabilising force. But only if we stop forcing it to masquerade as extroversion.

Self-Sacrifice as Virtue

Among caregivers, healers, educators, and service professionals, a quiet moral script often runs beneath the surface of daily life: *Good people give. The best give everything.* It is a script rarely questioned—because on its face, it appeals to deeply held values: compassion, commitment, generosity. But for sensitive individuals, especially those in relationally demanding roles, this internalised ideal of self-erasure is not simply unsustainable. It is corrosive. The belief that worth is measured by the extent to which one disappears for others is a subtle but potent psychological toxin—one that exhausts the body, fractures boundaries, and, over time, hollows out the very presence that service work depends on.

The roots of this narrative are complex. They stretch across history, religion, gender dynamics, and professional ethics. In Western culture, particularly in caregiving professions, the archetype of the noble martyr remains powerfully intact. The tireless nurse who never takes a break. The therapist who holds space long after their own resources are depleted. The teacher who works unpaid hours and carries the emotional weight of entire classrooms. These figures are not only normalised—they are *celebrated.* The problem is not that we admire their dedication. The problem is that we fail to see the cost. And worse, we build systems that rely on this self-disregard to function.

This dynamic is especially pernicious for sensitive people whose nervous systems are more porous and whose empathy often operates involuntarily. In service roles, they don't merely *care about* the suffering of others—they *absorb* it. And when the professional culture conflates overextension with ethical virtue, they find themselves caught in an impossible bind: to do their job well is to violate their body's boundaries. To protect their body is to risk moral guilt. This double bind creates a slow-burn form of internalised stress—a moral fatigue that mimics burnout but runs deeper. It is not just the nervous system that is frayed. It is the identity itself.

At the heart of this is a misunderstanding of what service actually requires. Contrary to popular belief, the effectiveness of caregiving is not proportional to the amount of personal depletion it involves.

On the contrary, sustainable service demands containment, clarity, and regular restoration. But these practices often get mislabelled. Boundaries are mistaken for coldness. Rest is mistaken for indulgence. Emotional neutrality is mistaken for disengagement. Sensitive professionals learn to override their signals of fatigue and fragment in the name of duty. Over time, their capacity to discern between *ethical service* and *pathological overgiving* deteriorates.

The consequences are cumulative. Physical symptoms—chronic fatigue, autoimmune flare-ups, migraines—begin to surface without obvious cause. Emotional bandwidth shrinks, making even minor interpersonal tensions feel overwhelming. Dissociation may become a survival strategy, creating a professional who is technically competent but energetically absent. In extreme cases, individuals exit the very fields they entered out of love. They walk away not because they lack devotion, but because the model of service they've inherited is one in which *being whole is incompatible with being good.*

Take the case of Dr Miriam L., a gifted palliative care physician whose presence was known to calm even the most distressed families. She was respected, admired, and always available—until she wasn't. After months of waking with dread, experiencing sudden memory lapses, and crying without clear reason, she collapsed in her kitchen one morning. The official diagnosis was adrenal exhaustion. But Miriam knew something else had collapsed as well: her sense of self-worth, which had been built almost entirely on being the one others could always count on. The moment she could no longer sustain that role, she felt as if she ceased to exist.

This story is not unusual. It reflects a pattern that plays out quietly in countless professionals across the globe—particularly women, and even more so those in under-resourced or emotionally intense environments. What complicates recovery is not just physical exhaustion but *identity foreclosure*—the terror of imagining who one is if not the overfunctioning, ever-available carer. Without a clear alternative model of relational responsibility—one that integrates presence with self-preservation—many sensitive individuals continue to equate value with vanishing.

To disrupt this narrative, we need a new language of service. One that honours empathy without demanding enmeshment. One that recognises that *presence is not synonymous with sacrifice*, and that effective caregiving does not require perpetual depletion. This means actively resisting professional cultures that shame boundary-setting, that measure commitment by unpaid labour, and that elevate endurance over discernment. It means modelling a kind of ethical leadership that is rooted in regulation, not martyrdom.

Ritualised retreat becomes essential here—not as a luxury, but as a structural need. Sensitive professionals must be trained not only in technical skills but in *energetic hygiene*: practices that help them metabolise emotional residue, discharge sympathetic activation, and re-establish inner space. This is not a soft skill; it is a survival skill. Without it, the nervous system becomes a sponge with no wringing-out mechanism. With it, the same sensitivity that once caused overload becomes a refined tool of attunement—sharp, clear, and sustainable.

Cultural reframing is also required at the systemic level. Workplaces must begin to design policies that support *humane engagement*: protected time for recovery, structural limits on emotional labour, and accountability mechanisms that don't penalise people for honouring their limits. The cultural stories we tell—of the hero nurse, the selfless teacher, the burned-out social worker—must evolve. Not by devaluing these roles, but by reclaiming the *full humanity* of the people within them.

At a philosophical level, the glorification of self-sacrifice is rooted in a deeper discomfort with vulnerability. We are often more comfortable with people who lose themselves for others than with those who openly state their limits. But for cultures to be psychologically mature, they must elevate models of strength that include softness, recovery, and self-awareness. Sensitive professionals are uniquely positioned to lead this shift—not by abandoning their sensitivity, but by *protecting it fiercely*.

This is not just a personal issue. It is a collective one. When the sensitive minds among us are depleted, our systems lose some of their finest instruments of perception, care, and wisdom. The cost is felt not only by the individuals who collapse under the weight of self-erasure, but by the communities who lose access to their nuance, discernment, and quiet strength. What we need is not more sacrifice. We need models of service that make *staying whole* a condition of continuing to serve.

Real-World Case: The Burnt-Out Nurse

By the time Elena finally took leave, she wasn't just tired—she was hollow. A registered nurse with fifteen years of service in a busy metropolitan hospital, she was known for her calm under pressure, her encyclopaedic clinical knowledge, and her uncanny ability to de-escalate even the most distressed patients. She rarely called in sick, often stayed beyond her scheduled shifts, and was universally described by colleagues as "reliable" and "strong." The problem was, Elena no longer recognised herself. The quiet after a shift became intolerable. Her partner noted she'd grown withdrawn and hyper-reactive. One morning, halfway through folding laundry, she sat down on the bedroom floor and didn't move for two hours. It was not sadness, exactly—it was absence.

Burnout in the medical profession is not new. But what Elena experienced was something more specific, more insidious: the slow erosion of vitality that occurs when a highly sensitive individual is systematically exposed to human suffering without sufficient energetic recovery. This is not about workload alone. It's about the unrelenting *relational exposure*—the dozens of small empathic interactions that require micro-adjustments in tone, gaze, posture, and emotional containment. For someone whose nervous system is finely attuned, each of these moments carries a subtle cost. Over time, these costs accumulate into a kind of psychological debt, one that cannot be paid off with a weekend off or a single day of rest.

Elena had always been aware that she was more affected by her environment than her colleagues seemed to be. She could sense a patient's distress before they spoke. She would often find herself replaying conversations hours after they ended, analysing tone and subtext. At first, this seemed like a professional strength. She was intuitive, thoughtful, responsive. Patients trusted her instantly. But this attunement had an underside. A patient's despair lingered in her chest long after they were discharged. The sound of alarms triggered a nervous jolt, even on her days off. Crowded corridors, subtle staff conflicts, or the unspoken tension between exhausted team members all seemed to lodge in her body. What others described as "just part of the job" began to feel like emotional residue she couldn't wash off.

What made this experience so disorienting was that Elena *wanted* to keep caring. She was not burnt out in the stereotypical sense of becoming cynical or numb. Instead, she found herself overly permeable—*too affected.* But the professional culture around her reinforced the idea that the only way to be of service was to push through. Resilience, in her environment, was not defined by recovery—it was defined by endurance. Colleagues wore their exhaustion like badges of honour. Breaks were skipped, self-disclosure discouraged, vulnerability masked with humour. To step back felt like betrayal—not just of her patients, but of her identity as a "strong nurse."

Elena's turning point came not from a dramatic breakdown but from a quiet realisation. During a mandated trauma debriefing session, a facilitator asked each participant to describe how their body felt after particularly difficult shifts. Most offered vague answers: "tense," "tired," "wired." When it was her turn, Elena heard herself say, without planning to, "I feel like I've been borrowed by everyone and returned in pieces." The room fell silent. She hadn't meant to be poetic. She had meant to be precise.

That moment catalysed something. She began to explore the concept of *energetic boundaries*—not as metaphor, but as literal, body-based phenomena. She learned that the nervous system cannot endlessly regulate other people's distress without consequence. Even positive interactions—when unrelenting—demand neurobiological processing. She started tracking her physiological responses in real time: the breath-holding during difficult family updates, the tight jaw after managing a combative patient, the shallow inhale after a quick lunch in the fluorescent-lit staff room. Her goal was not just to notice, but to interrupt.

Enter the micro-retreat. Elena did not have the luxury of long sabbaticals or spacious wellness retreats. What she created instead were *pockets of recalibration*—brief, deliberate interruptions to the cycle of overexposure. Before entering the ward each morning, she sat in her car and did three minutes of focused diaphragmatic breathing while holding a smooth stone that she only used during those rituals. On lunch breaks, she wore noise-cancelling earbuds—not to listen to music, but to reintroduce *silence* to her auditory system. After every shift, she journaled precisely three sentences: What did I absorb? What do I return? What do I keep?

These were not acts of indulgence. They were forms of neurosomatic hygiene. Over weeks, she began to feel shifts. The space between stimulus and response grew. She was less reactive, more clear-minded. Her empathy returned—but this time with boundaries. She discovered that *containment* was not the enemy of care. It was its precondition.

Colleagues noticed. One junior nurse asked how she remained so composed during a particularly difficult paediatric code. Elena didn't offer a self-help slogan. She simply said, "I stay regulated so I don't have to shut down." It wasn't a performance. It was a principle she had earned through practice.

Importantly, Elena did not view her new rituals as "extras." They were no longer optional. They were woven into the infrastructure of her day. She replaced her notion of strength as stoicism with a new ethic: *sustainable presence requires cyclical withdrawal.* Not permanent withdrawal, but intentional pauses. Her micro-retreats were not escape routes; they were *return rituals*—mechanisms to return to herself after being repeatedly pulled into the needs, emotions, and energies of others.

What Elena's story illustrates is not just a single recovery. It offers a replicable model for any sensitive professional working in high-demand relational environments. The solution to burnout is not to care less. It is to *care differently*. To recognise that even care has a rhythm—and that rhythm must include rests.

Micro-retreats are not substitutes for structural change. Hospitals, schools, and service organisations must do more to support the nervous systems of those on the front lines. But while we await systemic shifts, individual agency remains critical. Sensitive professionals must reclaim the right to calibrate their own input-output ratios, to ritualise their restoration, and to name their needs without shame.

Elena continues to nurse. She still works long shifts, still holds space for grief and healing. But now, she does so from a place of grounded clarity, not sacrificial depletion. Her patients do not receive less of her—they receive *more of her intact.* And that, perhaps, is the paradox of the sensitive professional: when they learn to stop giving themselves away, they finally become the most present version of themselves.

Chapter 4
Rest as Regulation: The Biology of Restoration

Rest is not a break from life's movement but the very ground that allows life to continue without fracture. For those with sensitive nervous systems—people who process deeply, feel keenly, and register subtleties others miss—rest is not indulgence. It is elemental, as non-negotiable as breath or water. Yet contemporary culture tends to flatten it into absence: a pause in production, a gap in activity, a nothingness. Rarely is it recognised as an active force, a system's way of governing itself with intelligence. This chapter insists otherwise. Rest is regulation, and regulation is not surrender but the body's most refined expression of self-leadership.

The design of the autonomic nervous system tells the story clearly. It is made to swing between poles: mobilisation and stillness, readiness and renewal. This fluidity—autonomic flexibility—is what makes resilience possible over the long arc of a life. But when stress is relentless, the pendulum falters. Sensitive individuals are often caught tilted toward sympathetic activation: the faint buzz of vigilance, an almost invisible tension, the body always braced to respond. This low-grade arousal, dismissed as "normal," gradually corrodes balance. Sleep slips, thought fogs, irritability rises, and fatigue thickens. No discipline or caffeine can permanently override it. What the system hungers for is not more drive but a reset—deliberate activation of parasympathetic pathways through structured, intentional rest.

This "reset" is not wellness jargon. It is tangible neurobiology. Heart rate slows, vagal tone strengthens, breathing steadies, inflammatory signalling recedes. Research has mapped how restorative states modulate heart rate variability, facilitate glymphatic flushing in the brain, and even reverse certain stress-driven genetic markers. This is not simply doing nothing. It is the body working at a subtler register, repairing itself at levels no conscious effort can reach. Rest is not an absence of presence—it is a different kind of presence altogether.

Perhaps the most startling evidence comes from the glymphatic system, that nocturnal network dedicated to cleaning the brain. While the lymphatic system clears the body, the glymphatic system washes the cerebral landscape, removing metabolic debris such as beta-amyloid plaques, which are implicated in neurodegenerative disease. Yet it functions fully only when the nervous system descends into deep parasympathetic states—when safety is felt, not theorised. For sensitive people, whose systems often bristle at ambient threat even in ordinary surroundings, that descent is not guaranteed. It must be designed. Ritual becomes necessary: external conditions arranged to coax the nervous system into surrender.

This chapter will trace what such design entails in practice. Retreat, properly conceived, is not luxury but intervention—an engineered descent into states where repair becomes possible. Sensory boundaries, predictable environments, trustworthy relationships: these are not eccentric lifestyle choices but essential prerequisites for parasympathetic engagement. And contrary to the popular narrative, resilience is not forged only through strain. Neuroplastic growth, the brain's ability to rewire itself, is potentiated by rhythm, not sheer exposure. Pressure without integration does not create strength; it carves trauma. Integration, by contrast, emerges when the brain is allowed to process in low-demand states.

Consider Jonas, a young technology founder whose life had become indistinguishable from his company's acceleration. By his early thirties, he had secured capital, built international teams, and achieved every metric of entrepreneurial success. But inwardly, his system was unravelling—sleep fractured, attention scattered, and his once-reliable intuition dulled. What altered his trajectory was not another "hack" but a reframing: he began scheduling micro-retreats as rigorously as board meetings. These were not indulgent escapes but stripped-down intervals in which his nervous system could reset. Within months, his perception sharpened, his judgement steadied, his interactions softened. Neuroscience offers the explanation: clarity is not forced by effort; it flowers when a system has been restored.

Rest, then, is not retreat from life but coherence restored to it. In a world that mistakes noise for engagement and speed for success, sensitive individuals must reclaim the authority to pace themselves by their nervous systems rather than by cultural clocks. This is not fragility. It is fidelity to design. Depth requires intervals; integration demands rhythm. And those rhythms are not barriers to achievement. They are what make achievement sustainable, humane, and worth carrying forward.

The coming pages will dismantle the myths that reduce rest to laziness or self-indulgence. We will examine the evolutionary role of restorative states, the biological markers that signal true recovery, and the practical architectures that allow rest to be embedded rather than postponed. More importantly, we will invite a reorientation: to see stillness not as vacancy but as a form of intelligence—an art the body already knows. For sensitive systems, vitality is not mined through willpower. It is restored through rhythm. And rhythm, by its very nature, is something one chooses.

What follows is both scientific and quietly radical: a reclamation of rest as sovereignty. Sensitive lives cannot wait until collapse demands it. Regulation must be woven in deliberately, as practice, as protection. Rest is not softness. It is reset—firm, decisive, and necessary. The question, then, is not whether the body asks for it, but whether we are willing to hear its call.

The Autonomic Reset

It is one of the great ironies of modern life that the very systems designed to protect us have become the source of our chronic fatigue. The autonomic nervous system—our body's primary stress and recovery regulator—was not built for uninterrupted acceleration. It was built for oscillation: a cyclical pattern of activation and deactivation, of mobilisation and repose. When this rhythm is preserved, the nervous system performs with remarkable efficiency, allowing for acute response to challenge followed by deep restoration. When the rhythm is disrupted—when sympathetic arousal becomes the baseline rather than the exception—health, clarity, and resilience begin to erode from the inside out. For sensitive individuals in particular, whose systems are more reactive to environmental stimuli and relational dynamics, the cost of living without an intentional recovery rhythm is not theoretical. It is physiological, cognitive, and emotional. What they require is not just rest, but *autonomic reset*—a deliberate return to biological balance.

The autonomic nervous system operates largely outside of conscious control, governing essential functions such as heart rate, digestion, respiration, and hormonal regulation. It is divided into two primary branches: the sympathetic nervous system (SNS), responsible for energising and mobilising the body in response to perceived threat, and the parasympathetic nervous system (PNS), which facilitates rest, digestion, and repair. In a well-functioning system, these two branches operate like a seesaw—each rising and falling to maintain homeostasis. But when the sympathetic branch remains chronically dominant, the PNS becomes underused, resulting in a cascade of problems: disrupted sleep architecture, systemic inflammation, poor immune function, impaired digestion, and cognitive fog.

The notion of *reset* implies not mere rest, but recalibration. It is the process of bringing a dysregulated nervous system back into alignment—not by shutting down, but by restoring the full range of autonomic flexibility. Flexibility, in this context, refers to the nervous system's ability to fluidly move between states depending on environmental demands and internal cues. This is a dynamic capacity, not a fixed trait. And it is trainable. What has emerged from the convergence of neurophysiology, somatic psychology, and contemplative neuroscience is clear: *autonomic regulation is malleable, and it improves with deliberate recovery rituals*. For sensitive people, this is not simply a helpful insight. It is a foundational strategy for vitality.

Consider heart rate variability (HRV), one of the most reliable biomarkers of autonomic health. High HRV indicates that the nervous system is agile—able to rapidly shift between sympathetic activation and parasympathetic recovery. Low HRV, by contrast, signals rigidity and depletion. Studies show that practices such as diaphragmatic breathing, yoga nidra, mindful movement, and time in low-stimulus environments can significantly enhance HRV, even in individuals with a history of stress-related dysfunction. But crucially, these practices are not effective when approached sporadically or reactively. What matters is consistency and structure. *The nervous system responds best to predictable signals of safety and rhythm.*

Autonomic reset, then, is not the same as taking breaks. It is a physiological event with specific markers: lowered cortisol, increased vagal tone, improved respiration depth, and enhanced interoceptive awareness. These changes do not arise from distraction or escapism, but from deliberate engagement with regulation-based behaviours. This includes non-sleep deep rest (NSDR) protocols, somatosensory grounding, or immersive solitude. What these interventions share is that they reduce novelty, lower environmental load, and increase the sense of internal coherence—all conditions that help sensitive nervous systems to re-establish balance.

One of the major barriers to reset is cultural. The prevailing belief that recovery equals weakness—or worse, indulgence—creates an internalised pressure to override bodily signals of depletion. Sensitive individuals, who often internalise unspoken emotional expectations from others, are particularly vulnerable to guilt when stepping away from constant engagement. But the biology tells a different story. Without deliberate reset, the body does not merely slow down. It begins to break down. Chronic sympathetic dominance has been linked to numerous disorders: cardiovascular disease, autoimmune dysfunction, anxiety syndromes, and even accelerated cellular ageing via telomere attrition. Autonomic reset is not optional. It is preventative care.

To illustrate the stakes, let us consider the clinical profile of a patient under prolonged sympathetic dominance. A mid-40s educator, highly attuned to the emotional needs of her students, begins to experience chronic insomnia, shortness of breath, unexplained digestive issues, and a flattened affect. Standard interventions—cognitive reframing, dietary changes, even medication—provide only partial relief. What shifted her trajectory was a structured regimen of autonomic reset: 20 minutes daily of guided parasympathetic stimulation through breathing protocols, 10 minutes of silence upon waking before any device interaction, and two hours per week in a sensory-reduced environment. Within eight weeks, her sleep quality improved, gastrointestinal symptoms diminished, and—perhaps most tellingly—her emotional range returned. She began to feel again, not just function. *The reset allowed her to re-enter life with responsiveness instead of reactivity.*

It is important to distinguish between collapse and restoration. Sensitive individuals often reach a point where the only way the nervous system forces a break is through shutdown—emotional numbness, social withdrawal, or physical illness. This is not restoration. It is emergency regulation. Autonomic reset, by contrast, is intentional and proactive. It honours the body's early signals rather than punishing it for its limits. And while many people reach for rest only after collapse, it is far more powerful when integrated into the daily ecology of one's life. Ten minutes of physiological sighing, five minutes of orienting to stillness, or a weekly half-day of tech-free solitude can yield disproportionate benefits when designed with precision. *The nervous system responds to cues of safety faster than it responds to words of reassurance.*

Critically, the reset process also involves *repatterning attentional habits.* The sympathetic nervous system is tightly linked to what is known as the salience network in the brain—the circuitry responsible for detecting threat and novelty. When this network becomes overactive, attention becomes fragmented and scanning replaces presence. Practices that redirect awareness inward (interoception), or toward rhythmically predictable stimuli (e.g., breath, sound, gentle movement), help downshift salience and re-anchor the self in embodied safety. This not only calms the body—it improves cognitive clarity. Sensitive minds, once reset, regain access to their full perceptual depth, rather than operating in a narrowed, threat-biased field.

What emerges from this process is not passivity, but capacity. A system that is regularly reset can handle challenge without slipping into dysregulation. It can navigate social complexity without emotional exhaustion. It can move between solitude and intimacy without either becoming overwhelming. For those in caregiving or leadership roles, this flexibility is critical. It means they can remain attuned without becoming enmeshed, assertive without becoming reactive, productive without becoming compulsive.

Ultimately, the case for autonomic reset is not philosophical. It is measurable, observable, and repeatable. The sensitive nervous system is not a problem to be fixed, but a system to be maintained with precision. And maintenance requires recovery—not occasionally, but rhythmically. This subchapter offers not just a lens, but a protocol. Because once we understand what the body is asking for, the real question is not whether we can afford to rest, but whether we can afford not to.

Glymphatic Flow and Brain Detoxification

It is not hyperbole to say that your brain cleans itself while you sleep. What was once speculative folklore—that rest restores the mind—now has a growing foundation in neurobiology. And at the centre of that foundation is the glymphatic system, a recently discovered mechanism that flushes waste from the brain with surprising efficiency. Unlike other bodily organs, the brain does not possess a traditional lymphatic system to remove cellular debris. Instead, it relies on this parallel infrastructure—a glymphatic network—that operates most effectively during deep, uninterrupted rest. For sensitive individuals, whose nervous systems often hover in hypervigilance and struggle to reach the deeper stages of sleep, this has profound implications. It means that their clarity, resilience, and emotional balance are not simply psychological matters. They are contingent on a physical cleansing process that requires access to specific physiological states. *Without sufficient glymphatic activity, the brain becomes less efficient, more reactive, and increasingly prone to overload.*

The glymphatic system, first characterised in 2012 by neuroscientist Maiken Nedergaard and colleagues, functions as a kind of neurological sewerage network. Cerebrospinal fluid (CSF) flows along the outside of blood vessels in the brain, entering the brain tissue through aquaporin-4 water channels embedded in glial cells. From there, it interchanges with interstitial fluid and removes soluble metabolic waste—such as amyloid beta, tau proteins, and other neurotoxic by-products—that accumulate during wakefulness. These waste products are linked to neurodegenerative diseases when allowed to linger. But under deep sleep, particularly in slow-wave non-REM stages, the glymphatic flow increases dramatically—up to 60% more efficient than during waking states. *This is not a fringe theory. It is a shift in how we understand the biological necessity of profound rest.*

Sleep, it turns out, is not a passive state. It is an actively orchestrated event in which the brain disengages from external processing in order to conduct internal maintenance. Crucially, glymphatic clearance is most robust when the brain's metabolic demands are lowest. This is why periods of deep rest—not merely unconsciousness, but physiologically regulated slow-wave activity—are essential. Light, fragmented sleep does not confer the same benefit. Nor does rest achieved through sedation, which often suppresses the brain wave patterns necessary for glymphatic activation. This presents a challenge for individuals who struggle with sleep onset or maintenance, particularly those with heightened sensory processing. *For them, achieving brain cleanliness is not merely a matter of getting to bed—it is about accessing specific, restorative neurophysiological rhythms.*

What exacerbates the problem is that many modern habits and stressors directly interfere with this mechanism. Irregular sleep schedules, late-night screen exposure, caffeine dependency, ambient noise pollution, and psychological rumination all conspire to reduce the likelihood of entering the slow-wave phases needed for glymphatic activity. Moreover, chronic stress increases norepinephrine levels in the brain, which constricts the glymphatic channels and inhibits fluid flow. The sensitive nervous system, which already registers subtle environmental shifts with high resolution, becomes even more impaired when these lifestyle factors are present. The result is a double burden: the mind becomes both overstimulated and under-cleaned.

One of the most striking findings in glymphatic research is that sleeping position also matters. Studies in rodents suggest that the lateral sleeping position—lying on one's side—promotes more efficient glymphatic transport compared to supine (back) or prone (stomach) positions. While human research is still emerging, preliminary imaging studies echo this orientation effect. Such detail underscores a broader point: *the brain's capacity to clean itself is exquisitely sensitive to subtle changes in internal and external environment.* This sensitivity is precisely what makes the system both powerful and fragile.

What does this mean in practical terms for the sensitive reader? First, it elevates rest from being a behavioural choice to a biological imperative. Second, it reframes cognitive fog, emotional irritability, and decision fatigue not as weaknesses of willpower, but as potential indicators of neuro-metabolic load. When the brain has not had the opportunity to conduct its nightly cleanup, thinking becomes less fluid, emotional thresholds narrow, and sensory thresholds drop. Third, it highlights the importance of protecting deep sleep—not just in quantity, but in quality. And for that to happen, *daytime regulation becomes critical.* Sleep is not an isolated nighttime event. It is shaped by the preceding 16 hours of stimulation, light exposure, stress response, and bodily movement.

The implications extend beyond individual wellbeing. From a systems perspective, professionals in high-demand, emotionally charged roles—clinicians, educators, caregivers—often accumulate glymphatic debt without knowing it. They push through cognitive fatigue, normalise sleep fragmentation, and adapt to suboptimal baseline functioning. Over time, the build-up of waste proteins impairs synaptic plasticity, reduces working memory, and limits creative thinking. In organisational cultures that reward perpetual output, this is viewed as burnout. But from a physiological perspective, it is closer to congestion: *a brain that has not been allowed to clean itself properly over extended periods.*

This insight aligns with emerging concepts in neuropreventive medicine, which suggest that interventions aimed at enhancing glymphatic clearance may reduce risk for Alzheimer's, Parkinson's, and other neurodegenerative conditions. Techniques such as sleep compression therapy, chronobiology-aligned light exposure, and transcutaneous vagal nerve stimulation are being explored as means to promote restorative sleep architecture. For now, the most reliable intervention remains optimising one's sleep hygiene and environmental conditions: darkness, cool temperature, minimal sound, consistent rhythms, and screen cessation at least 90 minutes before bed. *In essence, the same conditions that support sensitive nervous systems during the day also enable the brain's sanitation crew to get to work at night.*

Interestingly, recent research is exploring whether certain mindfulness practices may enhance glymphatic function indirectly. By downregulating sympathetic tone and promoting parasympathetic dominance, meditative states can facilitate the preconditions necessary for transition into deeper sleep stages. Even practices such as yoga nidra or body scanning—when practiced consistently—can shift the body toward a state where glymphatic activity becomes more likely. While the science here is nascent, the pattern is suggestive: *states of low-demand, high-awareness support the brain's regenerative processes more than states of passive distraction or overstimulation.*

To draw this back to the experience of the sensitive individual: if your brain feels slow, foggy, or easily overwhelmed, the problem may not be the complexity of your thinking but the debris clouding it. Glymphatic flow is not something we feel directly, but we live its effects. When it is functioning well, clarity, emotional range, and creativity return. When it is blocked, life becomes harder than it needs to be—thinking takes more effort, emotions linger longer, and the world feels just slightly louder. Recovery, then, is not indulgence. It is neurological hygiene.

Understanding the glymphatic system offers something else: a map for intervention that is grounded in biology, not guilt. The answer is not to be tougher, but to be more attuned. It is to treat your rest not as optional, but as an active investment in cognitive clarity, mood regulation, and long-term resilience. For those whose minds are already working overtime to process a noisy world, allowing the brain to clean itself may be the most intelligent decision you make all day.

Neuroplasticity Requires Recovery

Neuroplasticity, the brain's remarkable ability to rewire itself through experience, is often celebrated in the context of grit, persistence, and exposure to challenge. Yet what is frequently overlooked in this narrative is that plasticity is not purely about endurance—it is about integration. The nervous system does not merely reshape itself through stress or stimulation. It remodels itself through cycles of activation and recovery. *Without sufficient recovery, there is no true adaptation—only exhaustion masquerading as resilience.*

This has profound implications for highly sensitive individuals, whose threshold for arousal is typically lower and whose processing is more elaborate. For them, the popular mantra of "just push through" can backfire. Repeated exposure to overwhelming stimuli, without adequate time and conditions for recalibration, does not build tolerance. It entrenches dysregulation. In fact, when stressors exceed the nervous system's window of tolerance, neuroplasticity can turn maladaptive—reinforcing pathways of hypervigilance, reactivity, or shutdown rather than resilience. *True growth requires more than challenge. It requires an internal climate in which integration is biologically possible.*

The science of neuroplasticity supports this assertion. Research across cognitive neuroscience, affective neuroscience, and psychophysiology consistently shows that rest, sleep, and parasympathetic dominance are essential to the consolidation of learning and the recalibration of stress responses. Synaptic changes do not occur uniformly during stimulation. Many of them happen afterwards—during sleep, during stillness, during low-arousal periods when the brain has the bandwidth to process and embed new information. This is why even short "offline" moments throughout the day—brief pauses, quiet intervals, naturalistic movement—can have an outsized impact on long-term adaptability. *Plasticity is a process, not a moment. And recovery is its scaffold.*

Consider how athletes train. Periods of high intensity are always balanced with recovery, not merely to prevent injury but to enable muscular adaptation. The same applies neurologically. If you want a system to grow stronger, it must have space to repair and reconfigure. Sensory overload without recovery does not make the nervous system more robust—it erodes it. The concept of hormesis—the beneficial effects of moderate, intermittent stress—only holds when the stressor is bounded and recovery is sufficient. Without the latter, what's being built is not strength, but fragility.

Modern neuroscience increasingly recognises that stress-induced plasticity is context-dependent. For example, prolonged cortisol elevation can impair hippocampal neurogenesis and reduce prefrontal cortex function, diminishing working memory and emotional regulation. Conversely, environments that facilitate parasympathetic activation—such as those evoking safety, familiarity, or low social demand—can support structural and functional connectivity in brain regions associated with resilience. *In other words, your brain changes depending not only on what it encounters, but on how it is allowed to recover afterwards.*

Sleep, once again, becomes central. Deep non-REM sleep supports synaptic homeostasis—pruning irrelevant neural activity while strengthening salient pathways. REM sleep plays a role in emotional memory processing and affective flexibility. If sleep is disrupted, so too is the consolidation of neural learning. For highly sensitive individuals, whose sensory systems may be more easily disrupted by noise, temperature, or irregular schedules, this matters greatly. Recovery must be *intentional*, not incidental. The environment must be curated to honour the nervous system's needs—not simply hoped for at the margins of an overcommitted life.

This logic also applies to social-emotional learning. Exposure to emotionally charged or challenging relational contexts—conflict, performance pressure, difficult conversations—does not automatically produce maturity or wisdom. It may, in fact, reinforce defensive conditioning if the individual is not supported to reflect, regulate, and integrate the experience. This is particularly true in caregiving and helping professions, where emotional labour is high and reflection time scarce. The absence of recovery rituals here is not a luxury issue—it is a neurological liability. *Empathy without integration can calcify into empathic distress rather than deepen into empathic capacity.*

Therapeutic environments often illustrate this well. Sessions that offer catharsis or insight only support lasting change when the client has time and space between sessions to metabolise the experience. Pacing becomes crucial. Similarly, educational models that bombard learners with content but provide little time for reflection and digestion often produce shallow knowledge, not deep learning. Sensory and emotional input must be followed by cognitive and somatic processing. Without this, the nervous system becomes cluttered—not enhanced.

This same principle extends to digital environments. The constant stream of notifications, rapid content-switching, and algorithmically engineered novelty trains the brain to anticipate stimulation without rest. Neuroplasticity, in this context, becomes hijacked: the brain becomes wired for fragmentation, not focus. And yet, when individuals are given structured time offline—whether through nature immersion, tech-free retreats, or simply unstructured boredom—creative cognition and emotional range reliably return. *Recovery creates the space in which novel associations and deeper insights can emerge.*

One compelling line of research focuses on heart rate variability (HRV) as a physiological marker of adaptability. High HRV is associated with better emotional regulation, stress tolerance, and executive function. Importantly, HRV improves with practices that promote parasympathetic tone—such as mindfulness meditation, controlled breathing, and even safe social connection. These are not abstract lifestyle add-ons. They are direct contributors to a nervous system capable of responding flexibly to life. And flexibility—not numbness, not toughness—is the true signature of resilience.

Neuroplasticity is not about overriding the nervous system. It is about collaborating with it. That requires recognising the cycles of tension and release, effort and restoration, that govern its capacity to change. For highly sensitive people, whose internal landscapes are often more turbulent and richly textured, the stakes are even higher. Exposure alone will not teach the system how to handle complexity. What teaches the system is *rhythm*: the rhythm of activation and deactivation, of reach and return, of courage and rest.

This has ethical implications, too. When institutions glorify constant exposure—endless meetings, relentless connectivity, back-to-back engagements—they are implicitly assuming that adaptation happens without integration. That is a biologically incoherent assumption. It privileges the visible markers of output over the invisible foundations of capacity. Leaders and educators who understand neuroplasticity differently begin to structure environments differently: fewer inputs, more space, deeper trust in what the nervous system can do when not chronically overwhelmed.

In practical terms, this might look like integrating micro-recoveries throughout the day: moments to breathe, to pause, to disengage from the feed of inputs and return to one's body. It might involve building in decompression rituals after emotionally charged interactions. Or designing workflows with pulsation rather than constancy. For individuals, it requires reclaiming recovery as essential—not just as rest, but as the condition for transformation. And for culture, it calls for an upgrade in how we define productivity: not as motion, but as integration.

The bottom line is this: *if you want the brain to change, you must let it rest.* If you want resilience, you must create conditions for recalibration. Exposure without recovery is not strength-building—it is system strain. And for the sensitive mind, already finely attuned to its environment, this is not a philosophical nicety. It is a biological non-negotiable.

Real-World Case: The Entrepreneur's Second Wind - A tech founder discovers how structured retreat enables sharper decision-making and creativity.

By the time Arun Patel's fingers began trembling at the keyboard, it was already too late. The 38-year-old tech founder had spent the better part of a decade building a fast-scaling SaaS platform from the ground up—bootstrapped, lean, and obsessively optimised. From investor pitches to team sprints, late-night debugging to back-to-back user interviews, he had become the archetype of entrepreneurial stamina. Except that stamina, it turned out, was a brittle illusion. His mind, once hyper-analytical and clear, now felt like a fogged lens. Sleep eluded him, decisions felt paralysing, and his famed creative drive had collapsed into reactive task-switching. Colleagues described him as "distant" and "diffused." Privately, he feared he was burning out from the inside out. *The warning signs were not dramatic—they were subtle, cumulative, and ultimately systemic.*

What saved Arun wasn't medication or another productivity framework. It was a structured, recurring retreat. Not a sabbatical, not a vacation, but a deliberately designed container for restoration, sensory regulation, and deep thinking. It began as a desperate experiment and became a non-negotiable practice. Through it, he discovered something essential: *clarity is not the product of effort alone—it is the by-product of disengagement done with intention.* His story exemplifies how nervous system regulation, not ambition, is the critical hinge upon which creativity and decision-making turn.

To understand Arun's collapse, it's necessary to understand what was happening beneath the surface. Chronic hyperarousal—driven by ceaseless Slack messages, investor pressure, and his own internalised productivity schema—kept his sympathetic nervous system in perpetual overdrive. Initially, this served him. Alertness, intensity, urgency—they all fed the myth of founder brilliance. But physiologically, a body locked in fight-or-flight cannot sustain expansive thinking. It becomes preoccupied with risk, short-term payoff, and binary choices. The nuanced judgment required for innovation and leadership begins to atrophy. *There is a sharp cognitive cost to being constantly 'on'—especially for those whose nervous systems are more finely attuned to stress.*

What finally tipped the balance for Arun was not a breakdown, but a moment of sharp incongruence. In a product strategy meeting, he realised he could no longer track the logic of his own roadmap. The ideas were technically sound, but they lacked coherence. What had once flowed instinctively now required exhaustive justification. That week, he cancelled three meetings and booked a three-day solo retreat in a quiet forest lodge. No tech, no content, no optimisation plan. Just quiet walks, hand-written notes, silence, and sleep.

The shift was not magical—it was biological. On the second day, Arun felt something he hadn't in months: mental spaciousness. His thoughts slowed, not into dullness, but into precision. Insight surfaced unforced. Problems he had been hammering at for weeks suddenly clarified in his peripheral awareness. The paradox became obvious: *what he thought he was losing through disconnection—time, output, momentum—was exactly what he needed to regain them at a higher level.*

What Arun was engaging in, whether he knew it or not, was a full-spectrum autonomic reset. By withdrawing from digital stimulation and social demand, his system began shifting out of sympathetic dominance and into parasympathetic restoration. His vagal tone—responsible for calming physiological arousal—had space to strengthen. As his internal cues of safety increased, his brain could access prefrontal regions involved in abstract reasoning, foresight, and emotional regulation. These are not esoteric benefits. They are *prerequisites* for strategic leadership. And they don't emerge in meetings—they emerge in recovery.

After that first retreat, Arun made the practice regular. Once every six weeks, he structured a 48-hour off-grid interval. Not indulgent, but intentional: movement without performance, reading without annotation, journalling without outcome. These retreats weren't escapes from work—they were how he stayed sharp *within* work. What changed wasn't just his stress level—it was his leadership quality. His team noticed he was more grounded, more decisive, more available. Meetings became shorter but more effective. Creative sessions led to cleaner solutions. Rather than pushing through fatigue, he began anticipating it—and designing around it. *Retreat became strategy, not recovery.*

Critically, Arun's transformation didn't involve abandoning ambition. It involved redefining the fuel that ambition runs on. Like many founders, he had believed his edge came from grit. But grit without restoration becomes grind—and grind produces short-term throughput, not sustainable innovation. The nervous system cannot sustain high-level cognition under chronic load. This is a physiological fact, not a personal failing. Sensitive individuals—those with higher interoceptive awareness or greater emotional reactivity—are especially vulnerable to this mismatch. They don't lack resilience; they require different conditions to access it.

This reframes how we think about performance. It's not just about what we do, but how we regulate ourselves to do it. Decision fatigue, creative block, and strategic incoherence often signal not poor skill, but poor regulation. And regulation cannot be outsourced to technology or hacks—it requires time, space, and rhythm. What Arun reintroduced into his life was *rhythm*—a pulsation of focus and recovery, social engagement and solitude, output and integration. Without that, even the sharpest intellect dulls.

Importantly, Arun did not retreat alone indefinitely. He worked with a coach to structure his post-retreat re-entries, gradually reintroducing stimulation in a way that preserved coherence. He noticed that even small rituals—five minutes of quiet before team calls, non-negotiable evening shutdowns, device-free meals—acted as micro-retreats. These were not time-wasters; they were time-amplifiers. By the third quarter, company KPIs had improved—not because he had worked more, but because he had begun thinking more clearly, choosing more wisely, and leading from stability rather than compulsion.

The broader implication is stark. In knowledge economies, where output is increasingly measured in mental and emotional clarity, *our nervous systems become our infrastructure.* And like any infrastructure, they require maintenance—not only after burnout, but to prevent it. Structured retreat is not a privilege of the elite or the spiritually inclined. It is a functional tool for those whose livelihood depends on adaptive thinking. Whether you're running a tech company or leading a small team, if your nervous system is perpetually in defence mode, your mind will gradually lose access to its most powerful capacities: synthesis, foresight, empathy, originality.

For sensitive leaders especially—those who are more affected by noise, tension, and ambiguity—the stakes are even higher. They are often the ones who bring the most nuanced insights, but who also pay the highest cognitive toll for chronic overstimulation. Structured retreat, then, is not simply about wellness. It is about sovereignty. It is how intelligent people reclaim their nervous systems as assets, rather than liabilities.

Arun's second wind was not mystical—it was metabolic. By stepping away, he reclaimed access to the very faculties that had fuelled his rise in the first place. Creativity. Clarity. Perspective. Not because he tried harder—but because he *finally stopped trying long enough for his brain to reorganise.* This is the paradox every high-performing, sensitive mind must learn: restoration is not what you do when you're done working. It's what makes the work possible.

Chapter 5
Ritual vs. Routine: The Power of Predictable Sanctuary

Rituals are far more than ornamental customs or quaint personal habits; they function as neurological moorings. At their heart lies a remarkable convergence—sensory regulation, psychological safety, and the coherence of identity woven into one. The nervous system, especially when finely attuned as in sensitive individuals, is not driven by timidity but by an instinct for stability: it reads predictability as safety. And in a society that overwhelms us with constant flux, safety ceases to be preference—it becomes necessity.

Neuroscience in recent decades has only confirmed what ancient cultures knew without laboratory proof: rhythmic, deliberate practices—even the smallest—can recalibrate the body's stress response, soothe over-alert circuitry, and shift the system from survival into repair. Yet modernity has obscured this truth. Productivity culture has reduced ritual to superstition or consumerist novelty, severed from its deeper function—to steady the body and mind against unending disruption.

Routine, we might say, is duty-bound; ritual, by contrast, is dignified. It restores agency. For the highly sensitive, this is not a semantic distinction but a physiological one. Ritual becomes a shorthand to the nervous system: here, in this gesture or scent or sequence, you are safe. A candle lit before writing, a particular tune that meets the dawn, the way fingers close around a mug at precisely the same hour—such signals bypass the intellect and speak directly to the body. Mere routine, devoid of reverence, risks becoming another proving ground for performance, another way to tighten the screws of expectation.

To grasp ritual's power as sanctuary, we must look to the nervous system itself. The vagus nerve—messenger and mediator of parasympathetic calm—reads the world constantly for cues of safety or threat. Stephen Porges calls this neuroception: a wordless appraisal beneath awareness. The more finely calibrated this system, as it often is in sensitive people, the more urgent the need for consistent reassurance. Predictability, in this light, is not a deadening monotony. It is a form of medicine.

The chapter turns to the small but steady rituals that serve as these correctives. We might call them micro-rituals—fleeting but potent gestures that prime the system for restoration. A pause of three breaths before speaking. The striking of a match before reflection. The shared quiet of a tea poured the same way each morning. Their strength is not in elaboration but in repetition. They whisper to the nervous system: there is no crisis.

And yet, how resistant many remain. Because rituals are not easily measured, they struggle to earn legitimacy in an age ruled by metrics. A "good" day, by prevailing standards, is marked by visible output, not subtle rhythms. Pauses are indulgences, not investments. Even within wellness culture, rituals are dressed up as hacks to sharpen performance, rather than thresholds that guard against depletion. Thus, the body adapts to overstimulation without ever learning to feel safe enough to reset. The cost is dear: lives that run on the fuel of productivity but lack the sustenance of replenishment.

The sensitive nervous system bears this weight most heavily. Its very responsiveness to subtle shifts—tone, space, atmosphere—makes it prone to hidden accumulations of stress. Over time, that unnoticed load breaks surface as burnout, emotional volatility, disconnection. Healing does not arrive in grand gestures but in steady practices of self-stabilisation. Ritual is not a postscript to survival; it is the very ground that makes sustained engagement possible.

Here we come to the notion of psychological sanctuaries: those intimate, everyday refuges that the philosopher Gaston Bachelard might have called "immense in their smallness." They need not demand withdrawal from the world. Rather, they weave restoration into the weave of participation. A nurse in the corridor presses a pendant between her fingers before stepping into the next room. An executive draws breath with the familiar weight of a handmade cup before the next meeting begins. These are not trinkets. They are tethers.

And their strength lies also in their symbolism. The body and brain do not cleave physical from emotional reality so neatly. A familiar fragrance can tilt chemistry; a trusted gesture can slow the pulse. For those with heightened sensitivity, these signals—woven of texture, music, light—are more than comforts. They are languages, older than thought, that the nervous system hears fluently.

The subchapters to come guide the reader in identifying and shaping such rituals: how the nervous system responds to patterned sensory cues; how to design micro-retreats that grant sovereignty within the day; how specific sensory tools—weighted blankets, certain scents, repetitive movements—become portals to restoration when practised with precision and constancy.

We will also trace the story of one executive, who discovered that her resilience did not arrive through sabbaticals or escapes, but through tiny rituals woven into the flow of her workday. Her experience makes plain what this chapter seeks to establish: ritual is not evasion of responsibility but the very condition that enables it. Predictability, when anchored with care, becomes portable sanctuary.

In an era of relentless stimulation and performative pace, ritual is no mere luxury. It is a biological necessity. For sensitive minds in particular, it is a quiet rebellion—one that insists not on disengagement, but on a different mode of engagement: patterned, protected, personally consecrated. As the chapter unfolds, it extends an invitation: to see ritual not as relic or trend, nor even as routine, but as the scaffolding upon which the nervous system steadies itself.

Why Rituals Work at the Nervous System Level

The nervous system is not governed by logic. It responds not to what we *know*, but to what we *feel*. It interprets the world through a non-verbal code of cues—rhythm, tone, movement, temperature, scent, facial expression, and spatial predictability. This is neuroception, as coined by neuroscientist Stephen Porges: the brain's capacity to detect safety or threat below the level of conscious awareness. And for sensitive individuals, whose perceptual systems are finely tuned and constantly alert, this interpretive radar is not just background noise. It is the terrain on which their physiological wellbeing depends. In this context, ritual is not merely a behavioural luxury—it is a regulatory technology.

Unlike habits, which are often procedural and unexamined, rituals contain deliberate structure and symbolic weight. They are actions repeated not merely out of efficiency, but because their repetition *means something.* And this meaning—combined with their predictability—becomes a signal of safety to the nervous system. Just as unpredictability and chaos elevate cortisol and sympathetic arousal, structured, sensory-rich rituals cue the parasympathetic system to activate. The result: the body exits defence mode and re-enters a state of social receptivity, calm, and repair.

Consider a morning ritual that involves lighting a specific candle, stretching in a familiar sequence, and playing the same instrumental track. To an outside observer, these behaviours may seem arbitrary. But internally, each element becomes encoded as a safety marker. Over time, the nervous system learns: this scent, this sound, this rhythm, this space—none of it signals danger. And that consistent absence of threat becomes a powerful foundation for resilience.

There is a subtle but critical distinction between *doing* something and *returning* to something. Rituals function as returns—to an inner posture, a familiar landscape, a set of embodied cues that say: you've been here before and you were safe. This internalised familiarity lowers the perceived demand on vigilance systems, especially for those with heightened emotional or sensory sensitivities. The hippocampus, which helps form contextual memories, plays a crucial role here. When the environment becomes reliably associated with positive states, it reinforces neuroplastic pathways of ease rather than tension.

But to grasp why this matters, we must first reckon with how easily the nervous system—especially in the sensitive—becomes dysregulated. Sensory overload, emotional contagion, social fragmentation, and constant notifications bombard the vagus nerve with erratic input. The result is an autonomic system that struggles to distinguish urgency from noise. Without predictable counterweights, this hyper-aroused state becomes the baseline. Over time, individuals begin to live not from their values, but from their reactivity.

This is where ritual intervenes—not as escape, but as calibration. When a nervous system is offered repeated patterns that are low in demand and rich in sensory coherence, the dorsal vagal and ventral vagal branches of the parasympathetic system begin to collaborate rather than conflict. The person doesn't just feel 'relaxed'—they become neurologically available for connection, reflection, and creativity. In other words, ritual re-establishes the *conditions* under which healthy engagement is possible.

Modern science is only beginning to catch up with what contemplative traditions have long understood: that *structure is not the enemy of freedom; it is the precondition for it.* We see this in practices as varied as Japanese tea ceremonies, monastic liturgies, Sufi whirling, and secular mindfulness routines. Each provides a sequence of actions imbued with rhythm, sensory consistency, and symbolic relevance. Whether or not the practitioner uses the language of neuroscience, their nervous system is nonetheless being scaffolded into safety.

Critically, rituals do not require hours or ornate preparation. Their efficacy depends not on duration or external beauty, but on *repetition*, *sensory integration*, and *psychological ownership*. A five-minute ritual, if practiced with embodied attention, can have a greater regulatory impact than an hour of distracted self-care. The key is *association*—building a clear, consistent link between the ritual and the internal state it is meant to evoke.

Take, for instance, the use of ritual in trauma recovery. In clinical settings, trauma-informed therapists often introduce grounding exercises—touchstones of breath, movement, or sensory engagement—that clients can ritualise. These are not incidental; they are evidence-based interventions that allow the client's nervous system to tether itself to the present. Similarly, in high-pressure professional contexts, micro-rituals—such as three mindful breaths before speaking, or placing both feet flat on the floor while reading emails—function as psychological punctuation. They separate overwhelm from clarity, reaction from response.

The cultural misunderstanding of ritual—treating it as antiquated, overly spiritual, or unnecessary—is itself a product of nervous systems dysregulated by overstimulation and stripped of coherence. In Western productivity paradigms, what matters is efficiency and novelty. Rituals offer neither. They are slow, repetitive, and often invisible. But their power lies precisely in this invisibility. The brain learns through pattern. And the patterns we honour daily either stabilise our system or destabilise it.

One area where the science is especially clear is the impact of ritualised transitions. For many sensitive people, switching from one context to another—home to work, solitude to socialising, online to offline—creates friction. The nervous system interprets these gaps as disruptions. Rituals buffer those transitions. A closing ritual after work—tidying the desk, changing clothes, dimming lights—communicates to the body: the previous state is over; we are entering another. Without that signalling, the system stays partially braced, never fully arriving in any state, perpetually fragmented.

Even children's development supports this model. Predictable bedtime routines—bath, story, lullaby—help regulate the child's circadian rhythms, reduce cortisol, and improve attachment bonds. The same principles apply in adulthood. When sensory sequences are consistent, soothing, and autonomously chosen, they communicate safety in a language the body understands.

But rituals also have to be protected. The modern mind, shaped by perpetual distraction and micro-demands, is tempted to treat rituals as expendable. Yet every time we skip a ritual in favour of efficiency, we train the nervous system to privilege stimulation over restoration. Rituals must be reclaimed not as self-care hobbies but as *infrastructural acts of nervous system design.* They are, in this way, an ethical commitment—not only to self-regulation but to the quality of our participation in the world.

The emerging field of neuroaesthetics adds another layer of insight. Research shows that sensory environments—soundscapes, colours, textures—directly influence autonomic tone. Rituals that incorporate aesthetic attention (lighting a candle, using intentional gestures, choosing music with known calming effects) are not merely pleasing. They are *neurological interventions*. When layered with mindful attention, they form what could be called micro-sanctuaries—neural refuges from the chaos of ambient threat.

Ultimately, rituals work not because they are magical, but because they are biological. They compress chaos into coherence, time into rhythm, identity into agency. They are repeatable, resonant, and real—even when quiet, even when private. For the sensitive mind, whose inner world is easily flooded by external noise, rituals are not optional. They are non-negotiable technologies of return: to breath, to place, to body, to presence. Through them, the nervous system learns not just how to survive the world, but how to belong in it.

Sacred Micro-Spaces: Creating Psychological Sanctuaries

Restorative space is not merely a physical construct—it is a perceptual experience. For sensitive individuals, whose nervous systems register environmental cues with heightened intensity, the ability to regulate within a space is less about square footage or silence and more about *signals*. The real sanctuary is not a remote cabin or silent retreat centre, but the micro-space calibrated to communicate, *you are safe here*. This is not romantic idealism. It is practical neurobiology.

The concept of sacred micro-spaces challenges the modern presumption that recovery requires escape. Instead, it reframes sanctuary as a *designable experience*—one that can be embedded in the texture of daily life, even amidst the noise of children, colleagues, or traffic. These are psychological refuges forged through intentionality, sensory coherence, and symbolic continuity. They function as what might be called *retreat anchors*—places and moments that stabilise a dysregulated system not through withdrawal, but through well-structured engagement.

To understand their significance, we must first appreciate how the brain maps safety. As the polyvagal theory elucidates, the autonomic nervous system responds not to abstract ideas of 'calm' but to embodied signals—soft lighting, soothing rhythms, familiar scents, and spatial predictability. These cues, when consistently delivered, activate the parasympathetic pathways responsible for restoration and social connection. Without them, even a luxurious environment can feel subtly threatening. With them, even a cluttered flat can offer refuge.

Consider a woman who sets up a corner in her small apartment with a weighted blanket, a specific lavender spray, and an analogue clock. Every day at 4 p.m., she turns off digital devices, sits in that chair, and reads for twenty minutes. Over time, her nervous system learns that this context equals decompression. No travel. No ceremony. Just consistency. What she has created is a micro-space: a context that carries cumulative regulatory power because it is sensory-rich, psychologically bounded, and symbolically meaningful.

The act of design is itself therapeutic. Sensitive individuals often feel at the mercy of their environments, constantly negotiating noise, crowds, or unexpected demands. Micro-space creation flips this script. It allows for agency. The practitioner is no longer passively reacting to overstimulation but actively curating context. This shift—from reactivity to authorship—is foundational to nervous system resilience. It signals not only, *I can rest here,* but also, *I have a say in how I inhabit the world.*

Importantly, micro-spaces need not be physically separate rooms. They can be a specific mug, a certain kind of chair, a blanket that only gets used during rest breaks. The key is not opulence, but *association.* What matters is that these cues are linked—reliably and repeatedly—to internal states of decompression. In this way, the nervous system is not asked to summon calm in chaos. It is trained to access calm by stepping into a pattern it recognises.

One of the most elegant expressions of this is found in Japanese design philosophy, particularly the principle of *ma*—the conscious shaping of empty space as a container for presence. A tea mat, a tray, a niche—each becomes a vessel for attention. This aesthetic minimalism is not about reduction; it's about focus. When a space says one thing clearly, the nervous system doesn't have to sift through confusion. The message lands: *this is for you.*

Contrast this with the multitasking chaos of most contemporary homes and workspaces—blinking lights, cross-purpose surfaces, overlapping sounds. These spaces fragment attention and signal alertness. They are not inherently bad, but they are neurologically demanding. To a sensitive system already managing interpersonal load, they erode capacity. Sacred micro-spaces, by contrast, become rest stops in the overstimulated cognitive highway. Not by withdrawing from life, but by establishing moments of coherence within it.

Even the language we use matters. Calling a space sacred is not about spirituality—it's about *intentional sanctity*. The word says: this is not just a cushion on a chair; this is a threshold. Once I cross it, a different rule set applies. I move more slowly. I breathe differently. I let down my guard. For the high-performing executive, this could be a ritualised ten minutes with noise-cancelling headphones and a cup of herbal tea between Zoom calls. For the overstimulated parent, it could be stepping onto the balcony with bare feet for two deep breaths. The practice is not about scale; it's about signal density.

Technology, of course, complicates this picture. Our devices have a remarkable capacity to smuggle noise into sanctuary. Notifications, screens, and the implicit demand for instant response infiltrate even well-curated spaces. Thus, a true psychological micro-space often includes boundaries around technology—not as asceticism, but as necessity. One cannot truly exhale while being pinged. Sacredness requires protection.

But here lies an ethical tension: in a society where space and time are unequally distributed, what does it mean to recommend micro-sanctuaries? How do we speak about rest to a nurse working double shifts, a single parent in a crowded flat, or a student juggling multiple jobs? The answer is not to idealise privilege, but to democratise agency. Micro-spaces are valuable *because* they can be created in five minutes, in a corner, with household items. The revolution is not in the scale of the sanctuary, but in the insistence that even small spaces matter—and that even busy lives deserve coherence.

This reframing also shifts the cultural narrative around productivity. Instead of seeing rest as an interruption, we begin to see it as a platform. The five minutes in the micro-space aren't breaks from 'real work'; they are infrastructure for sustained cognition, emotional clarity, and relational presence. Over time, individuals who honour their micro-sanctuaries find that their capacity for strategic thinking, creative problem-solving, and interpersonal regulation expands. Not because they worked harder, but because they worked *rested.*

Case studies affirm this. In leadership coaching, for example, executives who incorporate structured micro-recoveries report better decision-making, lower impulsivity, and greater interpersonal empathy. In education, students who ritualise transitions into study mode through consistent environments—lighting a candle, playing the same instrumental music—retain more and procrastinate less. The nervous system, when given predictability, responds not with laziness but with *capacity.*

The principle is straightforward: when the environment becomes a partner in regulation, the self does not have to do all the heavy lifting. Sensory cues, spatial boundaries, and symbolic artefacts carry part of the burden. They say: *this is a place of restoration. You do not need to perform here.* That message, received consistently, reshapes the body's internal landscape. Not overnight. But reliably.

Ultimately, sacred micro-spaces are not indulgences. They are micro-interventions. In a culture obsessed with scale, they reclaim the small as significant. They honour the reality that nervous systems don't wait for ideal conditions—they respond to what's available. And what's available, when curated wisely, can become sanctuary. One cushion. One scent. One ritual. Repeated enough times to become a promise: *here, you are allowed to be whole.*

Embodied Symbols of Safety

Safety is not just a cognitive concept—it is a *physiological state*. The nervous system does not wait for permission from the thinking mind before initiating its response to perceived threat or refuge. It listens instead to non-verbal signals: the frequency of a voice, the rhythm of a breath, the scent in the air, the softness of light. In a society that overvalues intellectual processing and underappreciates somatic knowing, this fact is quietly revolutionary. Restoration, especially for sensitive individuals, cannot be reasoned into being—it must be *sensed.*

This is where embodied symbols of safety matter. These are not abstract ideas but tangible inputs—olfactory, auditory, tactile, and kinesthetic—that communicate directly with the nervous system: *you can let go now*. When used consistently and intentionally, they form a quiet but potent language. And unlike psychological insight or therapeutic strategies, which often require reflection and time, embodied cues deliver their message instantly. They bypass cognition and land directly in the body's neurobiological circuitry.

Consider scent. The olfactory system has a uniquely direct route to the limbic brain, which governs memory, emotion, and survival responses. This anatomical connection means certain smells—lavender, rose, sandalwood, or even a specific perfume worn by a loved one—can elicit a drop in heart rate, a softening of muscles, a return to breath depth. Scent does not just remind us of calm. *It induces it.* In one study conducted at Wesleyan University, participants who inhaled lavender oil before bedtime showed a significant increase in slow-wave sleep and reported greater morning energy. This isn't placebo; it's chemical signalling.

Sound is equally potent. The human nervous system evolved in an environment where certain acoustic qualities denoted safety: birdsong, soft human vocal tones, slow rhythmic drumming. The vagus nerve, a core component of parasympathetic regulation, responds especially well to prosody—melodic, non-threatening voice patterns. This is why lullabies calm infants and why chanting, toning, or even softly humming can restore adults. These are not spiritual practices by default—they are somatic tools. Tuning into particular frequencies, especially those that mirror the natural rhythm of relaxed breath and heartbeat, can entrain the body back into balance. In polyvagal terms, these auditory inputs shift us from sympathetic mobilisation into ventral vagal connection.

Movement, too, functions as an embodied message. But here we must be precise. Not all movement soothes. For sensitive systems already overstimulated, high-intensity or erratic motion can register as threat. The movement that regulates is often slow, patterned, and rhythmically predictable. Rocking. Swaying. Gentle yoga. Walking at a measured pace without devices. These actions provide proprioceptive feedback that reorients the body in space, communicates containment, and helps re-establish a coherent sense of selfhood. They remind the system: *you have boundaries. You are grounded. You are not being chased.*

This matters deeply in the context of social fatigue. Sensitive individuals are not merely "tired" after prolonged interaction—they are often *disembodied*, unable to access their internal cues or re-establish a coherent somatic baseline. In these states, verbal reassurance is limited in its effect. But a known scent, a particular texture against the skin, or a practiced somatic ritual can act as a doorway back to the body. It is not the complexity of the tool that matters—it is its familiarity and its integration into a consistent pattern of use.

This is why the concept of ritualised sensory tools is more than lifestyle advice. It is a strategy of neural conditioning. When scent, sound, and movement are paired regularly with safety and restoration, they become associative triggers. Over time, the nervous system learns to recognise the tool itself as a cue: *you are no longer under threat.* This is classical conditioning applied therapeutically—not to manipulate, but to restore.

There are cultural precedents for this. Consider the use of bells in monastic traditions, incense in Eastern practices, or rhythmic dance in Indigenous ceremonies. These are not decorative; they are regulatory. They serve to initiate state shifts—not just in individuals, but in collective physiology. They attune groups to shared rhythms and signal entry into a different relational space—one less governed by survival and more open to integration. These ancient tools persist for a reason. The body knows their language.

Modern neuroscience now confirms what these traditions long intuited. Safety is not taught; it is *experienced.* And tools that stimulate the vagus nerve—such as deep diaphragmatic breathing, slow vocalisation, and intentional sensory stimulation—do not simply feel good. They modulate inflammation, increase heart rate variability, enhance digestion, and improve executive function. That is, they repair. Not abstractly, but materially.

But this presents a challenge. In a culture of speed and cognition, embodied tools are often dismissed as indulgent, unscientific, or frivolous. Scented candles. Ambient music. A warm blanket. These are seen as superficial. Yet this perception fails to understand *the level at which restoration happens.* It is not through insight alone that a person comes back from dysregulation. It is through contact—with their body, with sensory constancy, with lived signals that do not lie.

There is also a quiet politics to this. When rest is reduced to luxury, or when sensory tools are commercialised into expensive wellness commodities, the core truth is obscured: *embodied safety is a human need, not a lifestyle preference.* A cup of tea sipped slowly in silence, a five-minute barefoot walk on grass, a particular fabric worn during decompression—these do not require wealth. They require only *permission.* And therein lies the deeper reframe. These tools are not add-ons. They are access points. Their power lies in their reliability and their integration into daily rhythms, not in their novelty or glamour.

For those in caregiving, service, or high-stakes leadership roles, this becomes even more critical. The more others rely on your presence, the more essential it becomes to anchor that presence in physiological regulation. And embodied symbols allow regulation to become portable. A particular essential oil carried during travel. A breath pattern repeated before meetings. A tactile object touched before difficult conversations. These are small interventions with profound nervous system implications.

This is also why rituals fail when reduced to performance. Lighting incense is not enough if the nervous system is still anticipating interruption. Wearing noise-cancelling headphones is ineffective if inner dialogue remains punitive. The tools only work when they are accompanied by *contextual congruence*—when the environment and intention match the message. Otherwise, the body remains guarded. It waits for the other shoe to drop.

Practically, then, the invitation is not to find the 'right' tools but to *build a reliable vocabulary*. Identify which scents consistently signal safety. Track which movements soothe rather than agitate. Notice which sounds soften the edges of vigilance. And most importantly, use them not as escape mechanisms but as signals of presence. These are not ways to check out. They are ways to check in—deeply and non-verbally—with the body's evolving needs.

This is where science and art intersect. The nervous system is precise. But it is also personal. What calms one person may agitate another. Vanilla may be a trauma trigger. Silence may feel oppressive. Bright light may feel exposing, while darkness may breed anxiety. Thus, the process of building one's own sensory toolkit is not formulaic—it is intuitive, experimental, and responsive. It is an act of inner attunement.

And attunement, ultimately, is the point. Not comfort for its own sake, but *coherence*. When the external environment consistently reflects and supports the internal need for regulation, the nervous system no longer has to fight the context. It can relax into it. And when that happens, something remarkable occurs: not just rest, but capacity. Sensory safety does not merely return us to baseline. It allows us to rise from it.

The greatest misunderstanding about embodied tools is that they are crutches. In fact, they are bridges—to the parasympathetic system, to creative flow, to relational attunement. In a hyper-verbal, over-analysing culture, they return us to the place where restoration begins: the body. And it is only from the body—regulated, resourced, and heard—that true clarity, resilience, and presence emerge.

Real-World Case: The Corporate Leader's 5-Minute Reset – How Micro-Rituals Between Meetings Restored Energy Without Sacrificing Ambition

It was a Tuesday afternoon in March when Rajiv Mehta—CEO of a midsize logistics technology firm in London—felt the signs that had become increasingly familiar: a tightening in his chest, a rising mental fog, and a sharp dip in executive clarity. These weren't isolated incidents. They were becoming patterned occurrences, particularly between his 14:00 and 17:00 meetings. No matter how invigorating the morning had started, by mid-afternoon, he was dragging himself through dense cognitive sludge. "I was performing," Rajiv said in retrospect, "but only just. My mind was alert, yet inaccessible. I was in the meeting, but rarely *with* the meeting." He had become a high-functioning ghost in his own calendar.

Rajiv's story is not extraordinary. In high-stakes environments where performance is the baseline, not the reward, executives like him are expected to sprint endlessly through decision-making, strategy, interpersonal politics, and crisis response—often with the emotional availability of a therapist and the stamina of a triathlete. For sensitive leaders in particular—those whose nervous systems are more responsive to environmental input—the cumulative cost of unbroken task-switching and social navigation often leads not to burnout in the traditional sense, but to a kind of strategic disembodiment. Functionality remains, but vitality fades. What Rajiv discovered—and what neuroscience now helps us understand—is that the body's stress-response architecture requires rhythm, not just resilience. And in his case, the key to restoring both clarity and stamina came not from overhauling his schedule, but from inserting a *ritualised pause* into the margins of it.

When Rajiv began experimenting with five-minute "micro-resets" between meetings, he wasn't indulging in wellness theatre. There were no Himalayan salt lamps or ambient playlists curated by lifestyle brands. It was clinical, intentional, and—most importantly—repeatable. He began by structuring a brief sequence triggered immediately after ending each Zoom or in-person meeting: close laptop, stand up, walk five paces away from his desk, stretch arms overhead while inhaling slowly for five seconds, hold for three, and exhale fully while letting his shoulders drop. He would then sit down, place one drop of eucalyptus oil on his wrist (the scent chosen for its ability to rapidly cue a shift in state), and take one full minute to observe his breath—three seconds in, five seconds out—without doing anything else. The entire process took fewer than 300 seconds. But the effects were cumulative.

After just two weeks of daily implementation, Rajiv began noticing that his energy levels no longer nosedived by late afternoon. More remarkably, he reported an uptick in idea fluency and lateral thinking—attributes often compromised when cognitive bandwidth is depleted by sympathetic nervous system dominance. He was, quite literally, rebuilding executive function by creating a predictable pocket of safety in a sea of strategic volatility.

What Rajiv stumbled into—through curiosity, desperation, and a growing interest in behavioural neuroscience—was the application of ritual as a tool for autonomic regulation. Unlike routine, which can become mechanical and cognitively flat, rituals evoke intentionality. They carry symbolic and sensory cues that create neural predictability. For the sensitive nervous system, such predictability is not mere comfort—it is biological *permission* to downshift into the parasympathetic state where regeneration can occur.

The science behind this is increasingly clear. The vagus nerve, often referred to as the body's 'brake pedal,' responds particularly well to cues that signal safety: slow exhalations, rhythmic movement, pleasant scents, and environmental predictability. When these cues are paired consistently with the same actions—such as Rajiv's wrist-scent and breathwork combination—they begin to build what neuropsychologists call "associative pathways." Over time, the nervous system learns that this sequence equals a state shift, reducing latency between stress activation and recovery.

Importantly, the potency of micro-rituals lies not in their length, but in their *contours*. What matters most is that the ritual is:

Predictable: Consistency creates neural efficiency.

Sensory-rich: Tactile, olfactory, auditory, and kinesthetic elements deepen the imprint.

Symbolic: A personal or professional meaning reinforces engagement.

Bounded: It has a clear beginning and end, giving it weight and coherence.

For Rajiv, the scent of eucalyptus came to symbolise a boundary between external demand and internal return. It wasn't just aroma—it became a *signal*, a trigger for a state change.

This reframing—of "ritual" as a biological utility rather than spiritual accessory—holds significant implications for how we think about productivity. The traditional corporate model, which privileges uninterrupted focus and heroic stamina, often assumes that recovery is the reward for performance, not the enabler of it. But what Rajiv's case illustrates, and what an emerging body of research supports, is that recovery must be embedded *within* the performance itself. It must be fractionally distributed, not just retroactively accessed.

Rajiv's transformation wasn't ideological. It didn't involve reducing his ambitions or rebranding himself as a mindful leader. What it *did* involve was the deliberate insertion of structure into transition—something that allowed his nervous system to re-establish coherence before plunging into the next interpersonal or cognitive demand. The ripple effect was tangible. Within three months, he reported not only fewer energy crashes but a noticeable improvement in team dynamics. "I was more present," he said. "And my team noticed."

The implications here extend well beyond corporate settings. Whether one is a clinician, educator, artist, or frontline worker, the capacity to shift state *deliberately*—not just collapse into it—is foundational to sustained presence and performance. Micro-rituals become what polyvagal theorists might call "portable sanctuaries": repeatable, embodied cues that teach the nervous system what safety feels like on demand. They don't require yoga mats or spa settings. They require discernment, discipline, and a recognition that *retreat is not withdrawal—it is recalibration.*

Rajiv's 5-minute reset might seem minor in the scheme of a CEO's weekly schedule. But that is precisely the point. In a culture that idolises grand solutions and sweeping reforms, it is the micro-patterns that often determine macro-stability. The nervous system is not asking for a revolution. It is asking for rhythm. And rhythm, it turns out, can be restored—five minutes at a time.

Chapter 6
The Physiology of Solitude: Healing in Silence and Space

We are quick to assume that solitude descends when connection falters. That silence is nothing more than the acoustics of loneliness. That time on one's own must be justified by output, filled with tasks, or distracted away. These assumptions, though dressed as cultural truths, are distortions—physiological ones, in fact—produced by overexposure to environments that confuse stimulation with aliveness. For those with finely tuned nervous systems, perpetually alert to the smallest shift in tone, volume, or emotional demand, solitude is not a deficiency. It is a necessity. And ignoring it does not leave one neutral—it leaves one biologically impaired.

In today's professional and social landscapes, where rapid response is praised and idleness carries suspicion, solitude often appears as retreat, as stepping back from life. Yet perhaps the opposite is true. Perhaps silence is not abandonment, but a precondition for genuine return. Space and quiet not as luxuries, but as prerequisites.

This chapter argues for a reframing of solitude—not as eccentricity or withdrawal, but as biological requirement. We were not designed for round-the-clock availability. The human brain cannot sustain uninterrupted exchange without consequence. The nervous system, especially in sensitive individuals, requires intervals of refuge—moments when external input ceases, so that repair and integration may occur. A muscle grows not under strain but in its rest phase; in the same way, experience becomes knowledge only when given space to consolidate.

At the centre of this lies a paradox often misunderstood: human beings are profoundly social, yet not endlessly so. Belonging is necessary, but so is disengagement. Our neurological architecture confirms this. The default mode network—the set of brain regions activated when we drift into reflection, memory, or imagination—only comes alive in the absence of external demands. It is here that empathy takes shape, creative leaps emerge, and emotional texture thickens. But this network is fragile, easily switched off by constant attention to screens, notifications, or conversation. A society that celebrates perpetual focus is, knowingly or not, silencing the very architecture that undergirds meaning and imagination.

The implications stretch far. Solitude is not passive idling—it is an active neurological condition, critical for learning, emotional elasticity, and identity formation. For those who feel the world intensely, neglecting solitude results in subtle dysregulations: irritability, shallow breath, foggy thought, reduced nuance in perception. These are often blamed on workload or poor sleep, but just as often, the missing ingredient is structured nothingness—deliberate, protected pockets of emptiness.

Language has not helped our cause. "Solitude" is too easily tangled with "loneliness," "eccentricity," or "failure to belong." But solitude, properly grasped, is not antisocial—it is pre-social. It prepares us to re-enter relationships with depth rather than reactivity. Without it, presence becomes performance, discernment gives way to reactivity, and the nervous system—overrun with unbuffered input—slips into chaos.

So what does healing space in silence actually mean? First, a recognition that solitude and isolation are distinct. The former is chosen, rhythmic, metabolising. The latter is imposed, erratic, corrosive. One reconnects; the other severs. Neuroscience makes the difference plain. Predictable, intentional quiet—away from screens and conversation—triggers parasympathetic activation, a physiological signal of repair. Isolation, by contrast, drives cortisol spikes, inflammation, and immune suppression.

For sensitive individuals, the need is even more urgent. Their systems hold onto stimulation long after others have brushed it off: a sharp word, flickering light, overlapping voices. Solitude allows this residue to dissolve, permitting the nervous system to downshift into calm, restoring subtlety of thought and emotional range. For them, solitude is less a luxury than a stabilising force.

This chapter traces how structured forms of solitude—silent retreats, flotation therapy, immersion in natural landscapes—produce measurable shifts in mood, cognition, and immunity. Yet one needn't seek exotic rituals. Solitude can be woven quietly into daily life: a closed door, headphones that deliver silence rather than sound, a deliberate digital blackout for twenty minutes. These gestures are not withdrawal. They are recalibration.

There is also value in sensory deprivation, paradoxical as that may sound. In float tanks, stripped of sound, light, even tactile sensation, the nervous system is not starved but relieved. Deprivation here is not punishment; it is permission. It grants the body space to process the unprocessed, to release what has been stored but not metabolised.

The chapter closes with a case study: a writer whose burnout stemmed not from lack of time, but from lack of mental space. Her restoration came not in a seminar or clinic, but during a solitary retreat in the Scottish Highlands. There, far from conversation and screens, she encountered something she had not heard in years—her own voice. What may sound poetic was, in fact, neurological: when external input ceased, her internal signal reappeared.

Solitude must be reimagined—not as escape from life, but as the medium through which integration occurs. Healing is not always about cutting back. Sometimes it is about removing the interferences that prevent healing in the first place.

Accordingly, the chapter explores:

– Why the brain's default mode network underpins creativity, empathy, and resilience, and how constant tasking suppresses it
– The physiological costs of uninterrupted stimulation, especially in sensitive people
– The recalibrating role of structured sensory deprivation
– How solitude can shift from perceived threat to biological ally

To crave silence is not weakness; it is memory. It is the nervous system recalling its conditions for strength. The aim is not escape but return: to face the world with perception intact, energy replenished, and nuance restored. Solitude, in this light, is not an absence. It is a form of care—a precise instrument for those who feel deeply. And it begins, not with withdrawal, but with permission.

The Myth of Loneliness – Redefines solitude as a vital nutrient for sensitive minds, not a problem to fix

For centuries, solitude has been mistranslated as a social failing. In today's hyperconnected culture, being alone often signals deficiency: of popularity, of productivity, or of emotional well-being. It is pathologised in subtle and explicit ways, from the pitying tone with which "loner" is uttered, to the wellness industry's fixation on togetherness as the universal salve. Yet for sensitive individuals—those whose nervous systems register and process stimuli more deeply—solitude is not merely a reprieve from social overload. It is a biological and psychological necessity, akin to sleep or hydration. The problem is not solitude itself, but the cultural narrative that treats it as something to be escaped, cured, or apologised for.

The framing of solitude as a problem is historically and psychologically loaded. Post-war psychology and the rise of individualism in the West created a paradox: while autonomy was celebrated, prolonged aloneness was increasingly viewed through a clinical lens, associated with social dysfunction, depression, or narcissism. Yet, this framing ignores a fundamental reality of how complex organisms recover and self-regulate. Just as cells regenerate in the absence of metabolic pressure, the human nervous system recalibrates most effectively in states of stillness, not performance.

This misunderstanding is especially costly for sensitive individuals—teachers, therapists, creatives, strategists, and caregivers—whose capacity to hold complexity and tune into subtle dynamics makes them particularly vulnerable to nervous system depletion. These individuals are often expected to stay "on" in environments that neither recognise nor accommodate the biological cost of constant engagement. The result is not only social fatigue but also a distorted self-perception: if solitude is shameful, then the need for it must be hidden or suppressed. This internalised stigma leads to guilt, overcompensation, and eventually, burnout.

Contrary to dominant assumptions, solitude is not synonymous with loneliness. Loneliness is a form of suffering rooted in disconnection and unmet relational needs. Solitude, when chosen and structured wisely, is generative. It provides space for neural integration, emotional digestion, and the kind of self-reflective processing that cannot occur in the presence of others, however beloved. Emerging neuroscience reinforces this distinction. Functional MRI studies have shown that the brain's default mode network—a constellation of regions linked to self-referential thinking and memory consolidation—is most active when we are alone and undistracted. This network is essential for insight, identity formation, and meaning-making. It requires silence, space, and non-doing—not another Zoom call.

Sensitive minds are often defined not just by emotional depth but by high environmental receptivity. Crowded rooms, conflicting tones, subtle facial micro-expressions—all register with amplified intensity. For such individuals, even benign social interactions may trigger micro-arousals in the autonomic nervous system: slight spikes in heart rate, shifts in cortisol, alterations in respiratory rhythm. These physiological changes compound over time, especially without adequate intervals of restoration. Solitude allows for the downregulation of sympathetic activity, re-engaging the parasympathetic branch responsible for rest, repair, and digestion. What looks like "doing nothing" is, in fact, neurobiological maintenance.

The myth that solitude equals deficiency is also economically reinforced. Productivity culture thrives on the assumption that value is demonstrated through visible engagement: talking, collaborating, networking, performing. Solitude, being invisible, is mistakenly equated with inertia. But there is a quiet cognitive alchemy that occurs when the external world is muted. Artists report their most fertile ideas arrive in silence. Therapists note their deepest insights arise between sessions. Leaders often make their most strategic decisions not in the boardroom, but in early morning walks, solo retreats, or silent commutes. These are not accidental by-products. They are the natural outputs of brains that have been given space to connect dots without interruption.

There is also a gendered and cultural component to how solitude is misinterpreted. Women, particularly those in caregiving or service-oriented roles, are often socialised to place others' needs before their own. Time alone is seen as indulgent, selfish, or a luxury rather than a necessity. In many collectivist cultures, communal engagement is idealised, while withdrawal is viewed with suspicion or concern. These narratives compound the shame that sensitive individuals may feel when they instinctively seek quiet over company. The pressure to perform sociability—even when it compromises internal regulation—is rarely questioned.

To dismantle this myth, we must first reclaim the language around solitude. It is not antisocial to need space. It is not pathological to crave silence. Solitude is not the absence of connection; it is a different mode of connection—one that is inward-facing, slow, and deeply reparative. In the same way that muscles need rest after exertion, the social brain requires intervals of disengagement to reset its regulatory functions. Without these intervals, our empathy becomes blunted, our cognition fogged, and our creativity stifled. Restoring solitude to its rightful place as a health imperative, rather than a social aberration, is essential for sustaining long-term wellbeing.

The practical implications are far-reaching. Organisations that want to retain high-functioning, sensitive professionals must begin designing workflows that honour periods of undisturbed solitude—not just during holidays but integrated into the daily rhythm of work. Educational systems that want to nurture depth and originality must stop conflating participation with performance. And individuals who want to sustain emotional clarity must learn to differentiate between solitude and isolation, and to build structured practices of alone-time that are restorative, not avoidant.

Take the example of Rina, a clinical psychologist in her early forties, whose entire professional life centred on being present for others. After fifteen years of full practice, she began experiencing what she described as a "loss of mental elasticity"—an inability to generate new insight, emotional numbness, and a growing resentment of client sessions. Initially, she interpreted these symptoms as professional failure or emotional fatigue. But after working with a somatically-trained supervisor, Rina began to see that what she lacked wasn't passion or skill, but space. Her calendar was airtight, her home life noisy, and even her vacations filled with social obligations. By carving out three hours each week for structured solitude—free of devices, conversation, or performance—Rina slowly began to feel her intuitive acuity return. The spaciousness restored not only her professional presence but her private joy.

This is not a call for retreat into permanent withdrawal. Human beings are relational creatures. But relational health depends on internal coherence. Sensitive individuals—those who tend to absorb, attune, and metabolise complex social cues—require more frequent and intentional solitude than others. Not because they are weaker, but because they are perceptually more permeable. The cost of ignoring this truth is not just burnout; it is self-alienation. We begin to see our biological needs as flaws to overcome, rather than signals to heed.

The final shift required is philosophical. Solitude is not a tool to be used only in crisis, nor a means to an end. It is a mode of being that reminds us who we are beneath the social mask. When approached with intentionality—supported by structure, rhythm, and self-permission—solitude becomes one of the most powerful instruments for nervous system regulation, creative renewal, and emotional integration. Sensitive people do not need to be more social. They need space to fully return to themselves—and from that wholeness, to engage the world with clarity and strength.

Let us reframe solitude not as a temporary refuge from an overwhelming world, but as a recurring ceremony of return. A practice that sensitive individuals are not merely entitled to, but biologically designed for. Because sometimes, the most intelligent thing a nervous system can do is to be alone. Quietly. Purposefully. And without apology.

The Default Mode Network: Why the Mind Needs Downtime

There is a curious paradox at the heart of human productivity: some of our most significant insights occur not while we are actively solving problems, but when we appear to be doing nothing at all. This is not a poetic assertion—it is a neuroscientific fact. During moments of quiet wakeful rest, when the mind is allowed to wander free from external demands, a particular network within the brain activates. Known as the Default Mode Network (DMN), this circuit is not idle or dormant. Rather, it is engaged in complex, integrative work essential for self-awareness, memory consolidation, creative ideation, and emotional regulation. Understanding how and why the DMN functions—and why it depends on uninterrupted downtime—is not just an academic exercise; it holds profound implications for sensitive individuals whose cognitive ecosystems are easily overloaded by relentless input.

To the untrained eye, someone sitting alone in silence may seem unproductive. In reality, their brain may be conducting some of its most meaningful operations. First identified in the early 2000s through neuroimaging studies, the Default Mode Network comprises interconnected regions including the medial prefrontal cortex, posterior cingulate cortex, and inferior parietal lobule. These areas light up when a person is not focused on the outside world—when they are daydreaming, recalling past events, envisioning the future, or engaging in internal self-talk. Crucially, DMN activity is suppressed during goal-directed tasks, but rebounds robustly during rest, especially in solitude.

This neurological rhythm reflects a broader biological truth: the brain requires alternation between activation and restoration, not simply to prevent burnout, but to support higher-order cognition. Many sensitive people report that after extended social interaction or focused work, they experience a kind of mental static—an inability to think clearly, recall information, or make decisions with ease. What they are describing is not weakness or inefficiency. It is the functional cost of DMN suppression. Without access to downtime, the neural systems responsible for sense-making, identity formation, and meaning-making are deprived of their operational window.

The modern world, unfortunately, is deeply misaligned with this need. Open-plan offices, back-to-back Zoom meetings, social media feeds, and ambient noise have colonised what were once periods of quiet reflection. The effect is a form of cortical crowding. Even when we're alone, constant stimulation prevents the mind from shifting into its default mode. The irony is bitter: in attempting to maximise cognitive output through continuous engagement, we often impair the very systems that make thoughtful engagement possible.

For sensitive individuals—whose nervous systems tend to register and process stimuli more intensely—this disruption is not merely inconvenient; it is corrosive. Without deliberate, protected intervals of rest, the DMN becomes underactive, which has been associated with symptoms such as anxiety, rumination, and cognitive fog. These are not personal failings. They are signs of a system in need of recalibration. Indeed, emerging evidence from neuroimaging studies suggests that individuals who engage regularly in contemplative practices such as meditation, silent walks, or structured solitude show more efficient DMN connectivity. They are not just "relaxing." They are maintaining the infrastructure of a reflective mind.

Consider, for example, a study published in *Nature Reviews Neuroscience*, which found that the DMN is implicated in both autobiographical memory and moral decision-making. What does this mean in practice? That our ability to remember who we are, and to act in alignment with our values, depends on periods when we are not externally distracted. In this light, solitude is not self-indulgent; it is moral maintenance. It allows us to integrate experiences, retrieve insights, and reset our internal compass. In its absence, we become not just overstimulated but disoriented—unanchored from our narrative continuity.

Equally compelling is the link between DMN activity and creativity. Unlike task-positive networks, which are responsible for focused problem-solving, the DMN appears to support associative thinking—the ability to connect disparate ideas in novel ways. This is why so many of our most original thoughts arise in the shower, on a solitary walk, or during idle moments. The brain is not idle. It is exploring, recombining, and incubating possibilities. It cannot do this, however, when perpetually yoked to linear output or external feedback loops. Creativity, in this respect, is less a flash of genius than a function of neural ecology—and rest is its native environment.

There is also a regulatory dimension. The DMN has strong connections with limbic regions that process emotion. When allowed to operate undisturbed, it facilitates emotional integration, helping us make sense of what we feel, rather than merely reacting. This is especially vital for sensitive people who often experience emotional states more vividly and complexly. Downtime enables them to metabolise these feelings, rather than suppressing or becoming overwhelmed by them. Without it, emotional resonance can tip into dysregulation or exhaustion.

This principle is echoed in psychotherapy, where insights rarely arrive during cathartic expression alone, but rather in the reflective space that follows—a space in which the DMN quietly assembles meaning. It is why techniques such as free association in psychoanalysis or unstructured time in narrative therapy remain powerful. They give the brain permission to default—to roam, revisit, and reintegrate without constraint.

None of this implies that focused, goal-directed work is harmful. It is vital. But it must be balanced by intervals of true, undisturbed downtime—not leisure activities that demand attention, but silence and solitude that allow attention to dissolve. The distinction matters. Watching a film or scrolling on a phone may feel restful, but often keeps the brain tethered to external stimuli. By contrast, lying on the floor in silence, journaling without direction, or simply staring out a window can restore access to the brain's default circuitry.

The practical takeaway is deceptively simple: we must architect our days to honour the default mode. For sensitive people, this is not optional. It is foundational. Rather than scheduling recovery as a response to overload, we must integrate rest as a precursor to resilience. Morning stillness before checking a device. Walking without earbuds. A closed door after meetings. These are not indulgences. They are strategies for safeguarding neural function.

In a world that equates busyness with value, choosing downtime can feel radical. But it is a rebellion rooted in biology. When we understand that the brain requires solitude to think clearly, feel coherently, and create meaningfully, we begin to reframe silence as service—not just to ourselves, but to our integrity, creativity, and discernment. The Default Mode Network reminds us that not all progress looks like movement. Sometimes, the mind does its best work in stillness.

The Science of Sensory Deprivation – How Reducing Input Recalibrates the Nervous System

In a world engineered for stimulation, silence has become radical. For the sensitive nervous system, which processes external stimuli with heightened precision, the endless influx of sights, sounds, and digital alerts is not merely distracting—it is biologically draining. Sensory overload is not a metaphor but a measurable state of nervous system agitation, and the antidote is not passive escapism but the strategic reduction of input. Sensory deprivation—once the domain of monastics and fringe experiments—is now emerging as a scientifically grounded method of deep restoration.

The nervous system, when overstimulated, behaves like a fire alarm on a hair trigger. It responds not only to threat but to novelty, brightness, volume, unpredictability, and even subtle interpersonal tension. Over time, the body becomes trapped in a loop of vigilance and reactivity. This is not sustainable. It is not even functional. What the sensitive brain requires is an interval in which the signal-to-noise ratio is dramatically tilted back toward signal. This is where sensory deprivation becomes not a luxury but a neurological imperative.

Historically, we have misunderstood the role of sensory absence. The absence of stimulation has been associated with boredom, deprivation, or psychological discomfort. Yet emerging neuroscience reveals something counterintuitive: when we reduce input, we don't shut down the brain—we free it to restore. When there is less for the senses to process, the brain shifts from defensive alertness to deep integration. It is in this quieter internal state that emotional processing, memory consolidation, and creative recombination flourish. In essence, we stop reacting and begin reorganising.

One of the clearest demonstrations of this comes from studies on floatation tanks. Also known as Restricted Environmental Stimulation Therapy (REST), floatation tanks remove nearly all sensory input: no light, no sound, minimal temperature variation, no tactile distraction. Participants float in a highly salinated solution that renders the body virtually weightless. The result is a neurophysiological shift. Within minutes, heart rate decreases, cortisol drops, and activity in the default mode network—the brain's integrative "rest mode"—rises significantly. Rather than shutting the system down, these sessions allow the nervous system to re-align with a baseline state that is often inaccessible in everyday environments.

The implications of this extend far beyond clinical research. In therapeutic settings, sensory deprivation has been shown to support treatment for anxiety, depression, PTSD, and burnout. But its benefits also extend to healthy, high-functioning individuals operating at cognitive or emotional capacity. Entrepreneurs, creatives, executives, and care professionals have increasingly turned to floatation, silence retreats, and minimalist sanctuaries not as indulgences, but as essential recalibrations.

This is not an abstract psychological phenomenon—it is embodied biology. When sensory input drops, the vagus nerve, which governs parasympathetic tone, is no longer chronically overridden by sympathetic arousal. Blood pressure normalises. Muscular tension releases. The enteric nervous system—often called the second brain—quiets digestive disruption. Sensory deprivation, then, is not merely the cessation of activity. It is the opening of space in which the autonomic system can return to balance. Rest here is not passive. It is deeply active on an invisible level.

Critics sometimes argue that removing stimulation is escapist or impractical. After all, we live in a connected world. Most people cannot disappear into a darkened chamber once a week. But the principle here is not to abandon life—it is to build moments of profound stillness into its fabric. Micro-deprivation is the adaptation. Turning off notifications for an hour. Sitting in an unlit room without music. Walking without a phone. Not as punishment, but as a nervous system offering. These interventions are not just symbolic—they are functional. They allow the limbic system to pause its scanning, and the prefrontal cortex to resume its executive oversight.

Even within traditional healthcare systems, this science is gaining traction. Hospitals and psychiatric wards have begun to experiment with sensory-reduced environments for overstimulated patients—especially those with trauma, autism, or acute anxiety. It turns out that less is not less effective. Less, when precisely applied, can be what allows the nervous system to finally repair itself.

This concept is not new. Ancient wisdom traditions have long understood that silence and sensory reduction are prerequisites for insight. Monastic cells, Zen gardens, desert fasts—all operate on the same physiological truth: that input must fall for inner signals to rise. The modern rebranding of these practices as "wellness" or "biohacking" obscures their more radical insight: the brain, when unburdened, knows how to heal.

But there is a cultural challenge. Sensory deprivation is often framed as uncomfortable, even threatening. Many people, especially in hyperproductive environments, find silence intolerable. This is not because it is harmful—it is because it reveals what distraction suppresses. In the quiet, we meet ourselves. And for those unaccustomed to this, the experience can trigger not peace, but unrest. The key is intentionality. When approached not as void but as nourishment, these moments become tolerable—and then transformative.

Importantly, sensory deprivation is not about disconnection from meaning. It is about allowing the nervous system to distinguish between what is meaningful and what is noise. In a world flooded with signals, this discernment is not intuitive. We must train for it.

We must make space for the system to remember its own rhythms. This cannot be done amidst perpetual input.

We must also consider sensory diversity. What is restorative for one person may be dysregulating for another. Some individuals with trauma histories or neurodivergent wiring may require graduated exposure to quietude, or prefer specific types of sensory reduction—darkness but not silence, solitude but not stillness. The one-size-fits-all model fails here. Effective sensory deprivation is highly individual. The goal is not uniform silence, but optimised input for recalibration.

Ultimately, the nervous system is not designed to operate under siege. Yet this is what modernity demands of it. Screens, schedules, social complexity—each adds cognitive and emotional load. If we never empty the cup, we are guaranteed to overflow. Sensory deprivation is the controlled emptying of the nervous system's inbox. It is a return to perceptual sanity, to equilibrium, to the possibility of resilience.

There is nothing weak or escapist in seeking less stimulation. There is, instead, something fiercely intelligent about it. For sensitive individuals especially, the capacity to pause—to deliberately limit sensory ingress—is not a withdrawal from life, but a re-entry on wiser terms. It is how we turn off the alarm, reset the system, and begin to hear the subtle signals that hyperstimulation drowns out.

We live in an attention economy. The greatest act of self-possession may not be focus, but its prerequisite—absence. The absence of noise. The absence of demand. The absence of needing to respond. And in this cultivated absence, we find what is essential. We restore not only our clarity, but our agency. Sensory deprivation is not an experiment. It is a return to baseline. And in that return lies not escape, but evolution.

Real-World Case: The Solo Retreat That Unlocked Creativity – A Writer's Structured Solitude and Cognitive Renewal

When acclaimed essayist and editor Julia K. locked herself into a weathered cabin on the edge of an unmapped Scottish coastline, she wasn't seeking inspiration—she was seeking silence. For nearly a year, her literary output had slowed to a crawl. Deadlines loomed, yet her paragraphs arrived like strained telegrams—tight, effortful, cautious. Despite decades of professional credibility, she found herself circling the same language patterns, defaulting to formula, writing from habit rather than insight. What was once intuitive had become mechanical. Her editors noticed. So did she. The more she pushed, the less emerged. Creative depletion wasn't a theory—it was a lived state.

Julia's condition, though specific in texture, is not uncommon. Writers, artists, and thinkers often speak of periods of psychic inertia—what's classically called "block," but more precisely understood as an exhaustion of the cognitive and emotional systems that make generative thinking possible. What Julia came to realise, after attempting multiple productivity hacks and content sprints, was that her issue was not output—it was nervous system saturation. The well wasn't dry. It was clouded. What she needed wasn't stimulation. It was subtraction.

Enter the solo retreat. But not a romanticised sabbatical of wine and wordplay. Julia's retreat was strategically designed to create conditions in which her sensory, emotional, and cognitive systems could down-regulate. She chose a remote location not for its aesthetic, but for its absence of cues. No traffic. No emails. No ambient chatter. She brought minimal technology—a notebook, a basic voice recorder, and a printed collection of essays she admired. No Wi-Fi. No screens. No performance metrics. She was not there to produce. She was there to restore signal clarity.

For the first 48 hours, she did almost nothing. Her mind fidgeted. Her thoughts scattered. The absence of noise did not at first bring peace—it amplified the chaos within. But she had anticipated this.

Part of her structure was to expect unease and not flee from it. This distinction is critical: structured solitude is not passive. It is boundary-rich and goal-oriented, but the goal is recalibration, not productivity. Julia walked twice a day along the coastline, ate simple meals, and observed strict digital fasting. Her rituals were sensory-based: steeping tea, lighting a candle at dusk, stretching barefoot. These became somatic anchors, reminding her body that it was no longer in a threat-saturated environment.

By the third day, something shifted. Her thoughts became less fractured. Internal chatter quieted. Words began to emerge—not as tasks, but as insights. She would scribble down phrases mid-walk. Snippets of dialogue arrived unforced. Paragraphs no longer felt like architecture—they flowed like recollection. Importantly, she didn't rush to capture it all. She resisted the impulse to convert insight into output. This is a mistake many high-functioning professionals make: equating clarity with readiness. Julia's structure protected her from this tendency. Creative germination was the aim. Not harvesting.

Her retreat lasted eight days. By the sixth, she had written the opening section of a new manuscript—not because she had to, but because it insisted on being written. The tone was different: less defensive, more porous. It was writing not for approval, but from coherence. Upon returning to her London flat, she reported sleeping better, speaking slower, and thinking with more vertical depth. Her writing rhythm had not only resumed—it had evolved.

So, what precisely was happening during Julia's retreat? From a neurophysiological perspective, several mechanisms were at play. First, the dramatic reduction in sensory and cognitive input allowed her amygdala to down-regulate. With fewer environmental triggers to scan for, the limbic system ceased its default vigilance, allowing prefrontal regions associated with executive function and abstract thought to reassert dominance. This shift is crucial for creativity, which requires both divergent thinking (idea generation) and convergent thinking (refinement and synthesis). When the nervous system is locked in survival mode, it defaults to binary logic. Nuance—the soul of creative work—cannot surface under cortisol siege.

Second, her structured solitude reactivated her Default Mode Network (DMN), the constellation of brain regions that becomes active when the mind is at rest. This network is essential for introspection, memory integration, and spontaneous imagination. It thrives not during active tasks, but in liminal space—walking, showering, gazing out of windows. Julia's daily walks and unscripted afternoons were not filler—they were essential periods of neurocognitive composting. Her brain wasn't idle; it was synthesising, patterning, resolving.

Third, the absence of external validation loops (no social media, no audience feedback, no analytics) freed her creative system from performative orientation. Instead of crafting sentences to impress, she began responding to internal cues—what felt true, rather than what sounded polished. This is a critical but often overlooked dynamic: *authentic creative voice is born not from output goals, but from internal coherence*. When that inner alignment is inaccessible, no amount of skill will substitute.

Julia's case also challenges dominant cultural narratives around productivity. In most high-performance industries, time alone is seen as inefficiency, and withdrawal as weakness. But the data tells a different story. Solitude, when structured with care and intention, becomes a crucible for recalibration. It is not escapism. It is optimisation. Julia's retreat did not diminish her ambition—it refined it. Her calendar, post-retreat, became more discerning. She reported saying "no" more easily. She became less interested in professional busyness and more committed to impact. Her solitude clarified not only her creative work, but the kind of life that work required.

This case also invites reflection on a broader societal problem: the collapse of spaces for thinking without reacting. Open office plans, algorithmic timelines, notification culture—all fragment attention and shorten the arc of thought. For sensitive creatives, the effects are especially acute. Structured solitude is not a luxury in such contexts. It is a countermeasure.

It is also scalable. Not everyone can disappear to the coast for eight days. But the principles can be adapted. Half-day digital fasts. Silent mornings. Walks without headphones. Designated no-output periods. The point is not replication, but integration. Julia's model is not prescriptive—it is illustrative. What matters is not the format, but the intention: to reclaim the inner space from which originality arises.

Critically, structured solitude is not about isolation. It is about differentiation. The difference between noise and signal. Between performance and truth. Between reaction and response. Julia's retreat worked because it was designed not to avoid her work, but to rediscover the context in which her work becomes possible.

In a professional landscape that rewards consistency, her experience reminds us that consistency without renewal becomes repetition. And repetition, over time, hollows craft into output. Structured solitude interrupts this erosion. It reconnects the thinker with the origin point of their ideas—not the algorithms, not the market, but the deep inner coordinates of curiosity, care, and coherence.

Julia did not return from retreat with a bestseller in hand. She returned with something rarer: her voice, unclouded. And that is the truest metric of creative success. Not audience size, not output speed, but the felt sense of alignment between what one creates and what one knows to be real. Her solo retreat was not a break. It was a re-entry—on wiser terms.

Chapter 7
The Five Pillars of Retreat Design

Despite the cultural fascination with rest, renewal, and all things "wellness," most people remain at a loss when it comes to structuring retreat in any meaningful sense. We speak often of taking breaks, practising self-care, or switching off, but such language barely scratches the surface of what an overworked nervous system truly requires. For those with finely tuned sensitivities—whether to sound, subtle shifts in social atmosphere, or the ebb and flow of inner states—generic advice is not only inadequate, it risks being counterproductive. Modern life, with its peculiar blend of overstimulation and disembodiment, has trained us to misread exhaustion as ambition, to confuse convenience with nourishment, and to label distraction as connection. What is missing—and what this chapter proposes—is not another vague prescription but an architecture for deep restoration: a design informed by neuroscience, somatic intelligence, and practical frameworks, where solitude, rhythm, and embodied awareness converge.

Retreat, in this sense, is not an escape hatch. It is precision work. A carefully considered configuration of time, environment, and sensory experience that allows for repair, integration, and the return of inner coherence. The model outlined here rests on five interlocking pillars—rhythm, containment, sensory literacy, movement, and integration. These are not theoretical ornaments but essential domains of regulation, each addressing a particular demand of the nervous system under pressure. When combined thoughtfully, they transform rest from a casual pause into a strategic mode of renewal.

Rhythm comes first, for obvious reasons. Every living system is rhythmic at its core—circadian patterns, ultradian cycles, the rise and fall of hormones. Yet modern life persistently overrides these patterns: screens that extend the day, emails that fracture ultradian rest, a culture that disregards the body's oscillations in favour of unbroken output. Re-establishing rhythm is less about scheduling than it is about listening. Where does your energy dip? At what times does focus naturally sharpen or scatter? When does the body ask to contract, and when does it crave release? To honour such signals is to reintroduce reality into one's sense of time. This, arguably, is the first act of retreat.

Containment follows. Without boundaries, rest dissolves. One sits down to "switch off," but the phone is within reach, or the laptop still open, and retreat quickly becomes indistinguishable from routine. Containment doesn't mean severity or asceticism—it means signalling, to oneself and to the nervous system, that this moment is of a different order. A candle lit before journalling, a shawl wrapped at the start of meditation, a closed door marking a shift in roles: these are cues that communicate safety and closure to the limbic brain. Psychologists call it contextual framing; the body experiences it as relief. Even a small ritual boundary can make stillness inhabitable.

The third pillar—sensory literacy—deserves more attention than it usually gets. We tend to treat the senses as aesthetic ornaments, when in fact they are the primary language of the nervous system. Modern environments, with their fluorescent hums and synthetic odours, bombard rather than soothe. By learning to read sensation with more discernment—the scratch of fabric, the resonance of sound, the weight of a blanket—we begin to curate experience not for style, but for nervous system tone. This is not indulgence. It is stewardship. To design sensory retreats, whether in a single corner of a room or in a larger sanctuary, is to give the body a vocabulary of safety it can trust.

Movement, the fourth pillar, is too often reduced to exercise metrics. Retreat requires something different: somatic reset. Practices such as restorative yoga, vagal toning, gentle rocking, or lymphatic stimulation work not by pushing limits but by signalling that the stress cycle is complete. They restore proprioception and invite the nervous system back into regulation. For sensitive individuals in particular, high-intensity exercise can act less as release and more as another form of strain. The goal here is not to burn, but to soften—to move in ways that speak directly to the body's need for reassurance.

And then there is integration, the final and most easily overlooked principle. Many people leave retreats refreshed, only to collapse back into patterns within days. Without a transition strategy, clarity evaporates. Integration is about preserving gains: tapering re-entry into social demands, setting boundaries to protect renewed energy, carrying fragments of ritual into ordinary life. It ensures that retreat is not episodic theatre, but an ongoing, functional practice.

These pillars are not meant to be sequential steps. They are design principles, interdependent and flexible. One person may discover rhythm through movement; another may begin with sensory shifts and find containment arising naturally. The strength of this framework lies precisely in its adaptability—it meets the diversity of nervous systems, cultures, and contexts without prescribing a single template.

Throughout the chapter, you will encounter examples that anchor the theory: a musician pacing her creative output according to seasonal cycles; a trauma therapist using containment rituals between sessions; a sensory architect reshaping his workspace to fend off burnout; an executive who discovered that twenty minutes of vagal toning steadied him before high-stakes negotiations. Each demonstrates retreat not as withdrawal, but as a deliberate design for presence.

There is no romance here of vanishing from life. Retreat, properly designed, is not about abandoning complexity but preparing to meet it with steadiness. In a time when novelty, noise, and demand press on every side, the ability to pause with intention, restore with precision, and return with coherence is more than self-care. It is a kind of leadership.

This, then, is the invitation: to architect your own restoration—not as a panicked response to collapse, but as a conscious investment in adaptability, clarity, and vitality. The mind may be assaulted daily, but it is not irreparable. Given the right design, it knows exactly how to recover.

Rhythm: Syncing with Biological Cycles

The modern calendar is a blunt instrument when it comes to managing the human nervous system. Most schedules are mechanical, transactional, and relentlessly linear. But biology is cyclical. It pulses, surges, pauses, and renews in patterns far older and wiser than digital alerts or weekly planners. Beneath the static of deadlines and artificial urgency lies a body tuned by evolution to rhythms of light and dark, wake and sleep, action and recovery. The dissonance between our internal clocks and external pressures is not just inconvenient—it is costly, measurable, and increasingly untenable. For sensitive individuals, who register overstimulation more acutely, alignment with personal rhythm isn't a luxury. It's a biological imperative.

There is no one-size-fits-all restorative schedule. Some bodies thrive on brief, frequent respites. Others respond best to immersive withdrawal followed by intense bursts of output. Yet regardless of variation, the nervous system relies on rhythmicity to predict safety. In neurobiological terms, safety is not an abstract state—it's an ongoing calculation, shaped by predictability and co-regulation. When the body recognises a rhythm, it relaxes its vigilance. When it loses that rhythm, it moves toward dysregulation, often without conscious awareness. The mistake is thinking that rest is something you earn or must squeeze in. The deeper truth is that rest must be built in—cyclically, intelligently, and in synchrony with your own physiology.

Consider the example of circadian rhythm—the most widely understood biological cycle. Governed by the suprachiasmatic nucleus in the brain, the circadian system regulates sleep, temperature, hormone production, and immune function. Disrupting this rhythm, even slightly, can impair memory, mood stability, metabolic efficiency, and emotional resilience. But circadian disruption is only one layer. Ultradian rhythms—those shorter-than-a-day cycles—regulate our need for breaks every 90–120 minutes. And infradian rhythms, like the menstrual cycle, modulate energy, mood, and inflammation across longer timelines. These patterns are not inconveniences to overcome; they are instructional blueprints for how we restore.

Restorative rhythm is not simply about timing; it is about design. For instance, a professional might unknowingly sabotage their nervous system by cramming all their recovery into a Sunday evening, then launching headlong into a week of depletion. Meanwhile, another individual might craft subtle rituals throughout the day—pauses for breathing, natural light exposure, or silence—which accumulate to sustain vitality. The difference isn't time spent, but how time is structured. *Intentional micro-patterning creates neurophysiological predictability*, which supports both psychological safety and cognitive efficiency.

Cultural narratives often reward those who "push through"—who override their body's signals in favour of external obligations. But this model, while briefly productive, is neurologically unsustainable. Burnout is not a moral failing or a matter of weak will. It is the body's final attempt to enforce rhythm after it has been ignored. Research from Stanford, Harvard, and the University of Helsinki consistently shows that chronic stress and overstimulation without sufficient rhythmic recovery are predictive of neurodegenerative risk, decision fatigue, emotional volatility, and even premature aging. The costs of ignoring one's biological rhythm are not philosophical—they are physiological, economic, and relational.

For sensitive minds in particular—those with heightened sensory processing, empathic intensity, or finely-tuned attention—rhythmic alignment offers not just restoration but amplification. When the nervous system trusts that recovery is imminent, it allows full engagement in periods of effort. This is not laziness disguised as self-care. It is *strategic oscillation*, a way of leveraging both activation and restoration to optimise function. A violin string cannot produce resonance if it is always taut. It needs release to maintain tone.

The industrialised world, with its obsession with output and optimisation, treats rest as an afterthought. But even peak performance frameworks—from elite athletics to military recovery protocols—are now designed around rhythmic cycles. The U.S. Navy SEALs, for example, incorporate rhythmic stress exposure and recovery phases into training to prevent dysregulation. Tech entrepreneurs are engineering work-rest intervals based on heart-rate variability data to avoid cognitive depletion. This is not sentimentalism—it's science-backed efficiency through biological literacy.

Yet understanding one's personal rhythm requires more than data. It demands attunement. Sensitive individuals are often told they are "too much" or "too fragile" for conventional demands. But what if sensitivity is simply accurate signal detection? What if their apparent fragility is actually an evolved capacity to detect when rhythm is off—when the system is approaching unsustainable patterns? Reframed this way, sensitivity becomes a guide, not a liability. A sensitive nervous system is often the first to register the costs of pushing too far, and the first to benefit from intelligent rhythmic recalibration.

Practical application begins with observation. When do you feel most alert? Most creative? Most exhausted? When is your emotional bandwidth highest, and when does it decline? Rather than fighting your patterns, begin studying them. Tools such as heart rate variability monitors, sleep tracking, and journaling can offer clues, but intuitive noticing is equally valid. Ask: what is the rhythm of my mornings? My week? My month? What restorative cadences are missing? What signals have I been overriding? *Self-regulation begins with self-awareness, and awareness begins with pattern recognition.*

Rhythm also plays a role in collective settings. Organisations and teams often fail not from lack of skill but from misaligned pacing. Meetings scheduled during collective energy dips yield poor outcomes. Creative sessions held at times of peak fatigue result in burnout disguised as innovation. Wise leadership integrates rhythm into team design: alternating intense collaborative work with protected deep-focus time; encouraging true disengagement rather than performative breaks. Leaders who design around human cycles unlock not just resilience, but sustainable brilliance.

Seasonality is another overlooked dimension. Humans are not static; we are seasonal beings. Energy ebbs in winter, surges in spring, consolidates in summer, and slows in autumn. This is not poetry—it's biology. Yet most systems expect a flatline of performance year-round. Sensitive minds often feel disoriented not because they are unstable, but because they are attuned to cycles their environments refuse to honour. Acknowledging seasonal needs—whether through adjusted workloads, solo retreats, or intentional slow periods—is not indulgent. It is essential.

Ritualising rhythm creates anchors in time that stabilise the nervous system. Whether it's a morning light exposure ritual, a weekly screen-free sabbath, or a quarterly silent retreat, these patterns inform the body that safety is predictable. This predictability is not restriction; it is containment. And containment creates freedom. *The paradox is that the more securely our rest is patterned, the more confidently we can extend ourselves when it matters most.*

Ultimately, retreat is not an escape from rhythm. It is a re-immersion in it. The goal is not to avoid effort or disengage from challenge, but to build a life scaffolded by cycles that restore what activation expends. When rest is no longer reactive but rhythmic—baked into the structure of days, weeks, and seasons—sensitive minds don't just survive. They sharpen, stabilise, and rise. And in doing so, they model a form of vitality that is neither frenetic nor fragile, but deeply, intelligently human.

Containment: Creating Ritual Boundaries – Establishing Psychological Containers That Optimise Rest

Among the most overlooked factors in designing restorative experiences is not time or technique, but containment. Not containment in the punitive sense, but as a psychological architecture—a protective, bounded space that tells the nervous system, *"You are safe now. You can let go."* In a world where overstimulation has become ambient and porous boundaries are culturally normalised, the absence of clear psychological containers can render even well-intentioned rest ineffective. A quiet room alone is not sufficient. The nervous system doesn't recalibrate merely through silence; it recalibrates when it perceives that nothing more is expected of it. That shift—from vigilance to surrender—is what containment enables. It is not an aesthetic flourish; it is foundational to recovery.

Containment can be conceptualised as a deliberate, sensory, and temporal frame that signals permission to pause. This is especially crucial for sensitive individuals whose attention is hyper-attuned to subtle social cues, potential obligations, or internalised narratives of productivity. Without a clear start and end to rest, many find themselves oscillating between guilt and hyperarousal, never fully letting down. The brain, lacking markers of safety, stays online—scanning, planning, rehearsing. Containment corrects this by acting as a perceptual gate: it communicates, *"This is different. This is held. This has boundaries."* When boundaries are clarified, rest can deepen. And when rest deepens, healing accelerates.

To understand the neuroscience behind this, it helps to consider the role of the amygdala—an almond-shaped structure responsible for threat detection. When a person enters a space that lacks clear signals of containment, the amygdala continues to monitor for cues of potential disruption. But when sensory cues—like consistent lighting, closed doors, warm textures, or familiar scents—are combined with structured time limits and intentional framing, the brain receives a coherent message: *"You are in a bounded environment where nothing will be asked of you. There is no need to prepare."* This message dampens sympathetic arousal and facilitates parasympathetic activation, especially when the transition into the container is ritualised.

Ritualisation is key. Containment becomes neurologically effective when it is repeated, predictable, and sensory-specific. For instance, lighting a particular candle, donning soft garments reserved only for rest periods, or playing a designated soundscape before beginning a reflective practice tells the nervous system what's about to occur. These signals serve as neurological cues—bridges between intention and biology. With time, they acquire symbolic weight: striking a match becomes more than a fire source; it becomes an embodied declaration of pause. And declarations, when trusted by the nervous system, are potent.

Importantly, containment is not synonymous with isolation. Nor does it require silence. A psychological container can exist within a bustling household or in a shared workplace if the cues are respected. Consider the example of a therapist who places a small stone figurine on her desk to indicate she is in a ten-minute reset. Her colleagues understand this as a non-verbal boundary. Over time, this signal becomes self-enforcing. Or the artist who begins each morning with five minutes in a sunlit corner of her flat, marked by a cup of green tea and the same three piano notes playing through headphones. These are not habits; they are boundaries with symbolic and somatic impact. They function because they communicate: *"This is a space with rules. I am not available in the usual way."* Even short but clearly defined boundaries can shift the physiology of access—when others step back, the self can step in.

There is also a relational dimension to containment. In communal or co-living environments, the integrity of one's psychological container often depends on shared understanding. This makes communication essential—not just as a courtesy, but as a co-creator of safety. Saying, "I'll be off-grid for an hour," or "I'll be resting with my phone off until 10," sets expectations and reduces internal anticipatory tension. Sensitive individuals, in particular, are vulnerable to the emotional noise of unspoken obligations. The mind keeps spinning not because it resists rest, but because it fears misstepping. Social clarity allows the nervous system to step away without guilt. Thus, containment is not just built with objects or routines; it is built with honest communication that reduces uncertainty.

But even among those who understand its value, containment is often resisted for one subtle reason: it demands a boundary with the outer world *and* with one's own inner compulsion to stay productive. Declaring a psychological boundary requires courage. It confronts internalised cultural scripts that associate boundaries with selfishness or laziness. It says, *"I am worth protecting, even from my own drive."* For many, this is where containment becomes a transformative practice. It is not merely a design principle; it is a reclamation of autonomy over one's attention, one's energy, and ultimately, one's healing.

Some may argue that fluid, spontaneous rest is more 'natural' than structured containment. But this view overlooks the way modern life has eroded the natural rhythm of pause. When inputs are constant and interruptions are endemic, the human nervous system is not merely stressed—it is *confused*. And confusion is a barrier to repair.

Containment doesn't impose order on rest; it *clarifies* it. It creates coherence. In an incoherent world, coherence is not a luxury. It is a biological requirement for restoration.

Consider the impact of containment through the lens of trauma-informed practice. For individuals with a history of dysregulation—whether from chronic stress, environmental chaos, or attachment disruptions—containers offer reparative experience. The brain learns safety not through logic, but through repeated, felt experiences of boundary and return. Creating a ritualised rest space, even for ten minutes, can begin to rebuild that trust. And trust is what allows the default mode network to activate, glymphatic cleansing to deepen, and neuroplasticity to take root.

Containment can be scaled. What works for a single moment can also work across time. One might designate Fridays after 6 PM as a sacred no-input period. Or design a monthly ritual of reflective solitude, preceded by the same set of cues each time. Over months, these become self-anchoring. The body recognises them before the mind even catches up. The ritual container becomes a place you step into—sometimes physically, sometimes only perceptually—and the nervous system follows.

To operationalise this principle, one must ask: *What signals safety to my body?* Not what looks restful, but what feels held. Is it dim light or natural light? Is it closed doors or open air? What textures soothe, what sounds disrupt? When do I feel least observed, least obligated? The answers to these questions become your design blueprint. From there, containment is not built once, but iteratively refined. It is an adaptive sanctuary—not static, but dependable.

Ultimately, containment is the hidden architecture behind effective restoration. It tells the nervous system where rest begins and where it ends. It gives permission not only to stop, but to stop without fear. In doing so, it offers something increasingly rare: *the ability to be fully present with oneself, without demand or distraction.* In a culture of blurred lines and open tabs, that is not a soft skill. It is a foundational intervention.

Sensory Literacy: Designing Retreat Aesthetics

We vastly underestimate the intelligence of our senses. While modern culture prizes cognitive prowess, emotional intelligence, and even somatic awareness, sensory literacy—our capacity to discern, select, and shape the sensory inputs that influence our inner states—remains largely untapped. Yet for sensitive minds, sensory environments are not neutral backdrops; they are active participants in mood, focus, rest, and vitality. The aesthetic context of a retreat—its light, texture, temperature, acoustics, scent, and spatial arrangement—can either soothe the nervous system or subtly keep it in a defensive crouch. The quality of restoration is not just a matter of whether one rests, but *how* the space supports the body in recognising that rest is allowed, safe, and beneficial.

To understand this, we must first shed the notion of aesthetics as decoration or indulgence. Sensory inputs are physiological signals, not frills. The human nervous system evolved to interpret safety or threat not just from overt dangers, but from the ambient qualities of space. A room filled with harsh lighting, unpredictable noise, or cluttered visual fields can trigger subtle vigilance. By contrast, environments with consistent patterns, muted textures, and gentle sensory gradients can cue the parasympathetic system into activation—sending the implicit message that restoration is safe. *Aesthetic coherence is not cosmetic; it is neurobiological.*

Consider the research on the "soft fascination" effect in environmental psychology. Naturalistic scenes—running water, dappled light, birdsong—engage the senses without overwhelming them, allowing for gentle attention that promotes cognitive replenishment. This is why walks in nature feel so distinctly restorative: they create the right kind of sensory stimulus—not dead silence, but calibrated input. Similarly, studies in healthcare design reveal that patients recover faster, require less pain medication, and report higher well-being when their rooms include access to natural light, views of green space, and thoughtfully selected artwork. These are not luxury details; they are evidence-based strategies for accelerating restoration.

The same logic applies to retreat environments, even on the micro scale. What many sensitive individuals need is not escapism, but a sensory field that does not provoke internal resistance. This might be achieved through soft fabrics that cradle the skin without itch or pressure, scent profiles that cue safety (such as lavender, cedarwood, or chamomile), and ambient soundscapes that mute sudden intrusions. Importantly, *designing for sensitivity is not the same as designing for silence.* For many, total quiet becomes a vacuum that amplifies internal noise. What restores is often a symphony of small consistencies: a flickering candle, a rhythmic fountain, the gentle creak of wood underfoot.

Yet sensory literacy also involves knowing what to *exclude.* Sensory overload is not always loud; it can be cumulative. A retreat setting cluttered with visual distractions or mixed-purpose functions (work desk, dining area, meditation mat) may send mixed signals to the nervous system. Creating clarity in spatial function—this corner is for rest, that surface is for creative play—helps the body anticipate what kind of state to prepare for. *Boundaries are not just behavioural; they are spatial cues encoded in layout and design.*

Sensory literacy also challenges the modern overreliance on visual dominance. In many environments, visual aesthetics are over-optimised while other senses are neglected or even irritated. Take scent: often used reactively to mask odours or add artificial freshness, it rarely receives the nuanced attention it deserves. Yet olfactory inputs are wired directly into the limbic system—bypassing the thalamus and reaching emotion centres without linguistic mediation. Scents can ground, rouse, comfort, or destabilise with extraordinary efficiency. The question is not whether your retreat space *smells nice*, but whether it smells *coherent* with the restoration it intends to support.

Similarly, sound has often been treated either as noise to cancel or music to add. But there is an in-between category that is critically valuable: *auditory predictability.* Gentle loops of ambient sounds, recordings of rain or wind, or even the rustle of leaves outside a window—all of these offer rhythmic continuity that aids nervous system downregulation. What matters is not silence per se, but whether auditory cues are *safe, consistent, and low in cognitive demand.*

Tactile input, too, should be consciously curated. How many retreat centres or personal sanctuaries have exquisitely arranged visual aesthetics, but offer scratchy bedding or awkward seating? For sensitive individuals, this is not trivial. The skin is the largest sensory organ and a primary interface between body and environment. Weighted blankets, soft organic fibres, and supportive textures are not indulgences—they are signals of containment, of the body being held.

Temperature and airflow also merit greater attention. An environment that is too cold or stuffy can subtly prevent full parasympathetic activation. Sensory literacy means tuning not just to what one sees, hears, or smells—but what the body feels as presence or absence of ease. Does the space invite a sigh? Does it let the muscles soften? These questions matter more than stylistic coherence or design trend.

Crucially, sensory literacy must also be personal. There is no universally "calming" scent, sound, or surface. What soothes one person might agitate another. One person's sense of sanctuary may involve rich textures and dim light; another may need crisp whites and morning sun. Sensory literacy is not about copying someone else's ideal—it is about becoming fluent in your own body's response patterns. *Restoration happens when space meets preference with precision.*

For this reason, the process of designing retreat aesthetics should involve experimentation and iteration. Spend a few minutes in a space and notice: How does your body feel after ten minutes? Has your breath deepened? Has your internal monologue softened? Are you distracted or drawn inward? These are not mood check-ins—they are diagnostic signals of sensory alignment or mismatch.

As the science of psychophysiology evolves, we are beginning to see how dramatically the environment can modulate stress, inflammation, sleep quality, and even immune response. The implication for retreat design is profound: sensory curation is not ornamental. It is foundational. When done skilfully, it allows the nervous system to enter a state it cannot will itself into through mindset or effort alone. *Design becomes a form of care.*

This is not to suggest that aesthetic perfection is required for restoration. Quite the opposite. The goal is not sterile minimalism or monastic deprivation, but intentional coherence. Spaces that reflect thoughtful arrangement and respect for sensory nuance—whether in a remote cabin, a city flat, or a five-minute reset corner in a workplace—can function as sanctuaries for recalibration.

In the context of a structured retreat, sensory design becomes the silent facilitator of transformation. It doesn't command attention, but it changes what is possible. Like a skilled stagehand, it sets the conditions for the main act—whether that act is rest, reflection, grief, or creativity—to unfold without interference. And for sensitive minds, these conditions are not just helpful. They are essential.

Movement: Somatic Reset Practices – Introducing Gentle, Science-Backed Movements for Recalibrating the Nervous System

There is a quiet intelligence embedded in the body that often outpaces the mind in sensing safety, signalling exhaustion, or seeking equilibrium. For those attuned to this intelligence—particularly sensitive individuals—the body becomes more than a vessel; it becomes an instrument of insight. And yet, in a culture that often privileges cognitive productivity over embodied wisdom, the subtle power of movement as a nervous system intervention is frequently overlooked. Not all movement is created equal. While high-intensity workouts and achievement-driven exercise regimens dominate mainstream wellness narratives, the somatic realm speaks in gentler, more deliberate tones. It is here, in the terrain of slow, intentional movement, that we find a profoundly underutilised tool for restoring balance, processing stress, and regulating emotional energy.

Somatic movement is not about burning calories or building muscle. It is about tuning into one's internal state—using physical motion to send safety signals to the brain and recalibrate the autonomic nervous system. This subchapter explores the compelling evidence behind why certain types of movement—grounded in sensory awareness, breath synchronisation, and rhythmic repetition—hold particular promise for those prone to overstimulation, burnout, or emotional fatigue.

Central to this conversation is the concept of interoception: the body's ability to sense its own internal signals. When individuals engage in mindful movement practices—such as Feldenkrais, Alexander Technique, or trauma-informed yoga—they amplify their interoceptive awareness, which in turn enhances their ability to detect and respond to subtle shifts in physiological state. From a neurobiological standpoint, this matters deeply. Interoception is tied to the insular cortex, a brain region integral to emotional regulation, decision-making, and self-awareness. By engaging in gentle, patterned movement, the nervous system is effectively given a structured opportunity to assess, digest, and modulate stored stress signals.

What makes these practices so powerful is their capacity to regulate the balance between the sympathetic and parasympathetic branches of the autonomic nervous system. During states of chronic stress or social exhaustion, individuals may find themselves trapped in sympathetic overdrive—racing thoughts, shallow breathing, and an inability to switch off. Somatic reset practices disrupt this loop by activating the vagus nerve, a central highway of parasympathetic function. This activation isn't hypothetical—it is observable, measurable, and increasingly well-documented. Heart rate variability (HRV), a key biomarker of autonomic health, tends to improve significantly after even brief exposure to slow, mindful movement. And unlike pharmacological interventions, these practices carry no side effects, no dependency risk, and offer cumulative benefit over time.

To ground this in lived experience, consider the case of a senior physician who, after two years on the pandemic frontlines, began integrating a ten-minute sequence of breath-led spinal spirals before entering clinical rounds. The result wasn't merely physical relief—it was a softening of his affect, a restoration of emotional bandwidth, and, according to his team, a noticeable shift in his ability to connect with patients. Another example: a high-performing executive who, rather than joining the 5am bootcamp culture of her peers, committed to a twice-weekly somatic micro-practice focused on pelvic stability and diaphragmatic breath. After three months, she reported not only reduced anxiety but a newfound sense of embodied presence during negotiations—her nervous system no longer registering boardroom tension as existential threat.

Critically, these practices are not prescriptive; they are invitational. What regulates one person may overwhelm another, which is why the cornerstone of somatic design must be personalisation. This is where the distinction between exercise and ritualised movement becomes crucial. In exercise, the aim is often external: output, appearance, measurable progress. In somatic reset, the aim is internal: integration, recalibration, re-entry into one's own skin. This inward orientation does not signify weakness or withdrawal—it is the very mechanism by which nervous system resilience is built. *It is not the stressor alone that determines resilience; it is the organism's capacity to discharge, reorganise, and emerge with coherence intact.*

This insight aligns with research in neuroplasticity and trauma recovery. For the nervous system to consolidate new patterns of safety and adaptability, it must be given non-verbal, bottom-up signals that it is safe to relax, safe to feel, safe to be. Movement is uniquely equipped to deliver such signals. When performed with rhythmic consistency and contextual meaning, even simple gestures—a gentle sway, a shoulder roll, a full-body yawn—can serve as gateways to parasympathetic dominance. These are not trivial motions. In somatic psychology, they are micro-acts of self-liberation, permissions granted at the tissue level that one is no longer under threat.

The role of environment cannot be overstated. Movement done in fluorescent-lit gyms or amid digital overstimulation may fail to achieve its regulatory potential. By contrast, movement rituals embedded in calming, sensory-aware environments—spaces with natural light, soothing textures, grounding scents—enhance the effectiveness of the practice tenfold. *The body senses its context before the mind can interpret it.* Therefore, the creation of sanctuary is a prerequisite for somatic reset. It is not just the movement that matters, but the field in which it unfolds.

From a design perspective, movement should be structured in cycles—preparatory, active, and integrative phases. Beginning with grounding (such as a body scan or gentle joint mobilisation), progressing through dynamic flow (like rocking, circling, or spiralling patterns), and ending with stillness or breath-based integration ensures that the nervous system is not merely activated but metabolically completed. This cyclical arc respects the nervous system's need not just for stimulation, but for closure.

In cultural terms, we are only just beginning to reclaim movement as medicine. Much of Western society remains conditioned to equate movement with performance. But in indigenous, ancestral, and Eastern traditions, movement has long served a psycho-spiritual role: a way to restore balance, express emotion, and commune with one's deeper rhythms. When modern science meets these ancient insights, the result is not mysticism—it is a recalibration of our assumptions. Sensitivity is not fragility; it is the capacity to register fine-tuned information. Somatic reset practices honour this sensitivity, offering it a channel through which it can express and resolve.

As this chapter continues, the reader will be guided through accessible, evidence-informed practices that require no expensive equipment or formal instruction. What they do require is attention—both to one's internal landscape and to the subtle cues the body offers when it is ready to move, ready to pause, or ready to restore. In this way, somatic movement becomes not a luxury, but a necessity. For the sensitive system, movement is not merely what we do. *It is how we return to ourselves.*

Integration: Re-Entry Without Collapse

It is not retreat that challenges the modern professional—it is the return. For individuals who have carved out a pocket of stillness in an otherwise overstimulating world, the act of re-entering daily life can trigger a subtle yet significant threat response. The nervous system, having downshifted into a parasympathetic state during structured solitude, is asked to rapidly upregulate—often without preparation or support. The result is not dramatic breakdown but a quiet misalignment: emotional volatility, cognitive fatigue, social reactivity, and somatic disorientation. This is the paradox of well-being in high-functioning adults. We teach ourselves how to pause, but we rarely learn how to resume with integrity. Integration, then, is not an afterthought. It is the final—and perhaps most critical—pillar of retreat design.

What makes reintegration challenging is not merely the intensity of external demands but the fragility of newly formed internal conditions. During a retreat—whether it spans a weekend or three weeks—the nervous system recalibrates its thresholds. Cortisol levels drop. Sensory filters relax. Internal narratives become more coherent. This is not simply psychological benefit but neurological reconditioning. Without careful scaffolding, this progress risks eroding under the friction of inboxes, meetings, small talk, and the invisible obligations of social identity. To re-enter wisely is to protect this neurological gain from unnecessary abrasion.

Research in stress physiology and neuroplasticity reveals a phenomenon often overlooked in mainstream wellness rhetoric: the nervous system does not switch states like a light bulb. It transitions in gradients. This is observable in the work of Stephen Porges, whose polyvagal theory highlights how ventral vagal tone—associated with calm engagement—requires both safety and predictability. A retreat offers both. Re-entry, by contrast, often removes both. The task, then, is to mimic the predictability of retreat in the structure of return. This is the architecture of integration.

One of the most underutilised strategies in integration is intentional delay. The compulsion to "catch up" immediately upon return—be it through emails, updates, or social obligations—is more cultural than biological. The brain, particularly the medial prefrontal cortex and hippocampus, continues processing reflective insights and somatic shifts long after retreat ends. Integrating these requires white space, not white noise. In practice, this means scheduling buffer time post-retreat—not as a luxury, but as a neurobiological necessity. A Monday morning meeting following a Sunday return may seem efficient; in reality, it undermines retention and re-entry integrity. One gains rest but loses the reset.

Integration also demands ritual closure. Just as a retreat begins with intentional entry—a welcome, a letting go—so too must it end with intentional descent. In therapeutic contexts, this is known as 'debriefing,' but outside of clinical settings, this can be more symbolic: journaling what was learned, walking the same path one entered upon, lighting the same candle used throughout the retreat, or creating a physical artefact—a sketch, a phrase, a playlist—that represents the internal shift. These gestures are not ornamental. They serve as embodied cues that signal the nervous system to prepare for shift. Without such cues, the transition becomes abrupt, dysregulating, and cognitively disorienting.

Social re-entry poses a more complex challenge. Many sensitive individuals report feeling emotionally porous or socially misaligned in the days following a retreat. This is not weakness but neurobiological vulnerability. The limbic system—especially the amygdala—has likely reduced its hypervigilance during solitude. Exposure to unpredictable social cues, even benign ones, can reactivate subtle threat detection patterns. To mitigate this, re-entry plans should include graded social exposure: reconnecting first with those who feel safe, known, and attuned before expanding to broader networks. If the retreat was deep, the reintegration must be slow.

One overlooked but highly effective intervention is sensory consistency. If the retreat featured certain scents, sounds, or textiles—lavender oil, Tibetan bowls, a particular shawl—bringing those sensory anchors into the re-entry space can provide continuity. This taps into the power of the olfactory bulb and auditory cortex to ground memory and mood. The brain does not distinguish between 'retreat time' and 'work time' on its own. It responds to pattern recognition. Repeating the sensory signals that accompanied restoration can support a smoother return to function without sacrificing inner coherence.

There is also a broader cultural frame to consider. We often assume that self-care ends where productivity begins. This binary is not only false, but also physiologically harmful. Integration teaches us that the boundary between restoration and performance is porous. A well-structured return can, in fact, enhance executive function, creativity, and interpersonal clarity. The key is designing re-entry not as a collapse into old rhythms but as a conscious extension of new ones. This may require renegotiating workflow, recalibrating deadlines, or communicating new boundaries with colleagues or family.

Integration, at its best, is not a return to who we were, but a recalibration toward who we have become.

Consider the case of a senior product strategist who took a four-day digital retreat at a forested retreat centre. During those days, she reported a 40% drop in her heart rate variability variability, clearer memory recall, and creative insights into a project that had previously stalled. However, after returning directly to an open office floorplan and a 9 a.m. strategy sprint, she experienced sharp fatigue, irritability, and disorientation—symptoms she initially attributed to jet lag. Only upon reflection did she recognise that the absence of a transition window had created physiological and cognitive whiplash. The lesson was not that the retreat had failed. Rather, it had worked too well to be discarded abruptly. Her next retreat included a 48-hour home integration buffer: no calls, structured journaling, soft music, early bedtimes, and re-entry into collaboration via asynchronous communication first. The difference was profound. Integration allowed the insight of solitude to become a stable upgrade, not a passing spike.

Ultimately, integration is a discipline of respect—respect for the body's pace, for the nervous system's needs, and for the mind's capacity to transform only when given room to reconfigure. When approached with intention, re-entry becomes not a threat but a threshold. A rite, not a regression. And this, perhaps, is the final promise of retreat: not just to step away from life, but to re-enter it with deeper alignment, greater precision, and a nervous system prepared not just to survive, but to stay regulated amid the pulse of the world.

Chapter 8
Micro-Retreats: Small Practices for Big Recovery

Modern life is nothing if not compressed. Meals are grabbed on the move, emails fired off between meetings, attention pulled into fragments by pings, alerts, and the endless slide of notifications. What erodes resilience is rarely the sheer weight of stress, but rather its unbrokenness—the absence of pause, of punctuation. This chapter addresses a hard truth: most people, even those who understand what the nervous system craves, cannot retreat into forests, monasteries, or even free afternoons with any regularity. Yet the nervous system does not insist on luxury. It does not need hours, or days, to begin repairing itself. It responds in cycles, in moments, in tiny cues. Micro-retreats, when designed deliberately and practised with consistency, emerge as one of the most elegant and pragmatic answers to the problem of chronic, cumulative overwhelm.

They are not escapes. They are interruptions. A recalibration rather than a vanishing act. Micro-retreats work because they inject choice into a day that otherwise runs on rails. They transform liminal spaces—the minutes before bed, the walk between buildings, the silence while a browser window loads—into portals. Through these portals, the body can soften: vagal tone can reset, cortisol can lower, attention can knit itself together again. If a traditional retreat is a sanctuary, a micro-retreat is a tuning fork—small, precise, yet capable of restoring resonance through the whole system when struck with intent.

At the core lies a deceptively simple principle: the nervous system cares more for rhythm than it does for duration. This is a pivot away from outdated notions of rest, which exalt time away as the gold standard. Consider the vagus nerve. It responds to patterned inputs—slow exhalations, humming, the pressure of grounding touch—none of which require more than a couple of minutes to shift autonomic state. This is not speculative wellness jargon but grounded physiology. Polyvagal research, respiratory studies, somatic psychology—all converge on the evidence that a body can tilt toward parasympathetic calm rapidly, sometimes in under ninety seconds. Later sections of this chapter will show how that 90-second reset is not a hack, but an application of biology translated into practice.

Still, these micro-retreats are not only about biology. Their true power depends on being woven into the texture of daily life. Take commuting. For most, it is a battleground of traffic and irritants. But approached differently, the commute becomes ritual ground: breath aligned to the rhythm of passing scenery, music chosen with care to entrain a calmer state, a moment of silent grounding before stepping into the next context. Or consider walking. Typically, it is functional, distracted. Yet reframed as micro-retreat, walking becomes contact—feet pressing earth, posture recalibrating, eyes widening to the periphery. Each of these signals whispers to the nervous system: safe, safe, safe.

Sensory literacy is another key—though one our culture has largely dulled. Many of us numb or filter sensory input simply to survive the static of modern environments. Yet sensory elements—scent, warmth, light, texture—are direct cues for safety. The heft of a blanket across the chest, the resinous scent of cedar, the low vibrations of a cello note—such things are not luxuries, they are tools of modulation. Designing micro-retreats with this awareness is less about decoration, more about engineering recovery through perception itself.

Evenings, in particular, tend to be botched. Instead of descent, there is collapse. Nervous systems still charged with sympathetic arousal are hurled into screens, fractured conversations, then abruptly expected to surrender to sleep. A micro-retreat reframes that liminal zone: small, reliable rituals that mark the close of relational demands and guide the body into night. No extravagance is required—only precision. Cooling air, softening voices, dimmed light—these are circadian cues that remind the body how to release on time, rather than out of sheer depletion.

The material here is not abstract. Consider the case of a public school teacher, navigating the sensory storm of an inner-city classroom. With no access to prolonged rest or pastoral retreats, she learned to insert slender practices between lessons. A minute behind a closed door, breathing with attention. A grounding hand on the wooden edge of her desk. A slow gaze through the window, shifting her vision from tunnel to panoramic. From the outside, invisible. Inside, transformative. These tiny punctuations gave her back composure, steadied her cognition, and restored her emotional balance. Stress remained, but now it could be metabolised.

Beneath the science, there is also provocation. What if rest is not something earned, but something reclaimed? What if human biology was never designed for long-awaited weekends or distant holidays, but for daily rhythm and frequent punctuation? The implications stretch beyond personal health into the design of workplaces, schools, and family life. To re-insert recovery as a natural pulse within ordinary time is to challenge the productivity gospel at its core. Yet this challenge is not rebellion. It is refinement: a demonstration that consistent, intelligent recovery makes everything else—cognition, relationships, creative effort, even moral reasoning—work more effectively.

What this chapter offers, then, is not a theory of rest but a reframing of intervals. It asks us to reconsider those fragments of time too often dismissed as negligible, and to treat them as potent sites of change. Within these pages, you will find the science of rapid state shifts, the layering of ritual, and the psychology of habit. From the mechanics of a single breath to the cultural ramifications of redefining work-rest boundaries, the tools are here—not merely to understand micro-retreats, but to practise them, and perhaps to teach them.

We do not, in truth, need more time. We need more returns. More punctuation, more interludes that preserve coherence before it unravels. What is offered here is not escape, but mastery. The quiet mastery of knowing that small hinges move heavy doors, and that in the space of seconds—if offered the right cues—the body can recall itself, the mind can sharpen again, and the self can begin anew: clearer, steadier, whole.

The 90-Second Reset: Rapid Interventions for Real-Time Regulation

It is easy to think of recovery as something that must be earned through rest, protected by boundaries, or scheduled into an already oversubscribed calendar. But that model is both outdated and biologically inefficient. The nervous system doesn't always need hours. In fact, when under acute stress, what it often needs is not time—but precision. The right sequence of cues, delivered in a narrow window, can interrupt an autonomic spiral and pivot the body back toward coherence. This is the power of the *90-second reset*—a compact, actionable, and science-backed method for momentary self-regulation designed to operate in the real conditions of modern life.

Why 90 seconds? This number is not arbitrary. Neurobiological studies on emotional processing, especially those informed by the work of Dr Jill Bolte Taylor and later supported by somatic therapies, suggest that the chemical lifespan of an emotion—meaning the physiological cascade it creates—lasts about 90 seconds unless it is cognitively re-triggered. This provides a narrow but powerful opportunity: if we can use that window to re-signal safety to the nervous system, we can pivot out of reactivity and into restoration without requiring major environmental change. This isn't about bypassing emotion, but about offering the nervous system alternative data—signals that say, *you're safe now, and it's okay to downshift.*

A well-designed 90-second reset includes three key components: a respiratory intervention, a vagal stimulation cue, and a grounding anchor. Each targets a different mechanism within the autonomic hierarchy, allowing for rapid recalibration. Let's begin with breath. Respiration is the only autonomic function we can consciously control, which makes it the most accessible lever for changing physiological state. The aim here is not merely to "breathe deeply," but to *breathe directionally*. Specifically, a longer exhalation than inhalation (such as a 4:6 or 5:7 breath ratio) promotes parasympathetic activation via baroreceptor signalling. This is well-documented in studies on heart rate variability and vagal tone. When this pattern is coupled with nasal breathing and diaphragmatic expansion, the body receives a direct message: threat has passed, energy can shift from mobilisation to repair.

The second component is vagal stimulation. The vagus nerve, running from the brainstem through the lungs, heart, and gut, is central to the body's rest-and-digest system. And it responds to specific types of input: vocalisation (such as humming or chanting), rhythmic movement (such as rocking or swaying), and cold exposure (like splashing cool water on the face or holding a chilled object at the neck). One of the simplest and most effective vagal cues is *humming at a low frequency*, which vibrates the vocal cords and surrounding tissues, creating gentle resonance through the vagal pathway. Combined with extended exhalation, this provides a compounding effect: breath slows the system, while sound soothes the vagus.

The third element is grounding. When the body is in sympathetic overdrive—heart racing, attention narrowed, muscles braced—it loses its sense of present-moment orientation. Grounding exercises restore this by re-anchoring attention to the immediate environment or bodily sensations. But not all grounding is created equal. The most effective methods use multisensory input: pressing the soles of the feet into the floor while noticing the texture beneath them, placing a weighted object (like a book or small bag) across the lap to simulate containment, or tracing an object with the fingers while describing its details silently. These exercises are not distractions—they are reminders to the sensory system that the environment is not currently dangerous.

When all three components are combined into a fluid practice, the effect is often profound. One example: an emergency room physician, accustomed to 12-hour shifts punctuated by trauma and interruption, developed a reset ritual that included closing her eyes between patients, taking three slow breaths with a soft hum on each exhale, and pressing her thumb and forefinger together while internally naming the temperature of the room. Ninety seconds later, her heart rate had lowered, her cognitive focus had returned, and she could enter the next interaction with clarity rather than cumulative depletion. The intervention cost nothing. It required no app, retreat, or permission. What it required was design, consistency, and precision.

Critics may argue that such brief interventions are superficial—that deeper healing requires therapy, reflection, and structural change. That's not wrong. But it misses the point. The 90-second reset is not meant to replace deeper work. It is meant to *make deeper work possible.* It interrupts spirals that would otherwise accumulate into burnout, dysregulation, or interpersonal harm. And in the moments where those longer processes are not available—during a difficult conversation, before stepping onto a stage, after receiving unsettling news—it is precisely this kind of immediate tool that prevents emotional hijacking and preserves integrity.

It's also worth considering how the 90-second reset contrasts with typical self-care narratives. Much of modern wellness still conflates rest with withdrawal, or ease with avoidance. But the reset is not about running away from stress—it's about metabolising it. It requires engagement, attention, and somatic literacy. It asks the individual to *notice their state*, choose an intervention, and stay with it long enough to feel the shift. In that way, it builds not just calm, but capacity. Over time, these small acts of regulation rewire the nervous system's default responses. They reduce allostatic load, improve emotional granularity, and increase the latency between trigger and reaction—opening a window where agency can re-enter.

From a social design perspective, the implications are significant. What if every schoolteacher had a 90-second reset between classes? What if frontline workers, executives, and caregivers had ritualised interventions instead of collapsing into fatigue? What if parenting manuals included breath and vagal tools alongside behavioural tips? The barrier is not knowledge. It is infrastructure. Most people are never taught how to regulate. They are taught how to suppress, delay, or discharge—but not how to interrupt gently and return. Embedding micro-regulation into daily life is not only a nervous system upgrade—it's a cultural correction.

There's also a deeper invitation beneath the technique. The reset, when practised consistently, becomes something more than an intervention. It becomes a *relationship*—to one's body, one's signals, one's moments of overwhelm. Instead of seeing those moments as breakdowns, they become cues. Data points. Opportunities for recalibration. And over time, a trust develops: that no matter how fast the world moves, you can return. That your system, when given the right input, knows how to come back. That safety is not only a condition—it is a skill.

This chapter does not ask you to master everything at once. It asks you to commit to one practice. Ninety seconds, once a day, designed with intention and delivered with presence. From that small hinge, the door of regulation opens. And what awaits on the other side is not perfection, but a nervous system that no longer confuses urgency with threat, stillness with danger, or collapse with rest. What awaits is coherence—earned, embodied, and just a breath away.

The Commute Sanctuary: Turning Transitions into Micro-Retreats

There is a hidden architecture to our days, largely dictated by the spaces between. Commutes. Elevators. Waiting rooms. The seemingly unremarkable thresholds between destinations that most people rush through on autopilot. But what if these liminal spaces—so easily dismissed—hold untapped potential for restoration, insight, and self-regulation? For sensitive minds especially, the moments *between* doing are not mere logistics. They are invitations. When thoughtfully reimagined, these interstitial fragments of time can become highly effective sanctuaries—quiet zones of reorientation that recalibrate the nervous system without requiring an extended break from daily life.

A growing body of psychophysiological research confirms what many neurodivergent and sensitive individuals intuitively sense: overstimulation does not wait for high-stakes meetings or loud environments to derail equilibrium. It accrues insidiously, in the background noise of relentless transitions. And while extended retreats or protected weekends may be out of reach for many, the nervous system does not require hours to begin re-regulating. It needs *intentionality*. It needs *micro-boundaries*. And above all, it needs permission to pause in the places we've long treated as neutral.

Reframing the commute as sanctuary begins with rejecting its usual framing—as wasted time to endure or multitask through. The standard default—doomscrolling, mentally rehearsing one's to-do list, or unconsciously replaying the day's irritants—only compounds stress. Instead, research from cognitive neuroscience and somatic therapy underscores that even a ten-minute walk or drive, when imbued with ritual cues and sensory coherence, can quiet the amygdala, activate the parasympathetic system, and usher in cognitive clarity.

One exemplary practice comes from the Japanese concept of *ma*, often mistranslated as "emptiness" but more accurately described as the meaningful pause that gives shape to the whole. A Tokyo-based creative director, interviewed in a qualitative study on sensory environments and mental recovery, described how she built her walk home around *ma* principles. No phone. No errands. No podcasts. Just the deliberate noticing of texture, temperature, and light. The path became a sensory corridor. Not performative mindfulness, but sensory citizenship. "I don't try to feel calm," she said. "I let the walk take responsibility for that." Her commute became an embodied feedback loop: her steps slowed, her jaw relaxed, and the mental white noise dimmed.

This process is not passive. It requires design. Just as architecture uses elements like thresholds, transitions, and finishes to shape experience, a sensory sanctuary in motion must be curated. Start with one anchor sense. In a car, this might be scent—perhaps an essential oil blend associated with rest. A few drops on a cloth tucked into the air vent can create a strong, non-verbal cue for the nervous system to shift from vigilance to release. The olfactory bulb is directly linked to the limbic system—responsible for emotion and memory—making scent one of the fastest ways to influence psychological state without cognitive effort.

For others, the sanctuary might be auditory. A dedicated playlist—not of stimulation or entertainment, but of coherence—can serve as a sound boundary. Music with 60–80 beats per minute has been shown to synchronise with the resting heart rate, creating an internal entrainment effect. Whether driving, cycling, or walking, the act of pressing play on this particular soundtrack signals "this is recovery time," offering a self-honouring ritual even in transit.

Some find visual containment most potent. A therapist who works with trauma survivors shared that she uses a small object—a soft textile square or a grounding stone—placed deliberately in her line of sight during rideshare commutes. She never touches it. Its presence alone serves as a tactile reminder that this moment is protected. "It's not just about calming down," she explained. "It's about reasserting that I get to decide what happens in my nervous system—even between appointments."

Critically, none of these practices are about distraction. They are about *integration.* Unlike numbing strategies that offer short-term relief at the cost of long-term fatigue, commute sanctuaries centre the body's intelligence. They ask: What helps me come back to myself? What makes this body feel like a safe place to inhabit again?

A common misconception is that carving out sanctuaries in such spaces requires detachment from the world—closing eyes, tuning out surroundings, or feigning meditative stillness. This is neither realistic nor necessary. Instead, what matters is *directionality* of attention. A teacher walking from one class to the next may not have silence, but she can choose to breathe in through her nose, feel her feet contact the floor, and exhale audibly, even just once. That single act—conscious breath paired with tactile grounding—can begin the shift from sympathetic arousal to parasympathetic presence.

Further validation comes from trauma-informed somatic approaches like polyvagal theory, which emphasise the importance of micro-practices for autonomic re-regulation. Dr. Stephen Porges' work shows that the vagus nerve—responsible for shifting us into states of safety—responds rapidly to small cues of predictability, rhythm, and self-directed agency. In the context of commuting, this means that rather than using the time to rehearse conflict or overanalyse productivity, we can leverage it as a laboratory for re-anchoring in physiological safety.

Case studies from high-pressure professions also reinforce the utility of micro-retreats in motion. An ICU nurse in London, working back-to-back twelve-hour shifts, began integrating three-minute commute rituals at the beginning and end of each day. In the morning, she would place a warm mug of tea in her lap and do a sensory scan of the cup—heat, scent, weight—before starting her drive. In the evening, she transitioned into silence and rolled the windows down, inviting wind and cool air as symbols of release. Her quality of sleep improved, and she reported a 40% reduction in end-of-day headaches. The commute did not get shorter. But it stopped being a stress amplifier—and became a container of agency.

What these practices share is not technique, but intent. The effectiveness of any commute sanctuary hinges not on the tools chosen, but the *message they send to the self.* You are allowed to pause. You are worth recalibrating. This is not wasted time—it is sacred margin.

There is also an ethical dimension here. In a culture that pathologises rest and prizes frictionless efficiency, reclaiming in-between time as a legitimate site of recovery becomes a quiet act of resistance. It models for others—especially younger colleagues or dependents—that care does not need to wait for crisis. That self-regulation is not indulgence, but responsibility.

As the pace of modern life continues to accelerate, with blurred lines between work and home, focus and interruption, urgency and exhaustion, the role of micro-retreats becomes not just practical, but existential. Without deliberate sensory sanctuaries, we default to what the environment dictates—often noise, fragmentation, and hypervigilance. But with care, even a five-minute drive can become a felt invitation into wholeness.

The most radical shift is not architectural. It is perceptual. It is the decision to see every transition—not as an inconvenience—but as a threshold. Not as wasted time, but as opportunity. When the commute becomes a sanctuary, recovery stops being something that only happens "later." It becomes something we inhabit, claim, and design—right here, right now, in motion.

Evening Decompression Rituals: Discharging Social Residue and Resetting the Nervous System

There's a particular quiet that descends in the hour after the world starts to dim—when work emails slow, traffic softens, and our bodies begin to sense a shift. For many, this time is squandered, hijacked by screens, leftover work obligations, or the inertia of overstimulation. Yet for those with sensitive nervous systems, the evening hours hold a critical, often overlooked opportunity: the chance to consciously transition from outer stimulation to inner coherence. What happens in the final two to three hours before sleep determines not only the quality of rest, but the nervous system's ability to truly reset. Decompression is not indulgence; it is infrastructure. And when designed intentionally, it becomes a cornerstone of sustainable energy, emotional regulation, and social resilience.

The modern nervous system is in a state of chronic vigilance. Constant input—visual, auditory, relational—leaves the body bracing long after the stimulus is gone. Even seemingly benign evening habits, like watching television or scrolling social media, reinforce subtle patterns of hyperarousal. For the sensitive mind, the effects are cumulative. Social interactions, particularly in performance-oriented or emotionally charged environments, create energetic imprints that linger. Without mechanisms to metabolise this residue, the system remains cluttered. Sleep onset becomes delayed, emotional reactivity increases, and resilience diminishes. What we call "burnout" is often an accumulation of unprocessed overstimulation.

Evening decompression rituals are the antidote. Unlike sleep hygiene, which focuses on optimising the sleep window itself, decompression rituals serve a transitional function: they shift the nervous system from sympathetic dominance (fight-or-flight) into a state of parasympathetic regulation (rest-and-digest). What distinguishes a decompression ritual from mere relaxation is its intentionality. These are not activities we stumble into; they are repeatable patterns, cued by structure, marked by sensory awareness, and anchored in the body. They carry a symbolic weight: this is the moment we stop performing and start restoring. They are boundary signals to the nervous system that stimulation is ending and safety is resuming.

The most effective decompression rituals involve three non-negotiable elements: sensory down-regulation, psychological containment, and somatic grounding. Sensory down-regulation refers to the process of reducing input across sensory channels—dimming lights, lowering audio volumes, using warm tones, removing visual clutter. This has immediate physiological consequences: pupil constriction signals the hypothalamus to slow down metabolic activity, while ambient soundscapes activate the vagus nerve and cue calm. Psychological containment involves closing cognitive loops. This might take the form of a written brain dump, a verbal check-in with a loved one, or a visualised mental archive—anything that signals to the brain that the work of the day is done and there is no need to keep problem-solving. Finally, somatic grounding restores body-awareness through physical anchoring: lying on the floor, doing gentle stretches, or engaging in slow breathing with tactile feedback (such as a weighted blanket or hand on the chest). These are not exotic interventions. They are simple, repeatable acts that restore safety at the level of the body.

Real-world examples of these rituals vary widely depending on personality, culture, and environment—but the underlying principles remain consistent. A high-stakes trial lawyer reported that after years of insomnia, he began a "dimming ritual" in which, at precisely 8:30 p.m., all overhead lights were turned off and only candles remained. He paired this with a curated playlist of cello music and a 10-minute yin yoga sequence. Within two weeks, his sleep onset latency halved. A social worker in a high-trauma school environment reported using essential oils in a warm shower immediately upon arriving home, followed by a strict 20-minute "no-speak" rule that allowed her nervous system to reset before family interaction. What both cases illustrate is that the ritual is less about the content and more about the signal: the act of choosing presence over performance, restoration over reaction.

There is a biological rationale behind this transformation. The shift from external engagement to internal regulation involves measurable changes in neurochemistry. Cortisol—the stress hormone—has a natural evening taper, but this taper is disrupted by ongoing cognitive arousal. Exposure to blue light, emotionally charged conversations, or even mild decision-making delays melatonin production and keeps the hypothalamic-pituitary-adrenal axis active. Effective decompression rituals reverse this trajectory. Slow diaphragmatic breathing increases heart rate variability, a key biomarker of parasympathetic activation. Sensory dimming lowers corticotropin-releasing hormone. The result is not only quicker sleep onset but deeper, more restorative sleep cycles. The nervous system is not just shutting down; it is being recalibrated.

Contrary to the myth of "unwinding" through passive distraction—streaming shows, drinking alcohol, or aimless scrolling—true decompression rituals are embodied, intentional, and predictable. They reduce novelty rather than introduce it. In fact, part of what makes them powerful is their ritualised repetition. The brain, particularly in states of chronic stress, craves predictability. Predictable routines cue neural safety signals—markers that allow the amygdala to lower threat detection and the prefrontal cortex to come back online. In this way, evening rituals become small acts of neuro-architecture: we are scaffolding calm, building safety into the structure of time.

Evening decompression is particularly essential for those in high-empathy or high-stimulus roles: teachers, therapists, parents, healthcare providers, and customer-facing professionals. These individuals often carry a "relational residue" that can linger far beyond the interactions themselves. Micro-reflections on conversations, perceived tensions, or emotional mirroring can leave their nervous system activated into the night. For such individuals, decompression is not luxury—it is emotional hygiene. Structured rituals protect against emotional carryover and reduce the likelihood of unconscious venting or dissociation. Over time, these evening practices can even create a sense of anticipated pleasure, rather than collapse. The brain begins to associate the end of the day with comfort, coherence, and reward.

There is also a deeper philosophical undercurrent to evening decompression rituals: they represent a refusal to let our final waking moments be dictated by demands we didn't choose. In reclaiming the evening, we reclaim the boundary between self and world, between effort and essence. For those with sensitive systems, this boundary is often porous—experience floods in, and it takes longer to metabolise. The evening offers a space to close the aperture, to return to the small sacred acts that remind us we are not machines designed for output, but organisms in need of restoration. And this, perhaps, is the most radical gesture in a culture that equates worth with productivity.

By consistently engaging in evening decompression rituals, we re-train the nervous system to expect closure, predict safety, and initiate recovery. The effects are cumulative. With time, what once required effort becomes reflex. The body learns the rhythm of rest. The mind loosens its grip. And sleep—true, replenishing sleep—becomes not an escape, but a return to baseline. For the sensitive, the introverted, the deeply perceptive, there is no substitute for this kind of restoration. It is not optional. It is a foundation. And it begins, quite simply, with how we choose to end the day.

Real-World Case: The Teacher's Classroom Sanctuary

By 11:15 a.m., the classroom felt like a battlefield. Thirty-two students, each radiating energy—some jubilant, some dysregulated, others quietly overwhelmed—swirled in a cacophony of shifting attention, minor conflicts, sensory distractions, and invisible emotional currents. For years, Ms. Eleanor Grant, a veteran public school teacher in an urban primary school, believed that the job required self-sacrifice above all: emotional containment, constant vigilance, and a pace of engagement that allowed no time for nervous system recalibration. She was praised for her stamina. Yet behind the commendations and performance reviews was a growing depletion—chronic headaches, mounting irritability, and a numbing disconnection from the very vocation she had once loved. What saved her wasn't a sabbatical or external intervention. It was a self-devised system of micro-retreats embedded inside the very environment that was overwhelming her.

Teaching in overstimulating environments—especially those involving children or populations with high relational demands—

places unique pressure on the nervous system. Unlike roles that allow withdrawal or segmentation of tasks, classroom teaching requires near-constant relational presence. Teachers must modulate their tone, read multiple emotional cues simultaneously, enforce behavioural boundaries, deliver content, monitor safety, and remain emotionally available—all in real-time. For sensitive individuals, this creates an internal contradiction: their attunement, which makes them effective educators, is also the very thing that leaves them most vulnerable to burnout. The capacity to notice everything becomes a liability when there is no time to process anything.

Ms. Grant's solution came after a particularly harrowing autumn term that left her on the edge of medical leave. She began exploring trauma-informed education models and encountered the concept of "regulated environments"—spaces structured not only for student safety, but for educator sustainability. While the literature focused mostly on classroom strategies for children, she began applying the same logic to her own sensory and emotional regulation. Her hypothesis was simple but profound: *If I can't leave the overstimulating environment, can I engineer micro-moments of sanctuary within it?*

She started with what she called the "60-second reset". At two predetermined times during the school day—just after morning break and again just before afternoon lessons resumed—Ms. Grant would turn off the classroom lights, step behind her desk partition, and conduct a brief regulation ritual. It included three slow, nasal breaths, eyes closed, feet pressed firmly into the floor, and a whispered phrase she had chosen for herself: "I am anchored." Though the practice took just one minute, the nervous system shift was palpable. Over the following weeks, she added other elements: a drop of lavender oil dabbed onto her wrist before the midday lesson block; a calming chime she rang at the end of lunch cleanup, which cued both her and her students into a new rhythm; a silent tea ritual conducted with a thermos and ceramic cup during recess duty. These were not escapes from responsibility—they were integrations of responsibility with restoration.

What made Ms. Grant's approach notable was its insistence on ritual and structure. These were not reactive coping strategies implemented during moments of collapse. They were proactive recalibrations, scheduled and repeatable, that prevented collapse from occurring. The power of the micro-retreat lies in this predictability. The nervous system, particularly in overstimulated adults, does not need grand gestures—it needs consistency and clarity. Each of Ms. Grant's rituals became a cue for parasympathetic activation. Her body began to learn that safety and stimulation could coexist—not because the environment changed, but because her interaction with it did.

This case also illustrates a broader truth often missed in institutional settings: *wellbeing is not the absence of stress, but the presence of tools that metabolise stress in real time.* Micro-retreats function as these tools—not because they eliminate demands, but because they offer the body a moment to re-centre, to remind itself of its own boundaries, and to renegotiate how it meets the world. Ms. Grant's sanctuary was not a physical space separate from her work—it was a rhythm embedded into it. And this distinction is crucial for anyone working in environments where traditional self-care practices feel implausible.

From a neuroscience perspective, these rituals were recalibrating her autonomic nervous system. By engaging the vagus nerve through breath and sensory cues, she was re-establishing parasympathetic dominance without needing to remove herself from the classroom. The consistency of her practice allowed for anticipatory regulation—her nervous system began downshifting pre-emptively, simply by recognising the upcoming ritual. This is a critical insight for practitioners in overstimulating roles: *the nervous system learns in patterns, not events.* A single act of rest may offer temporary relief; a repeated ritual changes the system's default settings.

Of course, such rituals did not eliminate the chaos of the school day. Students still tested boundaries. Noise still escalated. Institutional pressures still loomed. But Ms. Grant's relationship to those stressors transformed. Instead of reacting from depletion, she began responding from centredness. Over time, she also noticed her students unconsciously adapting to her new pace. Her calm became contagious. Transitions became smoother. The classroom climate subtly shifted—not because she enforced calm, but because she modelled it.

This case underscores an essential paradigm shift for sensitive professionals: rather than striving to be resilient *in spite of* their sensitivity, they can become resilient *because of* it—by honouring the cues their bodies give them, by designing environments that meet their needs, and by reclaiming agency over their rhythms of activation and rest. Micro-retreats are not concessions; they are technologies of self-preservation. And when done with intention, they become forms of leadership—showing others that it is possible to be both deeply attuned and energetically intact.

For those working in similarly demanding environments—be it healthcare, counselling, frontline services, or caregiving—this approach offers more than a coping tool. It offers a philosophy. That we do not need to wait for holidays or weekends to feel whole. That regulation can exist within the very spaces that deplete us. That a nervous system in a state of safety is not a luxury but a prerequisite for meaningful work. And that our capacity to serve others grows in direct proportion to our ability to retreat—frequently, briefly, and with reverence—into the sanctuaries we build for ourselves.

Chapter 9
The Somatic Compass: Listening to Your Body's Warnings

For many high-performing individuals, the first real sign of burnout is not irritability or fatigue but collapse. Not a figure of speech—collapse in the most literal sense: the body, pushed beyond its tolerance and ignored for too long, decides to withdraw cooperation altogether. This is not weakness. It is protest. And though it often appears "sudden," collapse is anything but. It is the culmination of a long, overlooked narrative: the stiff shoulders that never fully soften, the shallow breaths rationed across the day, the sleepless nights, the churn of digestion, the short temper disguised as urgency. These early chapters are routinely brushed aside, written off as quirks of temperament or the inevitable tax of ambition. Biology does not fail us here; our literacy does. We never learned to read what our bodies have been writing all along.

This chapter is an attempt to reclaim that literacy. It proposes that the body is not a final resort, the emergency brake pulled only when things go terribly wrong, but the first informant—the compass that notices imbalance well before the mind can frame it. For those living under high demands and in constant motion, this sensitivity is not indulgence; it is essential. The remarkable fact is that the diagnostic tools already exist within us. The task is not invention but attentiveness.

Interpreting these early cues is not a mystical talent. It is a skill that can be trained, refined, and applied with the same seriousness one might bring to financial analysis or case law. The belief that bodily awareness is soft, instinctive, or vaguely "woo-woo" is not only outdated—it is dangerous. Many professionals in intense roles—executives, clinicians, educators, parents—survive by severing awareness from sensation. It works, for a time. But what they suppress are not trivialities; they are signals. The twitch at the eyelid's edge, the clamped jaw, the chest that refuses a full inhale—these are not ornamental discomforts. They are coded messages, telegrams from the nervous system, sent ahead of a more drastic intervention.

At the centre of this work lies a simple but radical principle: the body speaks in pattern, not prose. Its language is repetition. Slight increases in resting heart rate, a growing habit of sighing, the jitter of legs that cannot be stilled, or a thinning sense of presence—none of these are random. Together they map out a nervous system in motion along a spectrum: sympathetic acceleration (fight/flight), parasympathetic collapse (freeze/shutdown), or the more elusive baseline of regulation. Once people can name their personal tells—tightness in the throat signalling fight, buzzing limbs hinting at flight, the flatness of freeze—they gain foresight. They can act before the system tips into freefall.

The implications are not small. Interoception—the brain's reading of internal bodily states—is increasingly recognised as a decisive factor in stress resilience, decision-making, even leadership. A 2021 University of Sussex study demonstrated that individuals with sharper interoceptive accuracy fared significantly better under pressure, showing less burnout despite operating in relentless environments. The method is not complicated. It begins with observation: tracking breath, pulse, muscular tone, temperature. Establishing a baseline so that deviations are felt, not guessed. From there, the body becomes not a mystery, but a map.

A core technique in this repertoire is the micro-check-in: ten-second pauses across the day to register breath depth, muscular contraction, and current energy. Readers will be invited to keep a "somatic log" for several days, marking physical shifts and pairing them with emotional or cognitive stressors. This is not narcissism; it is accountability. When the body realises its messages are being received, the nervous system itself recalibrates. The static quiets. The feedback loop stabilises.

Yet skill alone is not enough. There is cultural debris to clear. Many of us have inherited the tale that bodily fragility is shameful, that stoicism is noble, that exhaustion proves devotion. Such myths may have served productivity, but they have done violence to sustainability. The argument this chapter makes is unapologetically ethical: one cannot perform sustainably at the cost of self-awareness. The human system is not engineered for perpetual override. Ignore it long enough and it will make itself heard—in ways that cannot be ignored.

Consider a senior manager who, after multiple outbursts and a stern word from HR, began working with a somatic coach. What she discovered was striking: each escalation was preceded by specific physical cues—a burning in the chest, breath trapped in the upper lungs. By ritualising a simple protocol—pausing for sixty seconds before meetings, expanding breath, releasing tension—she rewired her leadership from volatile to deliberate. The intervention was small. The consequences were not. Her team noted greater clarity, steadier presence, more trust. She was no less driven, but far less combustible. That is the practical power of somatic literacy.

This chapter will guide readers through such literacy: how to catch depletion before it spirals, how to distinguish bodily fatigue from emotional withdrawal, how breath, posture, and cognition form a single feedback circuit. Different individuals manifest stress differently—some coiling into hyper-focus and taut muscles, others dissolving into detachment. The point is not to standardise responses but to personalise them. Regulation begins with recognition.

Even the extremities—too often disregarded—carry crucial intelligence. Cold hands, damp palms, flushed cheeks, alternating waves of heat and chill—none are incidental. They are the nervous system's shorthand for safety or threat. Learn to notice them, and with the right adjustments—grounding, paced exhalation, micro-movements—the body can be returned to steadiness before more severe interventions are required.

It must also be said: listening to one's body is not always comfortable. At first it is often the opposite. Years of suppression do not unravel without unease. Sensations may confront as much as they console. Yet this very discomfort is instructive. It points to the places where achievement has demanded disconnection, where adaptation has been purchased with authenticity. Healing, therefore, does not call for more discipline but for a greater willingness to feel what has long been silenced.

By the end of this work, the reader will have a functioning somatic compass: a set of interpretive tools, reflective practices, and daily protocols that decode the nervous system before it escalates into collapse or dysfunction. The great lesson is that resilience lies not in new technologies or productivity tricks, but in signals already embedded within the body—if only one is prepared to listen.

This is not about fragility. It is about precision. It is about learning the metrics of embodied leadership, and recognising the nervous system not as an obstacle to high performance but as its most subtle and powerful ally.

Decoding Early Signals of Exhaustion

Fatigue is rarely sudden. Most often, it accumulates quietly, disguised as minor irritations, small lapses in memory, a tightened jaw, or a slight aversion to conversation. Yet in a culture that reveres productivity and undervalues physiological awareness, these signals go unnoticed until they crescendo into burnout, illness, or emotional collapse. What if we reframed these subtle bodily cues not as inconveniences to be overridden, but as intelligent warnings—early whispers from the nervous system, urging us to course-correct before depletion takes hold? *Exhaustion is not the starting point; it is the consequence of signals repeatedly ignored.*

Somatic science has advanced a compelling hypothesis: the body knows before the mind admits. Long before someone consciously acknowledges they are "burned out," the body has already begun shifting into protective states. The shoulders curl inwards. The breath shortens. The voice loses resonance. Subtle inflammation rises. These are not aesthetic changes—they are early markers of internal overload. Interoception, the brain's capacity to perceive internal states, gives us access to a rich stream of data, but its value depends entirely on whether we're trained to interpret it. Without that literacy, we miss the moment when rest would have sufficed and instead arrive at the threshold where recovery becomes a necessity rather than a choice.

The cues are not universal in appearance, but their origin is surprisingly consistent. Fatigue manifests first in areas of high metabolic demand—the musculoskeletal system, the cardiovascular rhythms, and the executive functioning regions of the brain. A sensitive individual may notice a slowing of word recall or a blunted creative edge during meetings. A parent may snap at a child for a minor interruption and feel an unfamiliar surge of guilt. A teacher, having delivered the same lesson three times in a day, may find her breath caught shallowly in the top of her chest, even during silence. These moments are not failures of discipline or mindset—they are somatic data points indicating strain.

Understanding pre-fatigue cues demands rejecting the binary model of "fine" or "exhausted" and adopting a more graduated, nuanced vocabulary of internal states. In polyvagal theory, for example, the nervous system transitions fluidly through various modes of activation: ventral vagal (engagement), sympathetic (mobilisation), and dorsal vagal (shutdown). Each mode brings with it characteristic physical sensations and cognitive tendencies. The shift from ventral to sympathetic, for instance, may feel like a tightening in the throat or a sudden urgency to tick off minor tasks—behaviours that are praised in corporate culture but may, in fact, indicate the system is bracing for threat. If unaddressed, this mode often collapses into dorsal vagal withdrawal—fatigue, numbing, disengagement.

By learning to track these shifts, one becomes fluent in their own internal rhythms. Breath is often the first place to observe dysregulation. A steady, diaphragmatic breath signals balance. As stress mounts, the breath rises, becomes chest-based, and loses consistency. Tension migrates from the core to the periphery. Hands fidget. Toes curl. Shoulders rise. These are not just postural quirks—they are neurological compensations. Similarly, temperature fluctuations—cold hands or sudden flushes—may reflect vascular responses to perceived internal threat. Such signs precede what most people label as "stress" by hours or days.

Modern work patterns have only compounded the problem. Many professionals operate in digital environments where somatic cues are muted or ignored. Screens demand forward-focus, locking the eyes and spine into unnatural positions for extended periods. Fluorescent lighting distorts circadian rhythms. Notifications condition the nervous system into micro-spikes of alertness. In such a context, it becomes increasingly difficult to notice when exhaustion begins. People override fatigue because they're immersed in environments that reward disconnection from the body.

Recovery, then, must begin with retrieval—not of time, but of self-awareness. One way to practice this is through a method called "somatic check-ins." At regular intervals—upon waking, before meetings, after meals—pause to ask: *What am I noticing in my body right now?* Where is there contraction? Where is there space? Is the breath mobile or restricted? Is temperature stable or shifting? Over time, patterns emerge. Perhaps every Wednesday afternoon brings irritability. Perhaps caffeine changes digestion more than previously acknowledged. These micro-patterns offer insights that no app or wearable can provide, because they are direct signals from the living system itself.

Yet awareness is only the first stage. Once recognised, signals must be respected. That means building thresholds for action—not when collapse occurs, but when the first warning flares. This requires setting behavioural boundaries. If one's jaw tightens after three hours of screen time, then three hours becomes the upper limit, not a starting point. If sleep quality degrades after two nights of late emails, then the phone is turned off earlier—not when exhaustion peaks, but before it begins. In this way, *boundaries are redefined not as constraints but as recalibrations of respect for the body's intelligence.*

There is an ethical imperative here, particularly for leaders, caregivers, and those whose decisions affect others. When individuals ignore their own cues, they are more likely to ignore or misinterpret the signals of those around them. A dysregulated teacher misses the subtle signs of a student's distress. An overextended executive demands from employees what they have refused themselves: rest, spaciousness, dignity. The cost is systemic, not just personal. By contrast, leaders who model somatic listening create environments of psychological safety—not through slogans, but through nervous system coherence.

This brings us to a final but often underappreciated truth: pre-fatigue cues are not just warnings. They are invitations. Each flutter of anxiety, each heavy limb or dry throat, is a chance to turn toward the self, not away. They offer the opportunity to intervene early, to restore before repair becomes urgent. Learning to interpret them is not self-indulgent—it is strategic, relational, and profoundly human.

As exhaustion becomes more prevalent in our high-velocity, information-saturated world, the ability to detect its earliest signals is no longer optional. It is a form of psychological literacy. A nervous system fluent in its own needs does not just survive—it protects, adapts, and sustains. And for the sensitive mind—the one attuned to nuance, easily overwhelmed by noise, deeply moved by beauty—this capacity is not merely useful. *It is essential.*

Nervous System Mapping

To navigate the modern world without understanding your nervous system is like attempting to sail without knowledge of wind or tide. You may stay afloat, but you'll move blindly—pushed by forces you can't name, let alone steer. At the heart of emotional regulation, energy management, and resilience lies the ability to observe, interpret, and respond to the signals of the autonomic nervous system. Nervous system mapping is not a metaphor; it is a real, observable process that allows individuals to track how their internal state fluctuates across moments, environments, relationships, and demands. Done skilfully, it becomes the foundation of self-leadership: the ability to detect imbalance early, to return to stability efficiently, and to live from physiological integrity rather than reactivity.

Most people only notice their nervous system when it malfunctions—when panic grips the chest, when exhaustion leaves them hollow, or when social withdrawal becomes a refuge instead of a reset. But these experiences are not isolated incidents. They are the results of small, cumulative shifts in autonomic state. The body, in its exquisite intelligence, moves through patterns of arousal and regulation all day long. The problem is not that we experience dysregulation; the problem is that we so often miss its early stages. Mapping offers a way to track these internal currents with precision.

It requires no complex devices—only a willingness to tune into sensation, breath, posture, tone, and affect.

Polyvagal theory, developed by Dr Stephen Porges, provides a foundational framework for such mapping. It suggests the nervous system is not binary—calm or stressed—but hierarchical. The ventral vagal state supports connection, creativity, and calm engagement. The sympathetic branch prepares the body for action—mobilisation, urgency, fight-or-flight responses. The dorsal vagal state activates when overwhelm or defeat is perceived, resulting in withdrawal, numbness, or shutdown. These states are not abstract—they have physical signatures. And when you learn to recognise those signatures, you gain an astonishing power: to change your state by changing your input.

Begin with breath. Noticing whether your breath is slow and expansive, or shallow and rapid, is often the simplest way to assess nervous system tone. In a regulated state, the breath drops low into the belly. It is smooth, rhythmic, unforced. Under sympathetic activation, it quickens, becomes erratic or held. In dorsal vagal states, breath becomes faint or minimal—almost imperceptible. Next, observe posture. Regulation invites openness: shoulders broaden, spine lengthens, gaze lifts. In arousal, the body leans forward, muscles tighten, hands clench. Under shutdown, posture collapses, head drops, the body curls inward. These signals are not random—they are precise indicators of neurophysiological shifts.

Temperature is another subtle yet reliable cue. When arousal increases, blood moves away from the core toward the extremities. Hands may sweat. Cheeks flush. Conversely, during shutdown, extremities grow cold as blood flow is restricted. Similarly, vocal tone is a barometer. The ventral vagal state produces a warm, modulated voice; sympathetic tone becomes clipped, sharp, louder than intended; dorsal tone is monotone or withdrawn. Even eye contact fluctuates—accessible and steady in regulation, darting or avoidant in sympathetic, vacant in dorsal.

What makes nervous system mapping particularly relevant today is the speed and intensity of environmental shifts. A single hour might include a difficult email, a performance review, a triggering news story, and a demanding family text. Each of these encounters can jolt the nervous system. Without a tracking practice, we carry these micro-shocks without noticing the toll. But with awareness, we can intervene: a slow exhale after a jarring message, a gentle stretch before a hard meeting, a reset breath between errands. This is not indulgence. It is precision medicine for the modern nervous system.

Importantly, mapping does not just help individuals; it transforms relationships. When we know what sympathetic arousal feels like, we can name it before projecting it. Instead of blaming a partner for 'interrupting' us, we might say, "I notice my chest is tight and I'm clenching my teeth—I think I need two minutes to regulate before we talk." This is a profound shift. It decentralises conflict, bringing it back to the body where it often begins. It also models emotional maturity: the capacity to name state without needing to justify or explain it.

There are now structured tools that support this process. Some therapists and coaches use colour-coded tracking systems—green for ventral, yellow for sympathetic, blue for dorsal. Clients chart their states across the day or in response to specific interactions. Others use journaling methods, noting physical sensations, thoughts, and triggers in real time. Biofeedback tools and heart-rate variability monitors add data for those who prefer measurable metrics. But no tool is more powerful than regular self-attunement. Ask: What am I feeling right now? What is my breath doing? Where is my tension? Am I mobilised, collapsed, or open? These questions, repeated daily, build a map as detailed as any diagnostic scan.

It must be said that nervous system states are not moral categories. There is no 'bad' state. Sympathetic mobilisation is useful for action. Dorsal shutdown is protective when trauma hits. The goal is not to stay permanently regulated—it is to know where you are, to move through states with awareness, and to return to baseline more fluidly. Resilience, in this light, is not the absence of stress but the agility to recover. And mapping is the compass that allows that recovery to occur faster, earlier, and with more grace.

Consider the case of an executive who begins to lose motivation. Meetings drain him. Emails go unanswered. He feels foggy by mid-afternoon. A traditional model might call this burnout. But a mapped perspective offers nuance. Reviewing his state chart, he sees a pattern: after back-to-back Zoom calls, his system drops into dorsal. His voice flattens. His breath constricts. He's not lazy—he's physiologically shut down. With this data, he adjusts: 10 minutes of movement between calls, breathwork at noon, and no back-to-backs after 3 pm. Within two weeks, his tone returns, his output improves, and—crucially—he enjoys work again.

The value of nervous system mapping is cumulative. Over time, one begins to sense shifts before they escalate. This anticipatory intelligence prevents not only dysregulation, but also emotional harm. How many arguments begin not because of content, but because one or both parties are unconsciously dysregulated? How much creativity is lost because we misinterpret low energy as laziness instead of dorsal activation? How much potential is left untapped because we do not understand our internal environment?

In truth, mapping the nervous system is not just a self-care practice. It is a leadership practice. It is a parenting skill. It is a relational art. In any context that demands presence, empathy, or adaptability, it is foundational. And unlike most personal development frameworks, it is not abstract. You do not need years of study or advanced vocabulary. You need only the discipline to notice. To pause. To name what is felt. To honour what the body already knows.

As the nervous system becomes increasingly recognised as the seat of emotion, resilience, and connection, the ability to map one's states will become as essential as financial literacy or digital fluency. Not because it's trendy, but because it is how we navigate ourselves and each other—safely, skilfully, and with the dignity that awareness affords.

The Language of Tension, Breath, and Temperature

A body whispering before it screams—that is the premise upon which the language of biofeedback rests. Before burnout becomes visible, before a meltdown takes its social toll, the body transmits subtle, often disregarded cues: a tightening jaw, a shallow breath, a slight rise in core temperature. For sensitive individuals or those managing complex cognitive and emotional loads, fluency in this biological lexicon is not optional—it is preventative medicine. Recognising these early signs can mark the difference between functional sustainability and system collapse. The nervous system is constantly transmitting its internal state, not through metaphor or abstraction, but through measurable physiological signals. This subchapter explores how we can attune to these communications and make proactive decisions before our cognitive bandwidth is depleted beyond recovery.

The modern environment is structured for denial. Office lighting blunts circadian sensitivity. Open-plan spaces erase boundaries. Notifications hijack focus before it ever finds anchor. In such settings, the body's signals are not only drowned—they are actively devalued. Culturally, we have elevated cognition while trivialising somatic intelligence. Fatigue is often treated with caffeine, tension with distraction, and emotional flooding with more productivity. This has resulted in a generation of high-functioning individuals who know how to manage calendars and metrics, but not their own biology. Learning to listen to the body's language—its nuanced expressions of effort, strain, and overstimulation—reclaims agency over one's inner state. It is not about hypervigilance or self-absorption; it is about precision and choice.

Let us begin with tension, one of the most accessible yet misunderstood somatic signals. Muscular tension is not just a physical sensation; it is a form of internal messaging about unmet needs, boundary breaches, or sustained sympathetic activation. Jaw clenching, shoulder tightness, and gut rigidity are often the body's frontline responses to overwhelm, each mapping onto distinct emotional or cognitive stressors. For instance, chronic upper back tightness in desk workers may reflect not merely poor ergonomics but an unresolved state of defensive readiness. The nervous system is poised for conflict that never arrives—an argument imagined, a deadline looming, a fear unnamed. Tracking where tension initiates and how it migrates offers a sophisticated map of inner imbalance. This is not speculative. Electromyography (EMG) studies show that micro-changes in muscular tension correspond to fluctuations in emotional state long before verbal self-awareness catches up.

Breath offers another profound window into nervous system regulation. Unlike most autonomic functions, breathing is both involuntary and voluntary, making it a bridge between conscious awareness and unconscious state. Dysregulated breath—rapid, shallow, upper-chest breathing—is a hallmark of sympathetic dominance, the "fight or flight" mode. Conversely, slow, diaphragmatic breathing activates the parasympathetic branch, enabling restoration. But what matters here is not merely breathing technique; it is breath awareness. The average person breathes over 20,000 times a day, most of it unconsciously. Yet subtle shifts—a skipped inhale, a sharp exhale, a held breath before replying—can be read as data. Observing these nuances, without judgement, allows for micro-interventions before escalation. Therapists using Somatic Experiencing and trauma-informed breathwork increasingly employ breath tracking as both diagnostic and regulatory practice, precisely because of its immediacy and responsiveness.

Temperature, though less frequently discussed, is equally critical. Core body temperature, skin warmth, and extremity temperature can all indicate nervous system state. Cold hands and feet often signal vasoconstriction—a physiological hallmark of stress or fear. Meanwhile, facial flushing or a sudden wave of heat may indicate emotional flooding or unresolved sympathetic charge. Research in affective neuroscience supports this: studies using thermal imaging have shown consistent temperature patterning associated with specific emotions. Anger lights up the head and chest. Anxiety shows cold in the hands. Sadness cools the limbs. For sensitive individuals, or those living in chronically demanding environments, tracking temperature fluctuations can provide advance warning of impending dysregulation. One executive, profiled in a stress management study, noted that a sudden inner heat wave—unaccompanied by any external trigger—almost always preceded his worst professional outbursts. Learning to notice and label that early heat became a pivot point for behavioural change.

What unites tension, breath, and temperature is their immediacy and pre-verbal nature. These signals occur before conscious thought, before story, before justification. They offer raw data—uncoded, unembellished—about what is happening inside. The problem is not that they are too subtle; it is that we have not been trained to value them. We override, minimise, or distract, mistaking numbness for resilience. But resilience, in the context of somatic literacy, is less about endurance and more about attunement. It is the capacity to notice small shifts early enough to redirect the internal trajectory.

Developing this somatic fluency does not require special devices or complex protocols. It requires time, intention, and practice. Daily check-ins—pausing to scan the body at key transitions (before meetings, after difficult conversations, during commutes)—can build neural familiarity with internal cues. Naming sensations aloud ("My jaw feels tight." "My chest is warm." "My breath is shallow.") strengthens the neural networks that connect interoception to executive function. Over time, these practices enhance self-regulation, not because they eliminate stress, but because they allow for adaptive response before the stressor defines the experience.

Contrasting views within the field should be acknowledged. Some behavioural scientists argue that over-focusing on somatic signals can tip into rumination or even somatic symptom disorder. This is a valid concern. The key difference is between attunement and obsession. Attunement is grounded in curiosity and responsiveness; obsession is driven by fear and control. In high-functioning environments, the greater risk is not over-attunement but anaesthesia—the gradual detachment from embodied experience until the only feedback we notice is the loudest: illness, burnout, or breakdown.

A final layer to consider is cultural conditioning. In many professional or academic settings, bodily awareness is implicitly discouraged. Calm is equated with stoicism, and displays of somatic distress are pathologised. Women, in particular, are often socialised to ignore pain, push through fatigue, and mask physiological discomfort. Developing a healthy relationship with tension, breath, and temperature is therefore not just a personal act—it is a quiet resistance against disembodiment. It is the reintegration of the biological with the behavioural, the subjective with the scientific.

The nervous system is not a mystery to be solved; it is a language to be learned. Listening to its signals—tension tightening under the surface, breath hitching before speech, warmth rising as overwhelm nears—requires patience, not perfection. It offers, to those willing to hear it, a roadmap out of unconscious reactivity and toward conscious, embodied leadership of one's inner world. In a culture that celebrates intellect but ignores embodiment, learning to understand this language may be among the most radical acts of self-preservation available.

Real-World Case: The Manager Who Learned to Pause

By the time Angela M., a mid-level operations manager at a global logistics firm, sat across from her executive coach and whispered, "I think I might be broken," the signs had long been present. Tension headaches. Snapping at her team. An undercurrent of dread at the thought of another Monday. She wasn't new to pressure—she had climbed the ranks by outperforming her peers and was widely respected. But she had never learned to *pause*. Not in any meaningful, embodied way. Her body had been signalling for months that it was heading toward collapse. She, like many high-performing professionals, simply didn't know how to listen. What followed in the next six months wasn't a dramatic sabbatical or some Instagrammable lifestyle overhaul, but rather a quiet, structured cultivation of somatic awareness—one that would radically shift how she led, lived, and recovered.

Angela's story is not unusual. In fact, it's emblematic of a much larger cultural phenomenon: the valorisation of cognitive override. We reward the ability to push through discomfort, to suppress bodily fatigue, to delay rest. In the language of modern productivity, efficiency trumps embodiment. The problem is that our nervous systems were not designed to operate in constant overdrive. They are exquisitely sensitive calibration tools, continuously processing internal and external data, modulating between arousal and restoration. When we ignore their signals, we lose the ability to regulate effectively—and leadership under those conditions becomes not just unsustainable but dangerous.

For Angela, the tipping point came during a quarterly review. Her team's performance had lagged slightly due to system-wide changes beyond their control. She had already spent the week fielding late-night emails and micromanaging deliverables. By Friday morning, she was in what trauma-informed psychologists would identify as a state of high sympathetic arousal: rapid breathing, clenched jaw, inability to focus on nuance. When a junior analyst questioned a KPI on the team dashboard, Angela exploded—an outburst so sharp it left the entire room silent. She barely remembered what she said. But she remembered how her chest felt: tight, buzzing, like an electric wire about to fray.

That moment marked her entry into somatic coaching. Unlike traditional executive development programs focused on strategy and skills, somatic work attends to the *body's experience* of leadership. It starts with sensation—noticing the physiological cues that precede emotional escalation. In Angela's case, that meant learning how her body signalled early overwhelm: a narrowing in her field of vision, shallowness in her breath, and a particular ache in her left shoulder that always accompanied mental rigidity. These were not random discomforts; they were data. *The body speaks in micro-signals long before the mind declares a problem.*

Her coach introduced her to a simple daily practice: the structured pause. Three times a day—mid-morning, post-lunch, and pre-commute—Angela would stop for exactly 90 seconds. No emails. No Slack. She would place both feet on the ground, feel the contact of her chair, and scan her internal state: Was her breath deep or tight? Shoulders raised or released? Jaw clenched or soft? These pauses weren't intended as relaxation breaks. They were diagnostic. Over time, Angela began to anticipate emotional surges before they erupted. She could catch herself as tension started—not after damage was done.

What's striking is how little time this demanded. Somatic awareness doesn't require retreat centres or complex protocols. It requires the cultivation of *interoceptive accuracy*: the ability to detect and interpret internal signals. This includes not just dramatic signs like heart palpitations or nausea, but subtler sensations—temperature shifts in the extremities, micro-holding patterns in the spine, small changes in breathing rhythm. The modern executive's body is flooded daily with such feedback. Most are simply trained to ignore it.

Angela's transformation wasn't instant. But within three months, her direct reports noticed a shift. Meetings felt less tense. Her feedback became more measured. She didn't stop being demanding—but the quality of her demand had changed. Instead of transmitting her own dysregulation to others, she modelled containment. More importantly, she no longer needed post-meeting apologies to rebuild trust. Emotional blowouts, once weekly, had all but disappeared. Somatic intelligence had become a leadership competency.

What made the biggest difference? According to Angela, it was *language*. Before, she'd used abstract terms to describe her stress: "I'm overwhelmed," "I'm burnt out," "I'm fine." These labels were vague and reactive. Through somatic coaching, she began to describe states more specifically: "I'm in a high tone sympathetic surge," or "My system feels flattened—parasympathetic dominance." This precision didn't just improve self-awareness—it reduced shame. She no longer viewed her shutdowns as moral failures but as temporary states of nervous system imbalance. This shift allowed for earlier, more compassionate interventions.

This reframe aligns with contemporary neuroscience. The Polyvagal Theory, pioneered by Dr Stephen Porges, maps how the autonomic nervous system toggles between social engagement, mobilisation, and immobilisation. Leaders like Angela often operate in chronic sympathetic mode: high energy, high control, high reactivity. But without moments of recalibration, that system fatigues. The dorsal vagal state—associated with emotional numbing and disengagement—eventually takes over. Burnout, then, is not just a matter of stress accumulation; it's a failure to notice and respond to early shifts in nervous system tone.

One of Angela's most powerful tools became what her coach called a *somatic debrief*. After challenging meetings, she would take five minutes alone—not to ruminate mentally, but to ask her body: What am I holding? Where do I feel it? What would bring release? Sometimes this meant a stretch. Sometimes slow exhalations. Sometimes, simply lying down with legs elevated to cue a parasympathetic rebound. Over time, this became automatic. Her body, once muted by habit, now participated actively in her leadership.

Her story also offers a valuable caution: somatic practices must be integrated ethically. These are not quick-fix hacks for performance optimisation. They are relational tools—ways to stay connected to self and others under pressure. Angela was clear: somatic work didn't make her softer. It made her *steadier*. Her boundaries improved. Her clarity sharpened. What changed was the source of her authority: it no longer stemmed from control, but from coherence.

Today, Angela teaches her team to notice their own signals. She starts staff meetings with two minutes of quiet arrival. She's careful not to pathologise stress—acknowledging that pressure is real and sometimes necessary. But she now recognises that ignoring somatic cues is neither noble nor sustainable. It's a liability. In her words, "I still have hard days. But I no longer let my body become collateral damage."

Her case exemplifies a growing movement toward embodied leadership—one that doesn't sideline emotion, override sensation, or reduce resilience to grit alone. At its heart is a simple premise: *when we learn to pause, we gain access to wiser choices*. This is not about softness. It's about structural integrity—leading not just with skill, but with a system that can hold the weight of modern work without fracturing. Angela's story is not exceptional. It is repeatable. But only if we teach people to listen before they collapse.

Chapter 10
The Alchemy of Social Boundaries

There is, quietly but unmistakably, a revolution unfolding among the highly sensitive—those who once bent themselves into shapes that pleased others, absorbed the static charge of a room without protest, or wore a polished smile as camouflage for exhaustion. What is emerging is not simply a shedding of these old performances, but something braver: embodied sovereignty. Boundaries, in this sense, are not barricades of defiance but thresholds of resonance—lines that allow connection without depletion, intimacy without collapse. The cultural shorthand of "just say no," repeated endlessly in therapeutic slogans and self-help manuals, is too blunt an instrument for such delicate work. This chapter begins where the platitudes falter.

A boundary, after all, is not a wall. Nor is it a loophole for escape, an excuse for avoidance, or a declaration of permanent withdrawal. At its most vital, it is a living contract between body, mind, and environment: a threshold that says, *Here is how I remain in integrity with myself, while still being able to remain in connection with you.* This distinction matters especially for the sensitive, whose heightened emotional and sensory perception often makes conventional, one-size-fits-all strategies ineffective, even counterproductive. What they need is a more nuanced kit of tools—drawing on neuroscience, somatics, relational psychology, and contemplative practice.

So, this chapter is not in service of a sharper "no." It is about cultivating the capacity to recognise and trust the body's "yes"—to hear the barely perceptible shifts in breath, tension, or mood that indicate when presence is sustainable and when retreat is wiser. The practice here is less about defence than design: shaping interpersonal, physical, and energetic space so that restoration is not a rare accident but a reliable pattern. In other words, it is about the architecture of the self—constructed not in splendid isolation but within the tangled, pulsing landscape of human relationship.

First, the myth of heroic refusal needs dismantling. Boundary-setting is too often dramatised as the grand gesture—the emphatic refusal, the door slammed, the dramatic exit. Yet in lived reality, especially for those trained by culture to prioritise empathy and care-taking, the real work is quieter. It lies in prevention rather than crisis, clarity rather than confrontation. Neuroscience makes this plain: our nervous systems are ceaselessly scanning for cues of safety, and when those cues are absent, they shift into armouring or collapse. For the sensitive nervous system, waiting until rupture is already too late. What's required are rituals of maintenance—steady, repeatable practices that reduce the likelihood of overwhelm before it arrives.

Among the most neglected forms of boundary-setting is the energetic one. This may sound abstract, but it is not speculative mysticism; it is rooted in interoception, mirror neurons, and the science of co-regulation. Consider how instantly one can sense whether a crowded room welcomes or rejects. Or how a child, without a word spoken, knows when a parent's body is present but their attention elsewhere. Such knowing is not imaginary; it is data. The chapter explores how visualisation, intention, and subtle awareness can re-establish one's interior territory. Through deliberate practices, readers will learn to project a kind of perimeter of presence around themselves—wordlessly communicating: *I am here. I am whole.*

Of course, the point is not to bar out the world. True boundaries are porous, which means saying yes has its place—though not indiscriminately. Sensitive individuals tend to lean towards extremes: over-accommodating until they collapse, or withdrawing so completely that they forfeit nourishment from connection. Both postures deplete. Instead, what is needed is ritualised yes-saying—deliberate, embodied consent to engagements that add to vitality rather than erode it. This is not time management but energy management, more akin to tuning a violin than keeping a diary. One learns which invitations produce harmony and which strike discord. Yes becomes less about obligation and more about alignment.

The chapter grounds these abstractions in lived narrative. One story follows a mother, her days consumed by caregiving, her nights hollowed out by a grief she could not name—the erosion of her inner life. She discovered that boundary-setting did not mean rejecting her family, but reclaiming fragments of herself. A ten-minute meditation in the car before school pick-up. A frank conversation with her partner about the division of labour. Permission to leave the evening hours unproductive, open to rest. These micro-rituals shifted her from martyrdom to agency. Generosity, she realised, that excludes the self is not generosity at all.

Readers, likewise, will be asked to notice the everyday signals of overextension: the tone of voice that tightens when saying yes against one's will, the heaviness in the gut at overcommitment, the accelerated breath that accompanies endurance of too much. These are not moral failings but physiological flares. Learning to track them is part of somatic literacy—skills that prevent not just dramatic meltdowns but the subtler, slow-drip erosion of vitality.

Ultimately, this chapter proposes that boundaries are not separations but structures of sacred architecture. They allow connection to deepen rather than deplete, intimacy to become nourishing rather than exhausting. They outline where closeness can flourish and where solitude is indispensable. For the sensitive, this is not auxiliary knowledge but survival. Without it, every relationship risks draining the reservoir. With it, complexity in human connection becomes sustainable, even beautiful.

What unfolds here is not a tactical manual, but a framework for re-patterning presence itself. A re-education, deliberate and slow, in how to inhabit one's own space—physical, emotional, energetic—without apology. Boundary-setting, in this light, is nothing less than alchemy: the slow work of transformation, a practice that preserves what is essential and welcomes what restores.

The Myth of 'Just Say No'

The cultural mantra of "just say no" is often heralded as a beacon of empowerment, especially in conversations about personal boundaries. It's a phrase that's been championed in everything from assertiveness training workshops to mainstream self-help literature. But for many sensitive individuals—those who live attuned to the emotions of others, who feel the room before they speak, who absorb tone more than content—this advice lands less like liberation and more like a blunt instrument. It implies that boundaries are a matter of semantics, a clean verbal manoeuvre detached from context, consequence, and nervous system state. Yet the reality is far messier: boundary-setting is not a sentence we recite, but a skill we *embody*, negotiate, and refine in relationship with others.

For those with finely tuned nervous systems, boundary violations often register somatically before they are cognitively processed. The tightening in the gut when asked to stay late at work. The shallow breath during a conversation that feels too intense, too fast. The compulsive nod, followed by the internal resentment, when someone asks for yet another favour. In such bodies, the word "no" doesn't arise as a declarative stance—it must be cultivated over time as a physiological permission. To coach sensitive individuals into healthier patterns of relational self-protection, we must teach boundary-setting as an act of nervous system literacy, not simply verbal assertiveness.

What this requires, first and foremost, is abandoning the fantasy that boundaries are binary. The myth of "just say no" flattens the multidimensional reality of interpersonal dynamics. It assumes the speaker feels safe, regulated, and entitled to assert their limits. It assumes the recipient will respond with respect, or at least indifference. It assumes that saying "no" is a standalone event, not the culmination of years of unlearning and practice. But for those who grew up in households where boundaries were either punished or pathologised, or who belong to cultures where collectivism trumps individuation, "no" is never just a word—it's a threat to belonging.

What is needed is a relational model of boundaries, one that recognises them not as walls but as membranes. A membrane is semi-permeable: it allows in what nourishes and filters out what depletes. It shifts shape according to context, energy, and emotional bandwidth. This model invites us to assess our boundaries not based on what we should say, but on how we feel in real time. Do I have the internal spaciousness for this request? Can I offer this support without self-betrayal? Is there a way to connect without collapse?

Such questions, when practiced regularly, help construct boundaries from within—bottom-up, rather than top-down.

Consider, for instance, the simple act of receiving an invitation. In many workplaces and social settings, requests are disguised as obligations. "Can you take this on?" may be framed as optional, but it's delivered with a tone that implies expectation. For the highly attuned, that subtle mismatch triggers dissonance: they want to maintain harmony, but their body signals fatigue. In such moments, the ability to set a boundary hinges less on finding the perfect script and more on maintaining internal alignment. A soft "not right now" delivered with congruent breath and posture is often more effective than a brittle, rehearsed "no" spoken from disconnection.

Embodied boundary-setting begins with awareness of internal state. If you are dysregulated—flooded, frozen, or fatigued—your capacity to assert a need or limit shrinks. Neuroscientific research on co-regulation and polyvagal theory supports this: the autonomic nervous system, which governs our responses to safety and threat, plays a foundational role in relational communication. When we feel safe, our ventral vagal system activates—enabling social engagement, voice modulation, and flexible response. When we feel unsafe, we either mobilise (fight/flight) or shut down (freeze/fawn). Asking someone to assert a firm boundary while they're in a state of collapse is not only unhelpful—it's physiologically implausible.

This is why many boundary transgressions don't stem from a lack of willpower but a lack of regulation. Teaching people to set boundaries must include tools to stabilise the nervous system: breathing patterns that restore vagal tone, grounding exercises that re-establish somatic presence, and micro-movements that support emotional integration. Only from this place of embodied coherence can one assess, respond, and speak from clarity.

Another critical, often overlooked, element of boundary work is *attunement to relational context.* The assumption that every person or situation warrants the same type of boundary is a fantasy of control. In reality, some boundaries must be soft and ongoing, negotiated over time. Others require an immediate rupture or firm closure. What determines the appropriate response is not abstract principle, but moment-to-moment feedback from the nervous system, coupled with social intelligence. How does this person typically respond to limits? What power dynamics are in play? Is this a chronic pattern or a one-off misstep? Embodied boundary-setting is not rigid; it is responsive.

Take the example of Maria, a mid-level manager in a nonprofit organisation who consistently found herself absorbing other people's stress. Her reports came to her not just with task updates, but emotional unloads. For years, she struggled to maintain energetic separation, feeling drained by the end of each day. Initially, she attempted a cognitive fix—she rehearsed phrases like, "I don't have capacity for this right now," but her delivery felt wooden and anxious. Her turning point came when she worked with a somatic coach who helped her notice what "yes" and "no" felt like in her body. "Yes" came with openness in her chest, ease in her jaw. "No" came with tightening behind the eyes, a slump in posture. Armed with this data, she began tracking her cues in real time. Her boundaries became less about language and more about timing, pacing, and physical repositioning—standing up when conversations felt too long, ending meetings five minutes early to decompress, offering support only after checking her body's readiness.

What Maria discovered is what many sensitive professionals eventually realise: *boundaries are not what we tell others; they are what we are able to hold within ourselves*. This doesn't mean foregoing verbal communication, but it reframes speech as the *expression* of a boundary—not its origin. Without somatic congruence, the best scripts fall flat.

A final dimension worth examining is the social framing of boundaries as inherently oppositional. The cultural script suggests that to set a boundary is to risk rupture, to deny, to push back. But in practice, relational boundaries are invitations to sustainable connection. They tell others: here is what keeps me resourced enough to stay in relationship. When done with attunement, they do not shut people out—they make deeper presence possible. And for highly sensitive individuals, who often struggle to stay connected under stress, this nuance matters. Boundary-setting is not a retreat from relationship; it is the condition for authentic engagement.

To move beyond the myth of "just say no," we must replace simplistic maxims with layered wisdom. We must equip sensitive people with the tools to feel their limits before they speak them, to read their own body's data before they engage with others. We must normalise boundary repair—not just boundary enforcement—so that relationships can flex and evolve. And most importantly, we must honour that for many, the task is not learning to say "no," but learning to trust that their "no" will not make them unlovable. Only then can boundary-setting become what it truly is: not a performance of empowerment, but a daily practice of self-respect.

Energetic Boundaries: Invisible Shields

It is not always the volume of interaction that drains us—but its texture. Some environments feel heavy the moment we enter them. Certain people leave us inexplicably fatigued, even after brief exchanges. Others seem to commandeer space without ever raising their voice. Sensitive individuals often find themselves absorbing not only overt demands but subtle emotional frequencies, social micro-pressures, and the psychic residue of unspoken expectations. In this context, traditional advice about setting "clear boundaries" can fall flat. It assumes that all boundary violations are verbal, conscious, and negotiable. They are not. Much of the impact stems from the invisible—the felt, the sensed, the ambient. And it is here, in this subtler layer of experience, that *energetic boundaries* become vital.

Energetic boundaries are not mystical defences or imagined shields borrowed from spiritual clichés. They are intentional somatic and attentional practices that delineate where your energy ends and the external world begins—without having to announce it aloud. These boundaries are not expressions of aggression, but of clarity. They work below the level of speech yet above the level of unconscious reaction. They are perceptible to the nervous system long before they become visible to others. When done well, they shift the quality of presence you project: less porous, more coherent. Not closed-off, but sovereign.

Consider the subtle shift in posture that occurs when someone mentally "prepares" to enter a difficult room—chin slightly lifted, breath deeper, gaze steadier. Or the way a seasoned therapist marks the end of a session not just with words, but by adjusting their tone, their eye contact, and the tempo of their movements. These are not theatrical gestures; they are somatic cues signalling boundary. The body becomes the punctuation mark, and the nervous system takes the message more seriously than any verbal statement could deliver.

One of the most pragmatic ways to establish these energetic perimeters is through visualisation—specifically, *grounded visualisation*, anchored in breath and interoception rather than fantasy. Imagine, for example, a transparent membrane extending a few centimetres from your skin—permeable to kindness and curiosity, but filtering out urgency and coercion. Or a ring of light beneath your feet that widens each time someone's tone becomes manipulative or invasive. These images aren't "magic"—they're cognitive scaffolds that reorient your nervous system's boundary response, especially when verbal assertion is socially risky or contextually inappropriate. Over time, the body begins to treat these imagined perimeters as implicit cues, not conscious commands. *The more viscerally you inhabit your boundary, the less you need to defend it.*

The science here intersects with both psychophysiology and trauma-informed somatic practice. According to Stephen Porges' Polyvagal Theory, safety is not detected solely through language, but through tone, proximity, facial expression, and movement. The body constantly scans for "neuroception"—a subconscious reading of safety or threat. When energetic boundaries are unclear, the body often reads ambiguous social interactions as danger, even if the mind is telling us to "just be polite." That incongruence can generate long-term nervous system wear: chronic vigilance, adrenal fatigue, or emotional volatility. When boundaries are internalised somatically, however, *neuroception begins to recognise safety from within*, rather than waiting for external permission.

This distinction becomes crucial in high-stakes environments where over-verbalising boundaries may provoke defensiveness or retaliation. Take for example the case of Marlene, a healthcare administrator working in a fast-paced hospital environment. Her role required her to be constantly accessible—fielding demands from doctors, patients, and upper management. Initially, she tried to assert boundaries by setting stricter email hours and adopting more direct language in meetings. But she found herself emotionally exhausted, often absorbing the tension of every interaction. After working with a trauma-informed somatic coach, Marlene began practising subtle energetic containment strategies. Before walking into meetings, she would take 90 seconds to centre herself, visualising a calm inner sanctuary that could not be pierced by urgency. Instead of reacting immediately to requests, she would pause deliberately, allowing her body to register the request before her mouth responded. The result was not a dramatic confrontation—but a quiet change in the field. Colleagues began to approach her with more deliberation, sensing—without knowing why—that she was not as "available" to emotional overreach. *Her nervous system had learned to say no before her voice had to.*

There is also an important ethical layer to energetic boundary-setting: it is not a licence to disconnect or judge. Some people confuse "protecting their energy" with controlling their environment. But the purpose of energetic boundaries is not to repel others—it is to *stay intact while staying present.* This means recognising when your system is bracing unnecessarily, or when projection masquerades as perception. It means differentiating between genuine relational overwhelm and unconscious bias. Energetic boundaries are not walls; they are filters. Their power lies in precision, not in rigidity.

In group settings—particularly for facilitators, educators, and therapists—energetic clarity can be the difference between sustainable engagement and quiet burnout. Group dynamics often amplify porousness: emotions become contagious, and collective dysregulation spreads like static. A grounded facilitator who has consciously established an energetic perimeter can regulate not only themselves but the tone of the entire room. Their presence acts like a tuning fork: stabilising, anchoring, even when they say very little. *This is not charisma—it's coherence.* It is not about commanding attention, but containing reactivity.

The subtlety of this practice often causes it to be overlooked or dismissed by conventional approaches to personal development, which favour the explicit, the measurable, and the performative. But sensitivity to energetic cues is not a mystical temperament—it is an adaptive intelligence. It reflects an ability to track the field beneath the words, and to adjust your inner posture without explanation or apology. This form of boundary-setting is often most relevant for those who have historically felt unseen or overrun—those whose nervous systems were trained to attune to others before themselves. For such individuals, energetic clarity is not indulgent—it is reparative.

Of course, like any embodied practice, energetic boundary-setting must be cultivated gradually. Attempting to erect an energetic shield overnight often backfires, creating a brittle or hyper-defensive presence. The goal is not to armour yourself, but to become sovereign. This sovereignty is expressed not in dramatic gestures, but in the calm refusal to contort for comfort, to shrink for approval, or to mirror urgency. It is felt most acutely when you do *less*, not more.

Ultimately, energetic boundaries invite us into a different relationship with space—both physical and emotional. They remind us that not all presence must be shared, and not all stimuli must be absorbed. They teach us that withdrawal need not mean disconnection, and that presence need not mean availability. In a culture that prizes responsiveness over resonance, these invisible shields are a quiet act of refusal—*not against others, but in protection of one's own nervous system integrity.*

Ritualised Saying-Yes

For sensitive individuals, the ability to say no is often championed as the pinnacle of self-care. Yet an equally essential—though less discussed—skill is learning when and how to say yes. Not a yes rooted in compliance, people-pleasing, or obligation, but a yes that emerges from the body's wisdom, aligned with personal capacity, desire, and resonance. In this framework, *saying yes is not just permission—it is participation.* When offered deliberately, yes becomes a form of agency, a doorway into connection that nourishes rather than depletes.

Sensitivity is frequently misunderstood as fragility, but its deeper function is perceptual intelligence: the ability to register subtle relational, environmental, and somatic cues. This same sensitivity, however, can lead to chronic over-attunement—habitually monitoring external needs at the expense of internal ones. Over time, this compromises the body's ability to differentiate between voluntary engagement and socially conditioned performance. Without intentional practices, saying yes becomes automatic, not authentic. *The nervous system confuses endurance with consent.*

To reclaim the vitality embedded in a true yes, we must treat it not as a reflex but as a ritual—a micro-moment of inquiry, a checkpoint for coherence. This means learning to read the body's subtle language: Is the breath expanding or tightening? Is there warmth or contraction in the chest? Is the jaw relaxed or clenched? These physiological markers, often dismissed as background noise, are in fact the body's preliminary vote. They offer a quicker and more accurate verdict than cognitive over-analysis. And over time, they form the compass by which aligned engagement is discerned.

Contrast this with the experience of forced agreement. Most people can recall moments where they said yes while their body said no: accepting an invitation while already exhausted, committing to a favour despite feeling resentful, or staying silent when something felt off. The aftertaste of these interactions is not only fatigue—it is fragmentation. The internal dissonance creates a quiet erosion of self-trust. And because sensitive individuals often carry historical imprints of needing to maintain harmony or avoid conflict, they are more likely to override internal protest in favour of external ease. *Ritualising yes begins the work of re-patterning this dynamic—not through avoidance, but through embodied discernment.*

One method for creating this pause is the simple but profound practice of *delayed consent.* Instead of responding immediately to a request, invitation, or opportunity, allow a full breath cycle before speaking. This introduces a fraction of time where the body's signal can emerge—before it is drowned out by social reflex. If more space is needed, a respectful deferment—"Let me feel into that and come back to you"—buys time not for indecision, but for integrity. In this space, the sensitive person is not escaping responsibility but *anchoring it in self-alignment.*

But ritualised yes is not only about screening for safety—it is about honouring expansion. Some invitations awaken vitality. They may stretch comfort zones, but in doing so they reveal new layers of presence, joy, or connection. These yeses are often accompanied by a subtle lift in the body, a lightness behind the eyes, a rise in curiosity. For instance, a deeply introverted writer may find herself unexpectedly energised by an offer to speak on a podcast—not because it's easy, but because it aligns with a deeper truth she's ready to share. Her yes does not ignore fear; it includes it without letting it dictate the decision. *Here, yes becomes a developmental edge rather than a depletion trap.*

The difference between nourishing and draining engagement often lies in two overlooked variables: *timing* and *relational context.* A yes to the same request may feel enlivening one week and burdensome the next, depending on sleep, hormonal rhythms, or previous social exposure. Similarly, the same yes may feel safe in the presence of one colleague and extractive with another, based on how mutuality is held. For this reason, blanket rules about when to say yes or no are unhelpful. The nervous system does not deal in generalities—it reacts to precision. *Tracking those contextual shifts with granularity is what ritualised saying-yes trains us to do.*

This is where intention-setting and brief somatic check-ins become essential. Before entering a meeting, event, or call, taking even 30 seconds to articulate an inner intention recalibrates the nervous system's engagement mode. It shifts the posture from reactive to responsive, from compliant to co-creative. Intention need not be performative—"I will stay connected to my breath" or "I will track when I feel overextended" are often more powerful than lofty affirmations. These internal commitments become the energetic scaffolding that makes yes sustainable. They frame the social moment not as an imposition, but as a choice.

One sensitive leader I worked with—a director in a mid-sized NGO—used to leave meetings feeling inexplicably depleted, even when they went well. She was highly attuned, compassionate, and communicative. But she was also unconsciously attuning to *everyone.* Before every meeting, she began practising a three-part yes ritual: (1) scanning her body for signs of openness, (2) setting a clear intention—"I will engage, not absorb," and (3) defining a clear exit signal—a gesture or phrase she could use when she felt her system beginning to fray. Over time, she noticed that even difficult meetings felt less draining. It wasn't that she stopped caring. She simply began *caring with containment.*

There is also a broader philosophical layer to ritualised yes: it reclaims the sacredness of consent. Not just in romantic or sexual settings, but in all human exchanges. Every yes is a contract—spoken or unspoken—about time, energy, and presence. Sensitive people often struggle with this because their empathy overrides their instincts. But *consent is not only something we give others—it is something we give ourselves first.* When yes becomes intentional, it becomes a vehicle for intimacy, not obligation. It becomes a site of restoration, not sacrifice.

Critically, ritualised yes requires the presence of *no* in the background. It is the availability of refusal that makes acceptance meaningful. Without that backdrop, yes is not a gift but a default. This is why ritualising yes is not in contradiction with setting boundaries—it is a natural extension of them. The two are not opposing strategies but complementary intelligences. Together, they create a nervous system that is *both receptive and self-protective*—a system that can engage deeply without collapsing.

In professional environments, this discernment becomes essential for long-term sustainability. The high-performing employee who never says no eventually burns out, but so does the boundary-enforcing worker who withdraws too far. What is needed is *relational calibration*—the ability to sense which opportunities offer reciprocity, creative fulfilment, or meaningful contribution, and which ones drain by default. This level of discernment is not taught in time-management seminars, but it is core to any nervous-system-resilient workplace culture.

Ritualised saying-yes teaches us that presence is not binary. It invites a spectrum of engagement, held within the body's intuitive intelligence. It affirms that discernment is not cold or withholding, but deeply relational. It says that yes, when chosen wisely, can be as regulating as silence, as clarifying as solitude. And for those who are used to bracing, appeasing, or adapting in social life, this practice offers a new kind of power—quiet, embodied, and utterly transformational.

Real-World Case: The Parent Who Reclaimed Space

There is a quiet, often invisible cost to caregiving that many sensitive parents carry: the erosion of personal space not just in the logistical sense—time, energy, physical boundaries—but in the psychic and emotional realm as well. Nowhere is this more pronounced than in mothers who are both deeply attuned and chronically overextended. The narrative of unconditional availability, shaped by cultural expectation and amplified by internalised pressure, leaves little room for nuance. And yet, the restoration of self does not require withdrawal from love. It requires boundaries set from compassion—not only for others, but for the self who is always deferring.

When Maya, a 38-year-old mother of two, first began therapy, she was not seeking to set boundaries. She was seeking to survive. A former midwife turned full-time parent during the pandemic, Maya had internalised an identity built around competence, calm, and constant presence. Her children, aged 4 and 6, were bright, sensitive, and demanding in ways that often mirrored her own nervous system. Her partner worked long hours. Her parents were intermittently supportive but emotionally intrusive. Maya's life was full of care—given freely, generously—but she could no longer locate herself inside it. Her days blurred into a rhythm of caregiving tasks and quiet resentment. She wasn't angry at her family. She was vanishing in plain sight.

What brought Maya to the edge wasn't an event. It was the accumulation of micro-abandonments—the skipped meals, the phone calls taken while folding laundry, the shower she cut short because someone was crying outside the door. *No single moment felt like too much, but every moment demanded more than she had left to give.* When her therapist asked her where in her day she felt most like herself, she paused for a long time and then answered, "Maybe… between 1:00 and 1:07, when I sit in the car outside the preschool before pick-up."

That seven-minute window, it turned out, was not trivial. It was sacred. It was the only unclaimed time she hadn't offered up reflexively. And it became the anchor for her first true boundary—not a wall, but a pause. Her therapist helped her ritualise this moment into what they called a *daily boundary bath.* For seven minutes, she was unreachable. The rule was simple: no incoming demands, no multitasking, no emotional labour. Just breath, music if desired, a hand on her heart, and nothing asked of her body. This wasn't self-care in the superficial sense. It was nervous system triage.

What made this shift powerful wasn't its duration. It was its *intentionality.* By naming this micro-retreat and protecting it with both logistics and language—telling her partner and children "this is the time I'm charging my batteries"—she began rewiring the core belief that her availability was her value. She discovered that her children didn't collapse without her. They adapted. And perhaps more surprisingly, she did too.

Over the next few months, Maya began applying the same framework to other areas. She stopped taking unsolicited calls from extended family and instead offered scheduled times when she was emotionally resourced. She restructured the evening routine so that bath time was no longer a battle but a shared, quieter ritual that ended with a ten-minute solo stretch session for herself. She introduced a small sign—an amber stone on the kitchen table—that indicated she was "in space," a term her children learned to associate with quiet presence, not punishment or absence. *Boundaries, for Maya, became relational cues, not rejection signals.*

This case disrupts a cultural fallacy: that boundaries in parenting are inherently cold, distant, or selfish. In reality, they are relational recalibrations that protect connection by making it sustainable. Without boundaries, Maya's sensitivity became absorption. With boundaries, her sensitivity became discernment. She could notice when her child's tantrum was a bid for co-regulation versus a demand that would exhaust her further. She learned to differentiate between empathy and enmeshment. And this allowed her to respond—not react—with a clarity that served everyone in the household.

What is most compelling about Maya's transformation is not how much changed externally, but how much changed *somatically*. Before, she described a perpetual tightness in her shoulders and gut, a chronic feeling of being braced for the next ask. After months of boundary practice, she noticed her breath deepening without effort. Her posture softened. Her digestion improved. These weren't coincidences. They were physiological proof that her nervous system was no longer living in a state of unsignalled emergency.

Crucially, Maya did not wait for permission to reclaim space. She did not wait for her children to be less needy or her partner to be more available. She began with the smallest unit of autonomy she could access—seven minutes in a car—and expanded from there. This is a key insight for readers: *restoration does not require overhaul; it requires intention in microdoses*. The nervous system doesn't measure worthiness in hours. It responds to signals of safety and dignity.

There is a particular moral charge around maternal boundaries that complicates this work. Women are praised for being selfless and punished—socially, if not explicitly—for having needs. This is magnified for those who are sensitive, introverted, or prone to guilt. Maya had to confront the deeply ingrained belief that her needs would harm others. In truth, her unmet needs *were* harming others—not through malice, but through misalignment. Her burnout led to irritability, inconsistency, and a strained marriage. Setting boundaries didn't just help her; it improved the ecosystem of her home.

Over time, the ripple effects became clear. Her children became more resilient, not less. They learned that space could coexist with love, that repair was possible after rupture, and that asking for what one needs is not a betrayal—it's a skill. Her partner, initially sceptical, began to notice the impact and eventually adopted his own version of "space signs" on weekends. Maya's mother, long accustomed to frequent emotional unloading, had to adjust—but eventually developed more reciprocal habits when the dynamic no longer rewarded dependency.

This case illustrates a deeper premise: *boundaries are not barriers to relationship—they are invitations to conscious relationship*. When expressed with clarity and care, they do not create distance. They create structure, predictability, and trust. In families, this is especially vital. Children need attuned connection, yes—but they also need models of self-regard. What Maya modelled was not detachment, but differentiation. She taught her family that love is not measured by depletion, and that presence is most powerful when it includes the self.

There is no universal formula for compassionate boundaries in caregiving. But Maya's experience offers several transferable insights. First, start small. Second, name the boundary aloud—language gives structure to intention. Third, involve others not as adversaries, but as participants in a healthier system. And finally, anchor the practice in somatic feedback. The body will signal whether the boundary is real or merely symbolic. *If your breath doesn't deepen, the boundary isn't working.*

For sensitive readers, especially those in caregiving roles, Maya's case is not an anomaly—it is an invitation. It is proof that restoration is not a luxury reserved for those with spare time or fewer responsibilities. It is a necessity embedded in the fabric of sustainable caregiving. When boundaries are drawn with care, they do not harden the heart. They expand its capacity. They remind us that care offered from fullness is not just more effective—it is more human.

Chapter 11
Relational Recovery: Navigating Social Life Post-Retreat

To live well as a sensitive person in a relentlessly stimulated world is not simply about enduring intensity; it is, more profoundly, an act of conscious relational design. The nervous system does not miraculously stabilise once a retreat is over. Quite the opposite: it is in the aftermath—on returning to the hum and haste of ordinary life—that the subtler challenges of integration surface. For those with heightened perception, that threshold between withdrawal and re-entry often feels like standing on a fault line. One false step and the sense of renewal fractures. But this is not failure. It is a predictable tension within a social culture that struggles to legitimise rest, let alone recognise the intelligence embedded in retreat.

The task, then, is not to erect barricades around sensitivity, nor to abandon the relational world altogether. What is called for is the recovery of social life from a position of nervous-system literacy, relational bravery, and internal consent. Connection is reframed here not as default but as deliberate—a matter of discerned engagement, metabolised at one's own pace. True recovery begins not with escape from others, but with release from the reflexive habits of over-accommodation, shame-fuelled exposure, and compulsive caretaking.

Modern wellness narratives often cast solitude as a temporary detour, a pitstop before resuming a more sociable, "productive" self. Yet for sensitive individuals—those tuned to subtle energies and easily submerged by emotional cross-currents—solitude is not just remedy. It is a baseline. A calibration point. A frequency where one's own presence becomes audible again. The real difficulty emerges later: when this steadied system is required to navigate group chats brimming with subtext, layered social obligations, or that peculiar fatigue everyone feels but rarely names aloud.

What makes relational recovery so thorny is not a lack of relational capacity, but rather the absence of cultural models for intentional reconnection. Prevailing norms valorise availability, responsiveness, and uninterrupted momentum. For the sensitive psyche, such measures warp the very essence of connection. They assess closeness in terms that reward presence divorced from integrity. The result is a performance of belonging, one that appears sustainable but quietly drains the self.

A first step is to legitimise what so many misinterpret as pathology: the pendulum between withdrawal and return. This is not weakness. It is the nervous system's rhythm of regulation, a bio-intelligent ebb that makes sustainable flow possible. Ignoring it—forcing constant presence without pause—turns social life into theatre played on the edge of depletion. Just as ecosystems require seasons of composting, so too does the body-mind need intervals of digestion and reset.

From this understanding arises the idea of retreat-aware relationships. These are not lofty ideals for monastics or niche communities, but practical, workable frameworks for modern connection. In such relationships, silence is not interpreted as fracture but as reset. Space is not feared, but welcomed. Reconnection, when it happens, is intentional—consensual, paced, and transparent. The language shifts from explanation to embodied honesty: *I want closeness, but I need to feel myself again first.* Without apology, without pretence.

Of course, many sensitive people hesitate to voice such needs, not for lack of clarity but from exhaustion with explaining themselves in a world that equates withdrawal with avoidance. Here, ritualised reconnection becomes invaluable. Agreements can be co-created: a check-in message signalling readiness, a shared gesture marking return, even a pause-day reserved for no new commitments. Such rituals prevent the slide into isolation by weaving solitude into the fabric of belonging.

But discernment remains key. Cultivating nourishing circles is not a passive affair. One must ask not only who energises, but who can meet at one's present depth without confusion or demand. After retreat, even old friendships may jar at a subtle energetic level. The answer is not necessarily abandonment but recalibration—deciding who to see first, who to confide in, who to delay. A single ill-timed lunch can undo days of recovery. This is not fragility but precision, the nervous system working with exacting intelligence.

The cultural unlearning required is no less significant: dismantling the belief that belonging equals constant availability. Sensitive individuals frequently equate withdrawal with letting others down. Yet those who flourish post-retreat are those who uncouple worth from performance, and connection from guilt. They come to see relationship not as perpetual duty but as an exchange of mutual care—sometimes expressed in presence, sometimes in pause.

One story illustrates this beautifully: a circle of friends who began weaving collective retreat into their shared rhythm. Their version was not cohabitation but synchronised pauses—days of silence, time in nature, deliberate absence from the digital sphere. Retreat was no longer an emergency response to burnout; it became a preventive practice, a communal value. When they reconvened, conversation centred not on catching up but on what had shifted inward—dreams recalled, breath restored, clarity regained.

The central truth here is deceptively simple: your retreat rhythm is not a flaw to correct, but a pattern to respect. The point is not to resume performing the self that others once demanded, but to re-enter life as the one who has rediscovered themselves. Each return poses a choice: do I step back into the old choreography of compliance, or do I move forward from this steadier ground?

The work of this chapter is to furnish both the mindset shifts and the practical scaffolding for sustaining such integration. It offers guidance on making space without apology, on regulating through social contact rather than around it, and on building circles of connection that restore rather than deplete. The aim is not merely to endure social life after retreat, but to reclaim it as coherent, nourishing, and true.

Sensitive people are not frail links in the social web. They are the ones who interrupt destructive rhythms, who embody the intelligence of pause. Their cycles of retreat and return are not disruptions but recalibrations—signals that devotion to wholeness requires both presence and absence. In their rhythms lies a countercultural wisdom: that slowing, stepping back, and spacing out are not refusals of connection, but acts of fidelity—to the self, to integrity, and ultimately, to relationships strong enough to hold both silence and speech.

The Pendulum of Connection and Withdrawal

Modern society tends to celebrate constancy in social availability. The ability to respond quickly, maintain a vibrant network, and participate actively in community life is often interpreted as emotional health, commitment, and sociability. Withdrawal, on the other hand, is frequently pathologised—seen as avoidance, burnout, or even rejection. But for those with sensitive nervous systems—deep feelers, empaths, introverts, and neurodivergent individuals—this interpretation is both inaccurate and harmful. The rhythm of human connection is not linear. It pulses, oscillates, contracts, and expands. And it is in recognising and respecting this pendulum between engagement and retreat that relational wellbeing becomes possible.

To live in alignment with this pendulum is to reject the idea that connection must be maintained at a constant volume. It is to understand that intimacy deepens not through perpetual contact but through presence that has been metabolised, through re-entry that is self-chosen, and through boundaries that allow one to return to self before returning to others. In many sensitive lives, the greatest damage comes not from overstimulation itself, but from the *guilt* of needing space. This guilt is often internalised early—when one's need for solitude was misunderstood, or when time away from others was framed as selfish, rude, or emotionally distant.

But what if we considered withdrawal not as a failure to connect, but as a form of intelligent recalibration? The nervous system, especially in sensitive individuals, does not operate on willpower alone. It requires spaciousness to digest input, recover from overstimulation, and reattune to its own signals. When ignored, this need manifests as emotional volatility, social numbness, or a quiet, creeping resentment of relational obligations. People often blame themselves for these outcomes, thinking they are bad friends, disengaged partners, or socially dysfunctional adults. But these are not moral failings—they are signs of a cycle that has been interrupted.

Every healthy system has rhythms. The cardiovascular system has its diastole and systole. The respiratory system has inhale and exhale. The endocrine system has surges and plateaus. Likewise, the social system within each person has periods of openness and enclosure. To withdraw is not to sever—it is to gather. To connect is not to abandon oneself—it is to offer the self that has been freshly returned. But this truth is difficult to embody when cultural messaging prizes immediacy over attunement, and availability over authenticity.

The pressure to remain socially available is often exacerbated by technological immediacy. We no longer have the buffer of physical distance to honour natural rhythms of retreat. A message ignored for more than a few hours is interpreted as passive-aggression. A skipped invitation is read as a social slight. The digital world accelerates contact but often bypasses capacity. Sensitive individuals find themselves caught between wanting to respond and needing to decompress—between the value of connection and the cost of participation.

This tension creates what could be called *relational dysregulation*: when one's internal needs are out of sync with external expectations. This mismatch is not resolved by forcing interaction or by withdrawing entirely from the social sphere. It is resolved by internal permission—by recognising that the pendulum swing between connection and solitude is not an indulgence, but a necessity. *Normalising this cycle is an act of psychological hygiene, not isolation.*

Relational recovery begins with somatic honesty. Noticing when the body signals subtle cues of depletion—tightness in the chest during conversation, a sense of emotional flatness despite being "on", a creeping urgency to be alone even while smiling—these are all signs that the pendulum is beginning to swing inward. The earlier one listens, the shorter the withdrawal needs to be. But when ignored, the system is forced to compensate. The withdrawal then becomes dramatic, reactive, and confusing to others—not because it's excessive, but because it was delayed.

A useful reframe is to view withdrawal as a proactive, rather than reactive, practice. Instead of waiting until overwhelm mandates an abrupt disconnect, sensitive individuals can schedule small social fasts, pause-days, or "quiet blocks" after peak interaction. These periods allow the system to digest social input before it becomes residue. Even short respites—an hour of undisturbed silence between meetings, a screenless afternoon after a social weekend, a walk alone before re-entering group dynamics—can serve as maintenance, not repair.

Real-world applications of this approach are emerging across professional and personal domains. Consider a therapist who structures her client sessions in clusters, allowing an empty half-day midweek for recalibration. Or a teacher who knows that parent-teacher conferences require three hours of post-event solitude to restore clarity. These aren't luxuries—they are nervous system-informed design choices. When built into life rhythmically, they reduce the drama and unpredictability of forced retreat.

An equally important dimension is relational transparency. The pendulum of withdrawal becomes less charged when it's named and framed in relationship. Instead of disappearing without explanation, one might say, "I care about this connection, and I want to bring my full presence. To do that, I need space to reconnect with myself first." This kind of directness doesn't require a treatise. A few honest words, spoken without apology or defence, can create profound trust. People are far more willing to honour boundaries when they are offered without shame.

However, transparency also requires discernment. Not all relationships are mature enough to hold these truths. Some people will interpret withdrawal as abandonment regardless of how it's framed. In these cases, the work is not to over-explain, but to clarify one's own internal permission. External understanding is ideal, but *internal congruence is essential.* If the nervous system is sacrificed for the sake of social comfort, the connection will eventually collapse under the weight of unmet needs.

It is also vital to distinguish between *withdrawal from connection* and *withdrawal from relational stress*. Sometimes, what's needed is not less contact, but *different contact.* The presence of regulating relationships—those in which you feel met, not managed—can be profoundly restorative even in states of low capacity. These are connections where silence is safe, where there's no pressure to perform, where retreat is respected rather than resented. Learning to identify and invest in such relationships is part of maturing the pendulum's arc.

The wider cultural project must also shift. We need spaces—workplaces, communities, schools—where withdrawal is not pathologised. Where leaders can model regulated boundaries, where colleagues can say "I need a quiet hour" without social penalty, where children are taught that solitude is as natural as play. Sensitivity is not the problem. The problem is the pace, the expectation, and the absence of infrastructure for nervous system-aware living. When these are addressed, the pendulum doesn't swing wildly. It glides with clarity.

Ultimately, to honour the pendulum of connection and withdrawal is to honour the self that lives beneath performance. It is to declare that your presence in the world does not require the constant sacrifice of inner rhythm. You are allowed to disappear for a while, to choose quiet over commentary, to pause before rejoining the collective. And when you return—less reactive, more grounded, more truly available—you offer something rare: not just company, but *clarity*. Not just contact, but *coherence.*

Building 'Retreat-Aware' Relationships

Sensitivity, in its truest form, is not a defect to be managed but an intelligence to be honoured. It is the capacity to feel finely—energetically, emotionally, interpersonally—and to discern when those capacities are reaching their natural limit. Yet, for many sensitive people, the greatest strain is not the sensitivity itself but the social negotiations it requires. Saying no. Explaining silence. Justifying solitude. And most painfully, attempting to preserve relationships that don't respect one's need to step back. It is not the retreat that breaks the bond—it is the unspoken shame around it, the misinterpretation of the pause as rejection, and the cultural script that frames restoration as a deviation from relational norms.

To build a 'retreat-aware' relationship is to craft a container where one's rhythms are understood without excessive justification. It is to be seen not only when one is available, responsive, and present—but also when one is inward, quiet, and choosing space. Most relationships, by default, operate under assumptions of constant accessibility. This expectation, left unchallenged, slowly erodes the nervous system of the sensitive person who feels torn between the longing for connection and the biological imperative for recovery. If we do not interrupt these assumptions, we build connections at the cost of internal coherence.

What is required, then, is not better time management or more social stamina. It is a different foundation altogether—one where the language of boundaries is relational, not combative. Where one's need for solitude is not an act of distancing but of deepening. And where presence is offered not from depletion, but from sovereignty. The first step is internal: to dislodge the inherited belief that retreat is a problem to solve or a weakness to conceal. Retreat is not avoidance. It is integration. It is what allows presence to have weight.

But embodiment alone is not sufficient. There must also be communication. Clear, respectful, rooted in self-trust. Too often, sensitive people attempt to pre-empt disappointment by over-explaining or softening their truth. They offer disclaimers. They apologise for silence. They delay the boundary until resentment creeps in. But communication need not be a defence. It can be a calm assertion: "I care about this connection, and I also need to honour what keeps me grounded. That may look like space, quiet, or fewer check-ins—but it's not withdrawal from you, it's a return to me."

The difference lies in tone and timing. Retreat-aware relationships are proactive, not reactive. They normalise conversations around capacity before conflict arises. They allow both parties to understand what signals to look for: when someone is nearing overwhelm, when space is needed, and how reconnection can happen organically rather than through forced repair. This shared vocabulary transforms boundaries from barriers into bridges. The relationship learns to breathe.

One powerful way to facilitate this understanding is through co-created rituals. A sensitive person might introduce the idea of "pause days" in their week—predictable intervals where they intentionally minimise contact. Or they might use a mutually agreed-upon phrase that signals low capacity without inviting worry or interpretation, such as "quiet mode" or "off-grid for clarity." These small agreements remove ambiguity. They make space a known rhythm, not an emotional riddle.

Yet not all relationships will be willing—or able—to adapt. And this reality must be acknowledged without sentimentalism. Some connections, no matter how cherished, rely on performance, not presence. They depend on perpetual availability, and crumble when one dares to slow the pace. In these cases, retreat-aware living becomes an act of discernment: to see which relationships can mature with you, and which remain tethered to old codes of guilt and obligation.

Here, it is helpful to recognise the difference between relational compromise and relational self-abandonment. All meaningful relationships require some adaptation. But when the cost of connection is the erosion of self-awareness, the trade is no longer ethical. Retreat-aware relationships honour both sides. They acknowledge that everyone has different thresholds, and that emotional generosity must be rooted in energetic honesty. A friend who respects your "no" without demanding an explanation is not distant—they are attuned. A partner who notices when you need quiet and doesn't fill it with questions is not detached—they are wise.

These are the markers of mature intimacy: comfort with silence, flexibility around presence, and trust that withdrawal is not abandonment. Sensitive individuals, in turn, must resist the temptation to disappear without trace, to martyr themselves for approval, or to oscillate between over-engagement and total shut-down. Self-trust breeds relational trust. The more fluently you embody your own needs, the more confidently others can respond to them.

One often overlooked dimension of retreat-aware relationships is timing. Sensitive people often wait until they are at breaking point to draw the boundary—when the body is fried, the heart is frayed, and the mind can no longer articulate anything clearly. At that moment, communication tends to feel either explosive or avoidant. But if the boundary is expressed early—when the first signals of depletion appear—it lands as clarity rather than rupture. The earlier one names their edge, the less dramatic the edge becomes.

The cultural paradigm must also evolve. We live in a world that rewards hyper-socialisation. The person with the most group chats, the fullest calendar, the quickest response time, is often seen as the most relationally successful. But what if relational excellence included the courage to pause? What if depth replaced frequency as the gold standard? In a retreat-aware world, a text might read, "Thinking of you. No pressure to respond. Just letting you know you're held." A meeting might open with a genuine check-in: "What's your social capacity today?" A friendship might centre less around output and more around shared pacing.

The emerging neuroscience on co-regulation supports this. When two nervous systems are in contact, they influence each other's state. A dysregulated person cannot co-regulate another. But a person who has returned to themselves through intentional retreat brings a grounded presence that is inherently regulating. In this way, retreat-aware relationships are not only more sustainable—they are more healing. They shift from co-dependence to co-regulation. From obligation to resonance.

It is also worth stating: this work does not happen all at once. For many, learning to voice boundaries without shame is a developmental task. It requires unlearning years of people-pleasing, deconstructing familial scripts, and tolerating the discomfort of disappointing others. But the reward is profound. It is a social life built on mutual respect, not performance. It is relational rest, not just relational activity.

Ultimately, to build retreat-aware relationships is to choose a new blueprint. One where presence is not extracted but offered. Where space is not absence but sacred maintenance. And where the sensitive self does not shrink or harden in order to belong—but is met, understood, and given room to breathe. In these relationships, connection is not constant, but it is coherent. And coherence, for the sensitive nervous system, is the deepest form of safety.

Choosing Nourishing Social Circles — Teaches how to curate relationships that support sensitivity and retreat cycles

Some relationships drain us not because of overt harm, but because they chronically fail to honour our nervous system's thresholds. In modern discourse, we are urged to build social networks, expand our reach, and "never eat alone." But for the sensitive system—especially one attuned to nuance, pattern, and relational energy—indiscriminate connection is not neutral. It is costly. To function well, such individuals must move from merely "managing" social life to *curating* it with discernment. This is not social elitism; it is an act of biological integrity.

For sensitive individuals, the quality of a relationship often hinges not on whether it is "positive" or "negative" in content, but on whether it respects the rhythms of presence and pause, engagement and retreat. Most people are taught to assess relationships primarily by emotional metrics—do they make me feel good, safe, validated? But another, less conscious metric plays out simultaneously: *Does this relationship honour my need to regulate?* Does it allow the cycles of nervous system expansion and contraction that are critical for restoration? When that answer is no, chronic dysregulation accumulates silently, disguised as fatigue, resentment, numbness, or inexplicable withdrawal.

We must therefore rethink social connection not as a flat landscape of sameness, but as an ecosystem. Not every organism thrives in the same conditions. Some need sunlight and noise, others shade and stillness. When sensitive individuals try to force themselves to function in hyper-extroverted relational climates—group chats that never sleep, friendships that demand constant availability, partnerships without space—they begin to lose vitality at the source.

These individuals are not deficient. They are simply in the wrong environment.

There is no universal formula for what makes a social circle nourishing. What matters is not the size, structure, or frequency of connection, but its *energetic signature*. A nourishing social circle allows one to leave interactions more coherent, not more scattered. It invites reciprocity, not endless holding. It gives permission for retreat, not punishment for absence. These attributes are not always found in the relationships we inherit, especially in high-demand roles like caregiving, teaching, activism, or leadership, where social engagement is constant but rarely truly restorative.

The first step in curating nourishing social circles is therefore awareness. Most people never pause to evaluate their relational ecosystems through a nervous system lens. We ask: "Do I like this person?" "Are they kind?" "Are they loyal?" But we rarely ask: *"How does my body feel in their presence—before, during, and after?"* When we introduce somatic honesty into the process, patterns emerge. Some relationships bring tightening in the chest, shallow breath, or the compulsion to perform. Others bring expansion, exhalation, and quiet safety. The difference is not always about content; it is about resonance.

Many high-functioning, sensitive individuals override these signals for years—out of duty, habit, or the fear of being "too much" or "too sensitive." They silence the microdata of their inner world in order to meet external expectations of connection. But sustained suppression of these signals creates a costly detachment from one's own relational compass. Eventually, the body will begin to protest. The protest may show up as chronic fatigue, anhedonia, irritability, or the collapse into retreat that feels more like escape than renewal. At this point, social life becomes a threat to vitality rather than a source of it.

Reclaiming relational clarity begins with reframing. Choosing nourishing social circles is not selfish, antisocial, or cold—it is an ecological necessity. Just as a plant cannot thrive in hostile soil, a sensitive system cannot bloom in an environment that denies its natural rhythms. The task is not to become less sensitive. It is to become more attuned to what sensitivity reveals.

This involves a slow and steady realignment. Begin by identifying your "biological allies"—those rare individuals with whom you can be authentic without emotional labour, where silence is not judged, where space is not read as rejection, and where presence feels like a settling, not a bracing. These people may not be the ones you spend the most time with. They may not always be your oldest friends, your family, or your colleagues. But they are essential. They act as relational co-regulators, offering safe resonance and mutual nervous system attunement.

Equally important is setting boundaries with those who—though perhaps well-meaning—disrupt your cycles of retreat. Not through confrontation, necessarily, but through structure. That structure may look like not responding to every message immediately. It may look like declining social invitations without apology. It may mean redefining the pace, tone, or medium of your connection. And it may involve endings—not from cruelty, but from clarity. If a relationship chronically violates your nervous system's cues, then maintaining it becomes a form of self-abandonment.

One of the most overlooked practices in curating nourishing circles is *ritualised consent.* This means not treating every social invitation as an automatic yes or no, but running it through a deeper filter: *Does this invite align with my current capacity, values, and nervous system state?* Ritualised consent means pausing before committing. It means noticing whether the "yes" is emerging from a regulated centre—or from guilt, FOMO, obligation, or anxiety.

Crucially, we must normalise the fact that nourishment is contextual. A relationship that felt safe a year ago may no longer serve you. A connection that once exhausted you may, under new terms, become supportive. People change. Seasons shift. Sensitivities deepen or soften. Curating nourishing social life is not about perfection or permanence. It is about fidelity to your evolving capacity and truth.

Social sensitivity is often framed as a burden, something to be managed or corrected. But it can be a profound form of intelligence—if properly supported. It allows for deeper intimacy, greater presence, and the ability to sense dynamics that others miss. But it is only sustainable when the social environment honours that intelligence rather than demanding its suppression.

To curate nourishing relationships, then, is not simply to avoid "toxic" people or embrace "positive" ones. It is to live in right relation to your own physiology. It is to build a community architecture that supports coherence, not collapse. It is to turn social life from an energy drain into an energy exchange.

Ultimately, the work is not about isolating ourselves but *liberating ourselves from interactions that require self-abandonment to maintain.* Once that shift occurs, something remarkable follows: we don't just survive social life—we become enlivened by it. We find that connection no longer costs us clarity. It *amplifies* it. We discover that boundaries are not walls—they are channels for intimacy. And we learn, perhaps for the first time, that it is not only possible, but necessary, to build relationships where our nervous system feels safe enough to stay.

Real-World Case: The Friend Group That Learned to Pause Together – A group of friends integrates collective retreat into their social lives

Friendship, for many, is synonymous with constant availability. Be there. Show up. Say yes. The cultural script assumes that togetherness means proximity, and that silence—or absence—is a crack in the social bond. But this assumption collapses under the weight of sensitive systems, for whom connection without rhythm becomes dysregulating. In a world that expects constancy, this case study illustrates what happens when a group of friends rewrites the rules—not through conflict or detachment, but through *collective pause.*

The group in question consisted of seven individuals in their late thirties and early forties, most of whom met during graduate school and continued meeting regularly for over a decade. They came from different disciplines—psychology, design, education, journalism—

but shared one unspoken pattern: intensity. Their friendships were robust, intellectually engaging, and emotionally rich. Yet, over time, even those connections began to feel burdensome, not because of toxicity or misalignment, but due to *relational overstimulation.*

It began subtly. One member started postponing meetups with increasing frequency. Another stopped responding in group chats, only replying in direct messages. A third would arrive at gatherings but remain emotionally muted. There were no fights, no explicit grievances—only a creeping sense that the group's togetherness, once deeply nourishing, had become mildly depleting. They weren't falling out. They were *falling out of sync with themselves.*

The turning point came during a weekend retreat they had planned together in the countryside. The intention was rejuvenation. What emerged instead was a silent, collective burnout. By the second night, three of the seven had retreated to bedrooms early, citing vague exhaustion. Two others sat on the porch not speaking, just breathing. The hostess finally broke the silence with an observation that shifted everything: "What if we don't try to *do* anything tomorrow?"

That simple statement cracked the performance pattern that had encased their time together. What followed was an impromptu experiment: a day where each person followed their inner rhythms, without apology or explanation. Some journaled. Others walked alone. Some napped. A few sat near each other in silence. They shared only one agreement: no small talk, no group agenda, no forced togetherness.

What surprised them was not just the relief they experienced individually—it was the depth of connection they felt *collectively* once they reemerged that evening. One described it as "the most honest day we've ever had." Another said, "I didn't know I could be part of a group and still feel sovereign." They had, perhaps for the first time, encountered *mutual attunement through mutual pause.*

After that weekend, they decided to codify the experience—not rigidly, but intentionally. They introduced "silent zones" during group retreats. They designated check-ins to ask not just "How are you?" but "What's your bandwidth for connection right now?" They created optional group chats for practical coordination and separate, opt-in spaces for emotional processing. Most radically, they normalised *disappearing* for weeks—or months—without shame or the need for explanation. When someone resurfaced, the assumption was not guilt or explanation, but welcome.

This wasn't a move toward emotional minimalism. Quite the opposite. Over time, their relational depth grew because the underlying contract had changed. They were no longer tethered by obligation. They were *aligned by rhythm.* They honoured each other's nervous systems as legitimate indicators of availability—not as barriers to overcome.

From a psychological standpoint, what this group enacted was a live experiment in co-regulation without co-dependence. Each person became responsible for their own self-awareness, while also trusting the group's capacity to tolerate fluctuation. They weren't afraid of silence or distance because they trusted the integrity of the connection beneath it. And for sensitive individuals—especially those with a history of people-pleasing, social masking, or relational hypervigilance—this is no small feat. It is a redefinition of intimacy itself.

Critically, their transition wasn't seamless. There were moments of insecurity: "Am I pulling away too much?" "Are we drifting?" But these were addressed not through emotional urgency, but through shared agreements. One such agreement was the "retreat clause"—a simple, standing permission to step back from the group when needed, without social penalty. Another was "informed absence"—the practice of letting others know, briefly and respectfully, that one needed space. No justification required. Just the signal of *pause.*

Over time, these microstructures created a macro-shift. Their group stopped orbiting around availability and began orienting around *authentic capacity.* And what emerged was not just sustainability—but joy. Not the effervescent joy of peak experiences, but the quieter, steadier joy of being part of something that doesn't ask you to abandon yourself in order to belong.

This case, while specific, offers a replicable framework. The first insight is that *relational sustainability depends on rhythm recognition.* Most friendship models operate on linear, productivity-driven expectations—"we must keep in touch," "we should catch up soon," "don't be a stranger." But human nervous systems, particularly sensitive ones, don't work on calendar time. They pulse. They oscillate. They surge and retreat. And when groups learn to recognise and honour these rhythms collectively, burnout is not only prevented—it is *pre-empted.*

The second insight is that *absence can be a form of intimacy*. When space is granted without suspicion, a new kind of trust develops. It's the trust that says: I believe you know what you need. I don't require performance to keep loving you. I'm not scared of your silence.

And the third insight is that *collective retreat doesn't diminish connection; it refines it.* When friends pause together, not out of conflict but out of care, something deeper is activated: the shared value of attunement. This value transcends mere convenience or proximity. It becomes a relational ethic.

What made this group's evolution powerful was not the novelty of their structure but the maturity of their commitment. They didn't abandon each other to preserve themselves. They *transformed their way of being together* so that the self and the group could both thrive. This wasn't about self-care over connection. It was about *connection as self-care*—reimagined through a nervous system lens.

This case offers a compelling invitation to any group—be it friends, colleagues, or families—who want to move beyond the burnout of constant togetherness into the regenerative power of *mutual spaciousness.* It suggests that the future of healthy social life may not lie in doing more together, but in *resting more honestly alongside one another.* That sometimes, the most radical thing a group can do is *pause—together.*

Chapter 12
The Creative Surge After Retreat

Creativity is so often misconstrued as the fruit of relentless effort—an achievement forged through sheer determination, discipline, or the sudden spark of inspiration. But history tells a subtler truth. Some of the most profound creative leaps have not been born of strain but of stepping back. The painter who disappears into the countryside. The inventor who dozes off on his workshop floor. The writer who abandons the page in favour of a walk. We recognise these patterns, almost to the point of cliché, yet seldom do we pause to consider what they signify: retreat is not the enemy of creativity; it is the condition that makes it possible.

At the heart of this chapter lies a paradox that modern productivity culture resists acknowledging—that genuine generativity often begins in quietude. Contemporary bias tends to equate rest with avoidance, even laziness. Yet research and lived experience alike point to a different conclusion: intentional withdrawal creates fertile ground for breakthroughs. The sudden rush of imaginative clarity that follows a retreat is not accident but recurrence, a rhythm inscribed in our biology, psychology, and cultural memory.

Cognitive neuroscience now lends language to what artists and thinkers have long intuited. In states of rest—particularly when external noise diminishes and a sense of internal safety is restored—the brain activates what is known as the default mode network. This circuitry, tied to autobiographical reflection, associative thinking, and imagination, is not idle machinery. It is the backstage of the mind, where connections long buried resurface and disparate fragments coalesce into something coherent. Ideas ripen here, not through brute force but through a kind of spacious invitation.

Yet how rarely we are taught to trust this rhythm. Our conditioning insists on a binary: you are either producing or you are squandering time. Rest, in this view, becomes defensible only when reframed as recovery fuel for the next round of output. But what if rest is not the support act—what if, under the right conditions, it *is* the creative process?

This is where the language of "retreat" becomes indispensable. Retreat is not the same as collapse into passivity, nor is it an idle drift. It is structured pause, a deliberate enclosure of time and space that serves as an incubator. Whether that means a weekend in solitude, an afternoon free of interruptions, or a sabbatical carefully held, retreat establishes the boundaries that allow the psyche to let go of vigilance. It is a container where non-linear thinking can breathe.

We begin, then, by dismantling the seductive myth that pressure and stimulus are the truest companions of creativity. They are not. For sensitive minds—those attuned to subtlety, easily overrun by noise—spaciousness is not indulgence but necessity. Time and again, the greats have proven it. Jung retreating to his stone tower by Lake Zürich. Maya Angelou hiring anonymous hotel rooms to write in anonymity. Remove the static, and something elemental appears.

But retreat also intersects with more elusive states: the transitional moments around sleep, those liminal phases of hypnagogia and hypnopompia. Easily overlooked, these thresholds are abundant with fragments of vision and peculiar clarity. Edison and Dalí famously played with these edges—holding objects that would drop and wake them just as they slipped into dream-logic. In those few suspended seconds, the rational mind loosened its grip, and the unconscious offered its symbols unfiltered. Those who learn to court such states discover a seam of imagination unavailable to the waking grind.

Distinguishing collapse from orientation is essential here. Collapse is reactive, the body buckling after overstimulation. Orientation, by contrast, is chosen. It is the decision to value depth above velocity, resonance over performance. Retreat, understood in this way, is not an abdication of life but a rebalancing within it. For the burned-out, the blocked, or the dislocated, such recalibration is not accessory—it is the foundation upon which any real work can stand.

Retreat is not only an act of personal preservation but a design principle for a creative life. How might one shape environments to enable generative quiet? What rituals smooth the transition into and out of it? How can those whose systems register the world with particular intensity harness retreat, not as resistance, but as a way of living rhythmically with reality rather than against it?

Consider the case of a visual artist whose practice faltered under exhaustion. Instead of pushing harder, she reorganised her creative life around cyclical retreats. Quiet became her scaffold, not her escape. Her pace slowed, exhibitions fewer. Yet the depth of her work widened. Audiences sensed it. Retreat, for her, was not a delay but the very architecture of her integrity.

Practical frameworks will follow—methods for designing retreats that nurture creativity without requiring luxury or isolation. These are not escapes but intentional vessels where rest, play, low-stakes exploration, and gentle novelty interweave. From design theory to behavioural science, we see how variables—silence, time, sensory balance—can be tuned, particularly for sensitive or neurodivergent creators. Retreat becomes not rigid rule but adaptive art.

Of course, one must reckon with the cultural suspicion of retreat. In economies that commodify both work and imagination, withdrawal is often judged as waste or privilege. Yet to rest with intention is to resist that distortion. Retreat is not refusal but recalibration. It is the wager that creation born from wholeness serves more faithfully than output squeezed from depletion.

This chapter does not romanticise retreat as panacea for every creative block. It does, however, argue that for many—especially those who perceive and process with unusual depth—retreat is indispensable. Creativity is not a linear factory line; it is an organism with cycles. And some of its most luminous offerings emerge not in the grip of striving, but in the moments when one dares to put down the pen, close the studio door, and let silence do its unseen work.

By journey's end, readers will not only understand the neurological and psychological ties between rest and creativity. They will also have permission—firm, unapologetic permission—to design their lives so that silence ceases to look like absence and instead becomes the deepest kind of preparation.

Rest as Fertile Ground for Creativity

There is a cultural lie so deeply embedded in our collective psyche that it goes largely unquestioned: that creativity is born from pressure, busyness, and relentless effort. The image of the tortured artist, the burning-the-midnight-oil innovator, and the endlessly caffeinated founder populate our cultural narratives. But reality tells another story—one less glamorous, more subtle, and strikingly more sustainable. *True creativity thrives not in overstimulation, but in deliberate spaciousness.* Structured rest, particularly in the form of retreat, is not merely a way to recover from burnout; it is a method of engaging the brain's deepest creative faculties.

To understand why rest can become a crucible for innovation, we must first examine what creativity demands of the mind. Creativity is not simply the act of producing something new—it is the complex integration of seemingly unrelated elements into a novel synthesis. It draws from memory, emotion, pattern recognition, sensory association, and intuitive leaps. Under conditions of mental fatigue or continuous cognitive demand, these systems degrade. The mind narrows into functional survival thinking—useful for short-term problem-solving, useless for generative insight. In contrast, *restorative retreat reopens the perceptual field*, allowing diffuse attention to activate. This diffuse state, often mistaken for idleness, is precisely when the mind begins to rewire itself, find unexpected links, and reach beyond linear logic.

Cognitive neuroscience has provided increasingly robust evidence to support this claim. The default mode network (DMN), a set of brain regions that activates when we are not focused on the outside world, is strongly correlated with self-referential thought, imagination, and scenario simulation. When the brain is 'at rest' in retreat—walking alone, lying on a bed watching ceiling shadows, sitting in a field with no schedule—it is not doing nothing. It is *doing differently*. The DMN becomes metabolically active, allowing memory fragments, emotional impressions, and symbolic material to drift into consciousness. *This is the soil in which new ideas germinate.*

Historically, structured withdrawal has played a significant role in the lives of creators. Nikola Tesla engaged in ritualised solitude to visualise inventions down to the last bolt before ever picking up a tool. Virginia Woolf insisted on daily solitude not only for writing but for incubating thought. Even within high-performance fields such as design and engineering, structured disconnection has repeatedly been linked to innovation. IDEO, the design consultancy known for pioneering the modern innovation process, actively builds in undirected time to support creative incubation. When retreat is framed as strategy, rather than indulgence, its generative power becomes undeniable.

Yet, the power of retreat is not merely cognitive—it is also physiological. Prolonged engagement in high-arousal social or professional environments keeps the nervous system in a state of sympathetic activation. Cortisol remains elevated, heart rate variability lowers, and attentional flexibility suffers. In this state, the brain prioritises predictability and control. By contrast, parasympathetic states—induced through rest, low stimulation, and somatic downregulation—restore access to the prefrontal cortex and right-hemispheric functions linked to insight and intuition. Structured rest provides the biochemical foundation for lateral thinking. It is not merely about relaxing the body—it is about *reactivating the subtle circuitry that fuels original thought.*

There is also a moral dimension to consider. In a society that equates value with output, choosing to rest—let alone design structured retreats—can provoke inner resistance. Sensitive individuals, in particular, may feel guilt or self-doubt when stepping away from expected forms of productivity. But this guilt is not an ethical compass—it is a byproduct of cultural conditioning. When we allow ourselves to retreat with intention, we do not abandon responsibility; we *renew our capacity to meet it with clarity, depth, and originality.*

Structured retreats differ from casual leisure in one critical way: they are intentionally framed as generative containers. They create both time and psychological permission for the mind to enter altered states of perception. This does not require exotic locations or extended sabbaticals. A retreat may be as simple as a single day without digital input, a weekend with a journal and no expectations, or a walking practice designed not for exercise but for ideation. What matters is that the space is protected, and the nervous system is allowed to downshift. The benefits do not arise from the duration of the retreat but from the *quality of presence within it.*

Within such retreats, ideas do not arrive as neat outlines—they surface in fragments, metaphors, irritations, and dreams. They require patience and attunement. This is why retreat also cultivates the disposition necessary for long-term creativity: receptivity. In contrast to the ego-driven push for originality, receptivity allows something unexpected to emerge. It enables the creator not to direct the process, but to *witness it unfolding.* The mind moves from problem-solving to pattern-seeing, from effort to listening.

To illustrate this in practice, consider the case of a software engineer in a Fortune 500 company who, after several years of performance at the edge of burnout, began to experience what he described as "cognitive flatness"—a state in which even basic creative tasks felt dull. Rather than push harder, he designed a personal retreat: four days without screens, minimal talking, structured around long walks, journaling, and silence. On the third day, without prompting, a novel algorithmic structure he had struggled with for months suddenly surfaced in his mind. The problem had not been solved through conscious work—it had dissolved through deep neural reorganisation, only made possible by *letting go of the demand to solve it.*

Critically, the insight was not accidental. It was made possible by a structure—a deliberately cultivated environment that optimised the internal conditions for emergence. *Creativity is not the lightning bolt; it is the climate.* Structured retreat cultivates that climate. In this way, sensitive thinkers, introverted creatives, and reflective leaders can design lives that honour both their depth and their contributions. Instead of cycling between burnout and inspiration, they build a sustainable rhythm in which retreat and creation are not separate, but sequentially linked.

But the idea of retreat must be nuanced. It is not always comfortable. When the external noise is stripped away, internal material—doubts, griefs, unresolved tensions—can arise. Yet this discomfort is not a flaw in the process; it is the compost of creative renewal. *To rest is also to face.* The material that surfaces during retreat often becomes the very content from which meaningful creative work is made.

Writers find their voice not in the absence of struggle, but in the *stillness where struggle is seen clearly.*

Retreat also teaches scale. It reminds creators that not every insight must become a masterpiece. Some ideas will drift through like clouds—interesting, fleeting, unfinished. Others will land and ask for development. The discipline lies not in forcing ideas to arrive, but in recognising which ones are alive. Structured rest sharpens this discernment. It makes it possible to distinguish between the noise of mental chatter and the *signal of genuine emergence.*

For this reason, retreat is not only a space for creativity—it is also a training ground for creative wisdom. It teaches pacing, listening, non-attachment, and trust. These are not secondary traits; they are the foundation of sustainable innovation. In fields that reward speed, novelty, and external validation, retreat offers a radical alternative: *depth, integrity, and inner alignment.*

In the context of a society facing information overload, environmental degradation, and attention collapse, creativity is not a luxury—it is an imperative. But to meet that imperative with originality and coherence, we must first reclaim our capacity to rest. Structured retreat is not a refusal of responsibility. It is a *recalibration toward deeper contribution.*

In this light, rest is not a break from the creative process. It is its beginning. Its soil. Its rhythm. And when respected and protected, it becomes a quiet revolution—a way of creating not from urgency, but from *presence.*

Dream States, Hypnagogia, and Insight

There exists a narrow window between waking and sleeping where the ordinary rules of thought loosen and unexpected truths rise to the surface. This fleeting threshold, known as hypnagogia, has fascinated scientists, artists, philosophers, and mystics for centuries—not because it is mysterious, but because it is astonishingly productive. It is in this altered state that minds across disciplines have encountered breakthroughs that seemed inaccessible during conscious effort. Far from being a mystical accident, hypnagogia represents a powerful and reproducible state of consciousness in which the brain becomes uniquely suited to creative problem-solving, insight generation, and associative thinking. For the sensitive, thoughtful reader attuned to the rhythms of retreat, this liminal state offers not just intellectual novelty, but *a disciplined tool for ideation and emotional integration.*

To understand hypnagogia is to appreciate the neurological transitions that occur as the brain descends into sleep. During this passage, the dominant beta waves of wakefulness give way to slower alpha and theta rhythms, accompanied by transient visual imagery, auditory hallucinations, and fragmented thought-forms. This is not dreaming in the full sense—REM sleep occurs later—but rather *a fertile mental twilight where control and spontaneity co-exist.* In this state, the brain continues to process unresolved stimuli, recent memories, and latent emotional content, yet does so in ways less linear and more associative than in full waking consciousness. The result: pattern recognition untethered from rigid logic.

Artists have long intuited this state's power. Salvador Dalí famously used a technique whereby he would nap in a chair while holding a spoon over a plate. As he drifted into hypnagogia and his hand relaxed, the spoon would drop, wake him, and allow him to record the surreal imagery that had just begun to surface. Thomas Edison employed a nearly identical method, claiming it helped him visualise new inventions in their early stages. These anecdotes, often recounted as charming eccentricities, reveal something deeper: *insight thrives at the edges of awareness*, and those edges can be consciously cultivated.

But this phenomenon is not limited to artists. August Kekulé, the chemist credited with discovering the ring structure of the benzene molecule, arrived at his insight not through lab work, but through a semi-dream in which he envisioned a snake biting its own tail. Srinivasa Ramanujan, the Indian mathematician, claimed many of his theorems came to him fully formed in dreams. The common denominator in these examples is not passivity—it is *openness*. These thinkers entered states in which the analytical mind relaxed enough to allow subconscious patterning to rise into awareness.

Modern cognitive science increasingly validates what these historical figures sensed intuitively. Studies in the field of sleep research have shown that hypnagogic and hypnopompic states—transitional states around sleep onset and awakening—activate regions of the brain associated with default mode processing, emotional memory consolidation, and divergent thinking. In one study conducted at MIT, participants trained to solve a particular problem were significantly more likely to find creative solutions if they spent time in a hypnagogic state shortly after engaging with the task. Crucially, their success was not due to rest alone, but to the *transitional quality* of the state—a liminal awareness combining relaxation with residual cognitive intent.

For sensitive individuals and reflective creatives, this insight has major implications. Structured retreat, by design, often disrupts habitual overstimulation and creates internal spaciousness. In this quieter terrain, access to dream states and hypnagogic thresholds becomes more fluid. It is here that a shift occurs—not only in what the mind perceives, but in how it perceives. Instead of demanding answers, the retreating mind *invites emergence*. This distinction is critical. It marks the difference between creativity driven by force and that supported by inner alignment.

Importantly, hypnagogic insight is not merely about hallucination or fantasy. It often yields practical, structured content—solutions to technical problems, breakthroughs in narrative structure, elegant metaphors, or new conceptual frameworks. But accessing these insights requires that one suspend the inner editor. The egoic mind, trained to demand coherence, often interrupts before these fragments can form. The skill, then, is not just entering hypnagogia, but *staying present within it long enough to receive something meaningful without rushing to interpret.*

Some retreat practices are particularly conducive to this state. Yoga nidra, or yogic sleep, guides participants into a state between waking and sleeping, where body awareness fades and mental imagery arises spontaneously. Lucid hypnagogic writing, a technique involving journaling during the descent into sleep, allows for real-time transcription of subconscious material. Even more informal practices, such as lying on a sofa mid-afternoon and consciously observing the drift of thoughts, can create a bridge to insight—*provided the environment is free from interruption and expectation.*

The ethical and philosophical implications of this are worth noting. In a culture that prizes conscious willpower and analytical control, to value altered states as sites of wisdom represents a shift in epistemology. It acknowledges that *not all knowledge is consciously constructed.* Some truths are incubated in shadow, discovered through surrender, or whispered at the margins of sleep. To make use of these insights requires humility—not because they are irrational, but because they are not always immediately legible to the linear mind. This is not anti-intellectualism; it is *meta-intellectualism*: the capacity to recognise multiple forms of knowing and to discern when each is appropriate.

Of course, one must take care. Not every image or impression that arises in hypnagogia carries meaning. The mind, like a dream, can be noisy, strange, or chaotic. What differentiates productive insight from mental drift is *integration.* That is, returning to waking consciousness and applying discernment. What felt profound may, upon reflection, prove trivial. But often, amid the noise, *a pattern reveals itself*, one that resonates not merely intellectually, but somatically—felt as truth rather than inferred. That felt resonance is the signpost of genuine insight.

For those interested in practical application, it is possible to cultivate a personalised protocol. Begin with a retreat environment that supports nervous system downregulation—minimal stimulation, absence of digital interference, and a predictable rhythm. Choose a time of day when sleep pressure is naturally increasing—late afternoon or before bedtime. Lie down with the intention to observe, not sleep. Let the mind wander. Keep a notebook nearby, but avoid writing until something coherent begins to form. Upon reawakening, do not immediately re-enter stimulation. Instead, linger in the transition and allow whatever fragments arose to be considered, expanded, or set aside. *The power of hypnagogia lies not in manipulation, but in permission.*

In this way, dream states and altered rest become not just curiosities, but developmental tools—spaces in which the psyche rehearses, imagines, recombines, and reveals. The disciplined use of these states within retreat is not escapism; it is a way of courting deeper coherence. Where the rational mind falters, the subconscious often whispers. And when we are quiet enough, slow enough, and receptive enough, we begin to hear.

This is the art of insight at its most intimate: not extracted by effort, but received through attunement. And for those designing lives around cyclical restoration, hypnagogia becomes less a rare event and more a recurring portal—one that, when approached with reverence and curiosity, expands the range of what the mind can know, imagine, and become.

Retreats as Creative Incubators

Creativity is often romanticised as a spontaneous lightning strike—unpredictable, ungovernable, a flash of brilliance amid chaos. Yet for many sensitive and perceptive minds, the very conditions that provoke creative insight are remarkably predictable: stillness, slowness, safety, space. In this context, retreat ceases to be merely an escape from the pressures of daily life and becomes something much more generative—a deliberate container for the gestation of complex ideas, artistic work, and original problem-solving. A structured retreat, properly conceived, functions not as a withdrawal from productivity but *a redefinition of it.* It reframes the creative process as cyclical, embodied, and organically unfolding rather than continuously extractive or externally paced.

Modern culture rewards output and speed, which means much of what is created is derivative—products of stress, compression, or obligation. The sensitive person often finds this rhythm fundamentally misaligned with their deeper cognitive and emotional processes. It's not a question of talent or intellect, but of ecology. Some nervous systems need different conditions in order to access their best thinking. A retreat that blends rest with intentional incubation addresses this mismatch—not by asking the creative mind to perform on command, but by crafting a space in which it is *safe to wander, to gestate, to recombine, and to risk.*

The neuroscience of this is revealing. Studies show that insight often arises during default mode network activation—a resting-state in the brain associated with internal mentation, mind-wandering, and self-referential processing. These periods of non-task-oriented awareness are precisely what structured retreats prioritise. When the brain is not required to solve problems, it paradoxically becomes better at doing so. Creativity emerges not through focused effort alone, but through alternation—*cycles of focused engagement and diffuse relaxation.* Structured retreats intentionally amplify the latter, allowing the former to take root more deeply.

But not all retreats are equally generative. There is a meaningful distinction between rest that is merely passive and rest that is deliberately curated to foster emergence. A productive creative retreat is *not a vacation.* It is a design—a rhythm of solitude, contemplation, and optional creation, scaffolded by the recognition that new ideas often surface *between the moments we expect them.* These models are neither prescriptive nor rigid, but they are intentional. Their aim is not to force productivity, but to foster internal spaciousness from which novelty can emerge.

Consider three interrelated axes that make a creative retreat structurally effective: containment, contrast, and ritual. Containment refers to the boundaries that separate retreat from ordinary life—physical, temporal, and psychological. This might mean booking a cottage alone for four days, turning off digital access, and pre-arranging food so decisions are minimised. It could mean attending a curated group retreat with structured silence, optional communal meals, and long blocks of unprogrammed time. What matters is that the space *signals difference*—a temporary suspension of business-as-usual that cues the body and mind into a different rhythm of presence.

Contrast is equally essential. Many people mistakenly assume that doing "nothing" will lead to creative output. But paradoxically, the most productive retreats often oscillate between extreme rest and deep focus. A full morning of walking, napping, or meditating followed by a short, intense burst of writing or sketching tends to yield more breakthroughs than attempting to create continuously.

This alternation mimics the brain's natural energy cycles and honours the creative need for *both input and integration.*

Ritual is the final axis—those small, repeated actions that mark transitions, create psychological safety, and help tether the abstract to the concrete. For some, this might mean lighting a candle before a writing session, walking the same loop each morning to let ideas percolate, or closing the day with a journaling practice. These micro-rituals matter because they *signal intention.* They tell the subconscious mind: this time is sacred, this space is for something new.

Different models exist for structured creative retreats, each suited to varying temperaments and goals. The Solitary Incubator is perhaps the most traditional: a writer books a cabin and disappears for ten days. But within this frame, the rhythms vary. One model alternates: two hours of movement, two hours of rest, two hours of work. Another divides the day into "inputs" (reading, observation, wandering) and "outputs" (writing, composing, designing), with plenty of liminal space in between.

Then there is the Collaborative Retreat—used increasingly by interdisciplinary teams, artist collectives, or research groups. Here, the structure may involve co-working mornings in silence, shared lunches, and optional evening salons. The value lies in *parallel processing*—each person working on their own material, but in shared energy. Ideas cross-pollinate not through forced collaboration, but through proximity and resonance. When carefully managed, this can be a powerful middle ground between isolation and overstimulation.

A third model—the Cyclical Retreat—is designed for those who cannot step away for long periods but who can establish mini-retreats across the calendar year. These may be weekend intervals every two months, or five-day retreats quarterly. What makes them effective is not their length but their predictability. When the sensitive creative knows that restoration and ideation are built into the rhythm of their year, they experience less pressure to perform in periods of fatigue and more confidence that inspiration will return. *This removes the anxiety that creativity must always be available—and creates a sustainable model for lifelong generativity.*

Real-world examples reveal how powerful these retreats can be. A composer who spends one week per season at a rural monastery has written that her best work happens "between the walks, not at the piano." A design team from a start-up reports that a biannual retreat to the mountains, in which no laptops are allowed until 4pm, has led to more patents than any in-office brainstorming session. A high-performing academic with a chronic illness uses self-directed retreats as a way to "let her body set the pace for her mind," resulting in more original publications, not fewer. *The consistent thread across these stories is not relaxation but re-alignment*—a return to a state where inner clarity is again possible.

There are tensions, of course. The capitalist logic that underpins much of our professional lives often views retreat as indulgence or avoidance. But this view fails to account for the cost of unbroken productivity: burnout, creative stagnation, and shallow work. It also fails to appreciate that *real insight cannot be forced on a schedule.* Sensitive thinkers know this intuitively. Their nervous systems recoil from coercion and blossom under attunement. A creative retreat offers precisely that attunement—a space that doesn't command the muse, but invites it.

At its best, a structured creative retreat is not a break from life but a deepening into it. It is a stance—a commitment to listening before speaking, to allowing before editing, to receiving before generating. It reminds us that *creativity is not an energy we summon at will, but a conversation we enter into.* When we design spaces that honour that conversation—spaces marked by spaciousness, reverence, and rhythm—we find ourselves not only producing better work, but becoming more honest, more integrated, and more alive in the process.

Thus, retreat is not where creativity pauses. It is where it prepares. It is not absence from the world, but *a return to oneself*—from which better worlds can then be made.

Real-World Case: The Artist Who Found Flow in Stillness

When acclaimed visual artist Elinor Hart stepped away from the gallery circuit at the height of her career, many in her network were perplexed. After two decades of steady exhibition success, residencies, and commissions, her decision to "pause indefinitely" raised eyebrows. She wasn't ill. She wasn't retiring. She hadn't run out of ideas. In fact, it was the *surplus of demands and ideas* that had become the problem. Hart described feeling like "a technician of my own talent," fulfilling a schedule of deadlines and expectations with a growing sense of alienation from the work itself. What had once been an act of devotion was becoming a performance of competence. The technical polish was there, but the pulse had faded.

This dissonance is familiar to many creatives. There is a hidden cost to professionalisation—what begins as an intimate conversation between artist and medium often becomes diluted by the economies of visibility, market expectations, and linear output. For the sensitive practitioner, this pressure to remain publicly relevant can gradually erode the internal compass that first animated their work. Hart's recognition of this came not in a dramatic breakdown, but in a subtle, persistent hollowing—a recognition that *she was producing more than ever, but feeling less in each piece.*

Her decision to restructure her life around cyclical retreat was neither impulsive nor romantic. It emerged from a year of experimentation: blocking out calendar time without obligations, attending a silent retreat for the first time in her adult life, and working with a somatic coach to understand the physiology of creative depletion. What she discovered was not a need to escape the art world, but to *recalibrate her relationship with time, space, and inner listening.*

The model she eventually designed was deceptively simple: one month on, one month off. During the "off" month, she refrained from active production. No canvases. No sketchbooks. No meetings. She described this time as "slow sensory immersion"—walking, cooking, reading, and resting without extracting ideas or outcomes. It was not idle time; it was intentional emptiness. Importantly, she did not *prevent* creative ideas from arising, but she stopped *chasing* them. Any images or concepts that emerged during these intervals were noted quietly and stored, not acted upon.

The "on" months became periods of concentrated making, but with a key difference: they began not from conceptual planning, but from a somatic prompt. Hart would revisit the notes from the prior month and ask her body—not her market sense or professional ambitions—what it felt compelled to pursue. Sometimes that meant returning to motifs long abandoned. Sometimes it meant experimenting with unfamiliar materials without clarity on where it would lead. "The goal," she explained, "was not to build a collection but to build coherence with myself."

What followed was not only a personal renaissance, but a public one. Her next solo show, entitled *Intervals*, sold out in the opening week—not because she had rebranded, but because the work had regained a visceral, arresting quality that resonated. Critics noted the shift: the palette was softer, but the form more assured. There was space in the work—*not just negative space, but emotional spaciousness*—as though each piece had breathed before it arrived. The most repeated word in the reviews was "felt."

Elinor's retreat-based model challenges several dominant myths of creative productivity. First, it dismantles the idea that consistent output equals consistent growth. Her hiatuses—though visible to no one but her—became the *engine of her originality*. Second, it reframes rest not as absence but as incubation. By honouring non-linear, non-productive phases as essential rather than indulgent, she redefined success in terms of *integrity, not just visibility.*

This recalibration was not without tension. Friends questioned her reduced online presence. Her gallery initially resisted the biannual rhythm of new work. Financial uncertainty loomed in the early transition. But over time, what became evident was that *the sustainability of her practice improved as her nervous system stabilised.* She reported fewer migraines, more energy, and—most notably—a renewed sense of trust in her creative process. "I don't fear blank canvases anymore," she said. "I know that silence carries seeds."

A key insight from Hart's experience is that retreat is not only a response to burnout, but a proactive *ecological design.* She began thinking of her career not as a climb, but as a garden—something that required dormancy as much as bloom. This metaphor, while grounded in natural cycles, remained rigorously practical in application. She began to schedule her year as a rotation: two months of retreat (one full, one partial), three cycles of generative creation, one for editing and assembly, and one for exhibition. What looked like fragmentation was in fact *a return to seasonal intelligence*—a system that mimicked nature's own cycles of flourishing and fallow.

It's worth noting that Hart's creative retreats were not always solitary. She experimented with co-retreating—inviting one or two other artists to join her in shared silence, with optional evening conversation. These were not collaborations, but parallel incubations. She likened it to "two trees growing beside each other—not tangled, not separate." The presence of another creative nervous system, when intentional and boundaried, became a subtle amplifier of attention and mutual witnessing.

Critically, Hart's transformation was not only in what she produced, but in *how she experienced herself while producing.* She moved from extraction to reciprocity, from urgency to resonance. Her metrics of success shifted: instead of tracking sales or online metrics, she tracked aliveness. Was she sleeping well? Were her senses alert? Did the work feel necessary? These became her barometers—not as an escape from excellence, but as a *foundation for it.*

Her case speaks to a broader cultural need: the recognition that brilliance is not born from constant connectivity, but from calibrated alternation. Sensitive creatives in particular require *structures that legitimise withdrawal without shame.* When cycles of retreat are built into one's professional identity, the return to work becomes richer, riskier, and more meaningful. The "flow" so often sought in high-performance circles emerges not from pushing through fatigue, but from *cultivating the conditions in which insight can land.*

Elinor Hart's story is not a formula to replicate, but a provocation to reconsider. What if retreat was not what you earned *after* success, but what made success sustainable? What if the most innovative work came *not* from constant exposure, but from cyclical invisibility? And what if stillness was not a void to avoid, but the place where true artistic fidelity is found?

The artist who found flow in stillness did not do so by escaping the world. She remained in it—but on terms attuned to her nervous system, her inner timing, and her need for renewal. Her life, like her work, became less about proving and more about *presence*. And from that presence, the most honest creations emerged—not only for exhibition, but as *a practice of self-reclamation.*

Chapter 13
The Spiritual Dimension of Retreat

There is a truth that does not announce itself in the clamour of everyday striving. It does not compete with urgency or flourish in the theatre of performance. Instead, it lingers, often uneasily, in the intervals between doing and becoming. Some of the most enduring human transformations arise here—not through relentless action, but through retreat. And this retreat is not avoidance; it is alignment. Across centuries and cultures, the act of stepping away into silence, solitude, and surrender has never truly been about leaving the world. Rather, it has been a way of re-entering it with a deeper sense of coherence and responsibility.

What seems like stillness, when viewed through a spiritual lens, is something else entirely: a radical reorientation. Extended retreat, when shaped by contemplative or sacred intention, yields more than rest. It yields revelation. Unlike productivity retreats, marketed as ways to sharpen focus or unplug from devices, spiritual retreat asks for something more unsettling: the relinquishment of identity, the suspension of control, the probing of one's deepest convictions, and the possibility of insight that dismantles old certainties.

In monasteries, in desert caves, in forests and mountains, traditions as varied as Buddhist, Christian, Sufi, Stoic, and indigenous rites of passage converge on a shared conviction: retreat is not an indulgence, nor merely a therapy. It is a threshold. And the silence found there is not empty. It is charged—thick with encounter. What arises in those depths—God, source, soul, or self, depending on the tongue—rarely comforts, but invariably clarifies.

Our secular, performance-driven culture scarcely knows what to make of this. Silence is medicalised. Solitude, equated with loneliness. Withdrawal, dismissed as weakness. Yet, those who have crossed the austere terrain of spiritual retreat often describe it as the most unvarnished experience of their lives. Not because it produced outcomes to tally, but because it dissolved illusions they had not even recognised as illusions.

This chapter is concerned with retreat as revelation. We will look closely at how diverse traditions construct the architecture of sacred withdrawal: the framing of time, the insistence on silence, the use of symbols and rituals, and the transformations expected to follow. Importantly, these traditions do not stop at withdrawal. They also articulate philosophies of return, reminding us that solitude is never an end in itself but a recalibration for renewed participation in the world.

Take the Vipassana tradition. Ten days of noble silence are not imposed as punishment but offered as a portal. The silence does not erase the mind's chaos; it magnifies it. Past hurts, longings, and tangled patterns of thought rise to the surface—not to undo, but to be processed. The retreat itself is the container, and silence the mirror. One sees not what flatters, but what is true.

Or consider the Stoics. Seneca, for example, urged temporary retreats into voluntary hardship. For them, withdrawal stripped away illusions of wealth, honour, or comfort, returning one to the elemental. It was an exercise in moral lucidity, not self-pity.

Christian monasticism shaped another path entirely. For desert hermits and cloistered communities, retreat was not a pause but a life. Silence, work, and prayer fused into a lifelong rhythm. Solitude was not escape from God but communion with Him—an unbroken practice of becoming inwardly available to the divine.

Indigenous traditions complicate the picture still further. Retreat here is not detachment from the world but reconnection with it—through land, ancestors, wind, and fire. Vision quests, fasting, sweat lodges: these are not designed to repair the individual, but to erode the very illusion of separateness. Retreat, in such practices, is a rite of remembering one's place in the greater weave of life.

Taken together, these traditions reveal that spiritual retreat is anything but passive. It is active reorientation. And it is rarely tranquil. Many describe it as emotionally searing, psychologically dismantling. Without distractions or affirmations, one confronts grief, fear, shame, confusion. Yet it is precisely by traversing such thresholds that something else emerges: clarity, compassion, and a renewed willingness to shoulder the weight of what matters most.

These inner realignments are not confined to monasteries or mountains. They shape lives outwardly—transforming relationships, leadership, art, and public responsibility. In one case we will examine, a corporate leader returned from extended silent retreat with a wholly altered ethic: transparency, worker care, environmental responsibility—no longer brand slogans, but imperatives born of conviction. His is hardly an isolated story. The sacred dimension of retreat is not reserved for monks; it is accessible—and perhaps urgent—for anyone steering the machinery of modern life.

Yet one of the most overlooked aspects of retreat is return. If withdrawal is descent, then re-entry is integration. And re-entry is rarely seamless. Silence reshapes perception, but language and daily negotiation demand old habits. Communities have long recognised this. Christian practice, for instance, offers confession and communal reintegration. Buddhist retreats close with dharma talks to bridge silence back into speech. Indigenous traditions often use storytelling as a vessel to share and anchor what was glimpsed in solitude. Without such scaffolds, the wisdom of retreat risks dissipating.

The purpose here is not to homogenise these traditions but to distil their principles: the necessity of structured disconnection, the courage to face oneself without anaesthetic, the reverence for mystery, and the insistence that silence is presence, not absence. These are not relics. They are counterweights to our fractured, distracted existence.

In pushing against the cult of constant stimulation, spiritual retreat asserts a different logic: that the most decisive transformations often germinate in invisibility, that wisdom is not hurried, and that clarity is the fruit of surrender rather than control.

So this chapter extends an invitation. To take seriously the spiritual infrastructure beneath retreat—not for transcendence alone, but for fuller participation in the world. To recover retreat as moral restoration. To recognise silence as its own profound presence. And to ask, both as individuals and as communities: What do we become when we stop performing? What truths surface in the hush? And what clarity waits, patient and unbidden, if we dare to be still?

Sacred Withdrawal Across Traditions

Withdrawal, in its truest form, has never been about escape. It is not cowardice cloaked in silence, nor a retreat from reality. Sacred withdrawal—intentional, structured, and revered—has long been recognised across cultures not as an act of detachment but as a process of *realignment*. Long before modern wellness retreats and digital detoxes offered surface-level reprieves from overstimulation, ancient traditions understood that to withdraw from the world was, paradoxically, to return more whole to it. This insight—simultaneously spiritual, philosophical, and practical—sits at the heart of some of the most enduring wisdom lineages humanity has produced.

The Buddhist path treats withdrawal not as a temporary relief but as a core practice of liberation. In the Theravāda and Zen traditions especially, monastic retreat is a formalised and revered process—one that offers practitioners a structured environment to observe the mind without distraction. Noble Silence, observed over days or even months, is not simply about refraining from speech; it is about tuning inward with radical honesty. The silence becomes a crucible. With distractions stripped away, buried habits, cravings, and aversions rise to the surface. It is uncomfortable, often excruciating—but essential. The Buddhist model asserts that *insight arises only when habitual narratives dissolve*, and that such dissolution requires space, solitude, and slowness.

This model of sacred withdrawal is neither indulgent nor sentimental. Monastic life, though quiet, is not passive. It is structured, disciplined, and community-bound. Daily routines of meditation, mindful walking, and humble chores ground retreatants in physical presence. This is not escapism. It is a form of *radical participation in being*, without the filters of social roles and identity performance. When practitioners re-emerge, they do so not for applause or reintegration into status games, but with clearer perception and softened reactivity—what Buddhism would call equanimity.

The Stoic philosophers of Ancient Greece and Rome offer a contrasting but complementary view. For them, sacred withdrawal was not about monasteries or silence, but about perspective. Seneca, Epictetus, and Marcus Aurelius all recommended regular, intentional solitude as a means of fortifying moral clarity. They counselled that the wise person periodically withdraws from comforts, from society's scripts of success, and from the distractions of crowds—not to isolate, but to examine what is truly necessary. To walk in simple sandals, eat modest food, and reflect in silence was, for the Stoic, an exercise in philosophical resilience.

Where Buddhism frames withdrawal as a path to liberation from suffering, Stoicism treats it as a crucible for virtue. Both traditions, however, reject the modern impulse to pathologise solitude. Instead, they propose that time alone, whether in formal retreat or informal contemplation, is a *moral act*: one that fosters discernment, integrity, and the ability to act justly in a chaotic world. For both, sacred withdrawal is not a luxury but a discipline—one that builds the interior scaffolding required for wise re-engagement.

Christian monasticism formalised this intuition into an institutional architecture that still endures. From the desert fathers of the 3rd century to Benedictine monasteries and contemporary contemplative communities, Christian retreat practices reflect a theology of *return through relinquishment*. The Rule of Saint Benedict outlines a life of ora et labora—prayer and work—where withdrawal is not escape from worldly responsibility but a reorientation toward divine alignment. Silence, simplicity, and service form the triadic pillars of monastic retreat.

Yet unlike the asceticism often caricatured in popular imagination, Christian monasticism has long insisted on the *integration* of inner and outer life. Withdrawal from worldly noise is meant to deepen one's capacity to love—both God and neighbour. The rhythm of liturgical prayer, communal meals, and manual labour is not meant to sever ties with the world but to sanctify time itself. Retreat is the container through which monks confront their own pride, restlessness, and spiritual fatigue—and in doing so, find a centre sturdy enough to carry back into the world.

Among Indigenous cultures, sacred withdrawal is often interwoven with the natural world in ways that diverge significantly from institutionalised models. Vision quests, sweat lodges, and fasting ceremonies are common across diverse Indigenous traditions, yet they all share a core belief: that to be human is to be in relationship with land, ancestors, and spirit. Withdrawal here is not about stepping away from the world, but about *rejoining it more consciously*. The isolation of the quester is not one of abandonment but of connection—to birdsong, wind, stars, and the felt presence of guidance larger than self.

Indigenous models of retreat do not typically isolate the self from the cosmos. Instead, they remind the practitioner that *the self is part of the cosmos*. This relational spirituality shifts the very premise of withdrawal. It becomes less about renunciation and more about recalibration—an embodied remembrance of right relationship with community, ecology, and the sacred. When the young person returns from their vision quest, they do not re-enter life with a self-help insight or a productivity hack. They return *with responsibility*—to bring back what they've learned and offer it in service to the collective.

Across these traditions—Buddhist, Stoic, Christian, and Indigenous—a pattern emerges. Withdrawal is sacred not because it severs, but because it *purifies*. It clarifies the noise from the signal, the persona from the presence, the inherited script from the inner call. These traditions do not glamorise solitude, nor do they romanticise silence. They respect both as tools for transformation, *not ends in themselves*. And they all emphasise that the purpose of retreat is not perfection, but presence. A truer kind. A kind uncoiled from the tensions of pretending, performing, or protecting.

The challenge today is that modern life is calibrated to erode the very conditions these traditions hold sacred. Attention is monetised. Rest is distrusted. Silence is filled before it can reveal. In this context, sacred withdrawal becomes not just an ancient relic but a radical counter-practice—one that resists the dehumanising tempo of modernity by reasserting the sovereignty of interiority.

Importantly, sacred withdrawal is not elitist. It is not reserved for those who can afford five-star wellness retreats or month-long sabbaticals. The traditions we've explored offer diverse entry points. A quiet hour each morning in mindful reflection, a weekly fast from digital engagement, a day of solitude in the woods—these can be as transformative, if held with intention, as a monastery stay or desert pilgrimage. *It is not the grandeur of withdrawal that sanctifies it, but the orientation of the heart within it.*

The final thread that unites these traditions is the arc of *return.* Sacred withdrawal is never meant to be a static state. Its fruits are not hoarded but shared. The monk re-enters conversation. The Stoic rejoins civic life. The vision quester brings back their insight for the tribe. The Buddhist returns to a world now seen with more compassion and less grasping. The re-emergence is what completes the arc—not as a return to the same, but as an emergence with *changed presence.*

What can we learn, then, from these traditions of sacred withdrawal? That solitude is a training ground for compassion. That silence is a method of listening beyond language. That returning, after true retreat, is not about catching up—but about *showing up* differently. And that perhaps the most sacred form of withdrawal is the one that allows us to come back—not just to the world, but to ourselves.

Silence as a Mirror — Explores how extended retreat allows individuals to confront core fears and truths

Silence is often misunderstood as absence: of noise, of connection, of meaning. Yet in its most potent form—especially within the context of structured retreat—silence is not an empty void but a fiercely illuminating presence. For centuries, contemplatives across cultures have understood that when the external world grows still, the inner world speaks more clearly. But what it says is not always easy to hear. Extended silence, sustained over days or weeks, tends to strip away our social masks and intellectual distractions, revealing beneath them a more primal, less curated self. For many who enter silence in retreat, the initial experience is not peaceful—it is confronting. Unstructured time, paired with the absence of conversation, exposes thought patterns long buried under productivity and politeness. Worries emerge without their usual camouflage; ambitions sound shrill; internal criticisms grow louder before they dissolve. *In silence, what we most avoid within ourselves becomes inescapable.* That confrontation is precisely where the transformative power of retreat begins.

In modern society, where communication is constant and noise ubiquitous, the experience of sustained silence is almost radical. Yet silence has been the medium of insight for figures ranging from Buddhist monks in remote Himalayan monasteries to early Christian desert fathers, from Stoic philosophers in ancient Athens to contemporary psychotherapists guiding clients through sensory withdrawal. Across all these traditions, silence is not valued for its aesthetic appeal but for its capacity to act as a psychological mirror—a reflector of subconscious terrain that is otherwise difficult to access. Importantly, silence in retreat is not imposed so much as chosen. Unlike situations of involuntary isolation, structured silent retreats offer a framework: time-bound, intentional, and oriented toward insight rather than withdrawal for its own sake. *This structure enables silence to feel like a space of refuge rather than deprivation.*

Neuroscience lends support to what spiritual traditions have long intuited. Studies in contemplative neuroscience reveal that extended periods of silence and meditative reflection engage the brain's default mode network—a region associated with self-referential thinking, autobiographical memory, and introspective insight. During retreat, especially when external stimulation is reduced, this network becomes more active in a way that allows people to observe their own narratives with unusual clarity. A 2016 study at Massachusetts General Hospital found that participants in a week-long silent meditation retreat exhibited not only improved mood but also measurable changes in brain connectivity related to emotional regulation. *Silence gives the mind both space and permission to rewire itself.*

But neurobiology alone does not capture the lived texture of silence. For many retreat participants, the first few days evoke restlessness. Without conversation, performance, or distraction, one is left to face the momentum of years of internalised tension. A corporate lawyer, attending her first ten-day silent Vipassana retreat, described the experience as "emotionally brutal for the first three days—I wanted to leave every hour. But then, something shifted. I started to see patterns in my mind I had never slowed down enough to notice. I wasn't broken—I was just constantly running." Her report mirrors countless others: silence first magnifies discomfort before it births insight. The insight is often not cerebral, but felt—something closer to a deep remembering than a discovery. *This kind of knowing cannot be forced; it can only be uncovered.*

In retreat settings, silence also functions interpersonally, even when no words are exchanged. In a silent retreat, participants often eat, walk, and sit in proximity to others, forming what some scholars have called "relational stillness." There is a shared commitment to non-verbal presence, and over time, this can produce an uncanny intimacy. Paradoxically, many retreatants report feeling more connected to others during silence than they do in ordinary conversation. Why? Because without speech, the usual defensive postures—jokes, justifications, status games—fall away. The self one brings to silence is not the curated social self but the vulnerable, unguarded one. This makes space for compassion, both toward oneself and toward others. *When we are no longer trying to be heard, we begin to listen—not just to others, but to the parts of ourselves we had long silenced.*

The psychological implications are profound. Silence interrupts the default of constant self-affirmation and performance. For people who are highly sensitive or prone to overstimulation, this break is not only welcome but often essential. The overstimulated nervous system, when allowed to settle into silence, often begins to release trauma-held patterns not through dramatic catharsis but through slow, embodied awareness. A therapist who specialises in somatic trauma recovery noted that several of her clients, after attending silent retreats, reported breakthroughs that years of talk therapy had only gestured toward. "It's not that the silence fixes anything," she observed, "but it creates a container where deep material can surface gently, without needing to be explained immediately." *Insight, when not rushed into language, often deepens.*

There is also a spiritual dimension, difficult to quantify but unmistakable to those who experience it. In silence, many report a sense of contact with something larger than the self—what mystics have called the divine, the ground of being, or simply truth. Whether this is interpreted theologically or not, the felt sense is consistent: silence reveals a kind of inner spaciousness that is not available in everyday busyness. Philosopher Blaise Pascal wrote that "all of humanity's problems stem from man's inability to sit quietly in a room alone." That statement, often quoted as a critique, is in fact a diagnosis. Our discomfort with stillness is not because silence is empty but because it is too full—it reveals too much. *And yet, it is precisely what we most resist that has the potential to restore us.*

Of course, not all silence is healing. Silence that is enforced, isolating, or rooted in fear can retraumatise rather than transform. This is why the context of retreat matters: the boundary, the framing, the support structures. A well-held retreat includes check-ins, ethical frameworks, and trained facilitators who understand that silence can evoke pain before it brings peace. There is a responsibility to distinguish between solitude and abandonment, between quietude and suppression. The difference lies not in the absence of sound but in the presence of care.

What, then, does silence ultimately offer? Not a romantic escape from the world, but a clearer view of it—from the inside out. Silence strips away the artificial urgency of modern life and reminds us that attention is finite and precious. It reveals how often we fill space with sound not to connect, but to avoid. And it offers, if we are willing to stay with it, a chance to come home to ourselves—less adorned, more honest, and paradoxically, more available to life. *In the end, silence does not change who we are; it allows us to meet who we've always been, without interruption.*

The Mystery of Re-Emergence — Illuminates how retreat opens pathways to personal transformation, resilience, and renewal

Retreats are often described in terms of departure—pulling away from the demands, conversations, and rhythms of daily life. But the deeper story lies not in the act of withdrawing, but in the moment of return. What happens when a person re-enters their ordinary world after a period of deep retreat? How do they carry forward what was discovered in stillness into the friction of relationships, deadlines, and obligations? These questions mark the threshold of re-emergence, a phase far more psychologically complex and spiritually significant than it is often given credit for. If retreat is a kind of cocoon, re-emergence is not merely a return to the status quo—it is a reconstitution. Not necessarily visible from the outside, but internally unmistakable. *A well-held retreat doesn't leave a person where it found them; it alters their perceptual framework, and re-entry demands conscious integration.*

The difficulty is that the external world rarely adjusts to accommodate a changed interior. The demands are the same, the inbox still full, and the people around us may expect the familiar version of who we were before we paused. And yet, for many, the inner narrative has shifted in ways that are not easy to articulate. A person returns with altered priorities, new sensitivities, or an unshakable sense that the life they left behind now feels misaligned. This dissonance between internal evolution and external expectation is one of the most delicate phases of retreat work—and one that determines whether insight deepens or dissipates. *Re-emergence requires more than resilience; it requires translation—of silence into speech, of inner knowing into outer action.*

One of the great challenges of this phase is the loss of what philosopher John O'Donohue called "threshold space"—that liminal territory between two states of being, where the old has fallen away but the new is not yet formed. Most of modern life is structured to bypass these thresholds, to prioritise closure over ambiguity. Yet it is precisely in this in-between that transformation takes root. The individual who emerges from retreat is not instantly renewed; rather, they begin a second, slower process of metabolising insight into identity. A senior consultant who returned from a two-week silent retreat described feeling "subtly disoriented for days. Not in a bad way, but I kept asking myself: why did I agree to that meeting? Do I actually care about this project? It was like someone had recalibrated my compass, and suddenly everything was up for review." This recalibration is the essence of re-emergence—not a dramatic reinvention, but a quiet reordering of what feels true, tolerable, or necessary.

In therapeutic settings, this phase is increasingly recognised as one of vulnerability. After deep internal work, a person is often more open, more emotionally permeable. If they return to a high-pressure environment or relationships that dismiss their newfound insights, they may experience a kind of cognitive or emotional whiplash. Some report feelings of grief—not because the retreat was painful, but because ordinary life feels painfully shallow by comparison. Others encounter guilt: how can they hold onto their clarity while also participating in systems they now perceive as dysfunctional? This tension between insight and integration must be acknowledged, not pathologised. *The post-retreat landscape is fertile ground—but only if cultivated with care, community, and patience.*

One effective strategy for navigating re-emergence is the ritualisation of return. In monastic traditions, silence is often broken ceremonially, with chants, shared meals, or guided reflection. These acts mark the shift from solitude to society, and offer the nervous system a chance to transition with dignity. Contemporary retreat centres are beginning to adopt similar frameworks—structured re-entry dialogues, digital re-engagement protocols, or follow-up circles—so that participants can articulate what has shifted before being swept into routine. A former teacher who attended a month-long contemplative retreat said her most lasting change came not during the retreat itself, but in the twelve weeks after, when she committed to a daily journal of post-retreat insights. "That writing helped me notice which parts of myself wanted to disappear again, and which ones were asking to stay."

There is also a deeper metaphysical dimension to re-emergence, one that aligns with wisdom traditions across cultures. In many indigenous cosmologies, the pattern of withdrawal and return mirrors the cycles of nature—seasons, moons, migrations. The human psyche, too, follows such rhythms: expansion follows contraction, presence follows absence. The retreat is not an interruption of life, but a necessary rhythm within it. The re-emergent self is not a new self, but a remembered one—stripped of compulsions, clearer in purpose, more congruent with deeper values. *This is not self-improvement in the conventional sense; it is self-return.*

What complicates this process in modern contexts is the societal suspicion of inner work. A person who says they've just spent a week in silence, or ten days meditating in the woods, is still met, in many circles, with curiosity tinged with discomfort. The dominant cultural narrative privileges action over introspection, productivity over pause. To re-emerge with less urgency, more softness, or a desire for simplicity can feel subversive. And yet, precisely because of this cultural resistance, those who re-emerge from retreat bear an important role: to embody alternative rhythms. To model that clarity is not achieved through speed, that wisdom is often born of stillness. *Their re-emergence becomes a quiet act of cultural counter-narrative.*

There are also neuropsychological shifts that underlie this process. Research in contemplative neuroscience indicates that even short retreats can lead to changes in brain regions associated with compassion, attention, and emotion regulation. But those changes stabilise only when reinforced by post-retreat practices. Daily routines, relational boundaries, and intentional pauses serve as anchors. A leadership coach who guides executive retreats noted that clients who commit to small but consistent rituals—five minutes of breathing before meetings, technology-free evenings—are far more likely to sustain their post-retreat insights. "It's not about replicating the retreat," she says, "but about protecting the space it created, even as life resumes."

Re-emergence also carries ethical weight. A retreat, if well-held, tends to dissolve some of the egoic identities that organise modern life. Professional labels, social roles, even long-held opinions often feel thinner after a period of silence and solitude. The question that arises is not merely "what do I do now?" but "who am I now, and how do I want to live?" The person who returns to their workplace, their family, their community with these questions alive is not simply restored—they are reorganised. The most profound retreats do not produce grand epiphanies so much as subtle rearrangements of priorities. A parent might become more patient. A manager might stop micromanaging. A partner might listen more, fix less. *These micro-changes, born of inner shift, ripple outward in ways that slowly remake the social fabric.*

Yet, re-emergence is not without loss. The clarity of retreat cannot be preserved in its entirety; some of it inevitably dissipates. Life, after all, makes demands. But the goal is not preservation—it is embodiment. Can the insights of retreat find traction in movement, in conversation, in compromise? Can the silence of the forest translate into a more intentional presence in the boardroom? Can the inward compassion cultivated over ten days find its way into how one speaks to a child, or writes an email? These questions cannot be answered abstractly—they are lived into. *Re-emergence is not an event, but a practice.*

Perhaps this is the final mystery: the retreat does not end when we pack our bags and rejoin the world. It ends only when what we glimpsed in stillness is allowed to shape how we move through noise. And that may take months, even years. The path of re-emergence is a second retreat—less quiet, more visible, and no less sacred. It demands not only the courage to step away from life, but the deeper courage to return to it changed—and to let that change matter.

Real-World Case: The CEO's Silent Awakening – A corporate leader finds moral clarity and re-aligns his leadership after a silent retreat

The transformation didn't begin with a crisis, though the signs had been gathering. For years, Richard Evans, the CEO of a rapidly expanding tech consultancy, had been regarded as the embodiment of high-performance leadership. He delivered results, drove investor confidence, and maintained an image of ethical intelligence that earned accolades from boards and media alike. But beneath the polished exterior, Richard was contending with something far less stable: a creeping sense of disconnection—not just from his work, but from himself. Decisions that once felt clear now arrived clouded. Conversations with his executive team felt hollow. He caught himself wondering, privately and increasingly, whether the pace and priorities of his work life reflected any real alignment with his values.

"I was winning at a game I hadn't chosen," he later said. "And I didn't know how to stop without breaking everything."

When a close friend and fellow entrepreneur invited Richard to attend a ten-day silent meditation retreat, his immediate reaction was scepticism. He'd never meditated before, nor had he ever spent a day—let alone ten—without speaking. But something in the invitation unsettled him in just the right way. He said yes. The retreat was held in a remote part of North Wales, organised by a centre that followed Vipassana principles. No phones, no reading, no talking, no eye contact. For someone who led by conversation and charisma, this was a radical stripping away. "I thought I would be bored. What I didn't expect was how loud everything inside me would become once the world went quiet."

By the third day, Richard began to notice the patterns. Not of breath or body—that would come later—but of mind. The justifications, the internal debates, the reruns of meetings and forecasts and arguments that had long passed. What surprised him most was the way moral discomfort, previously a background hum, now came forward like a siren. "I saw with painful clarity how many decisions I'd made from fear. Fear of being outpaced. Fear of losing credibility. Fear of being seen as soft." These insights weren't abstract reflections—they were visceral, almost physical. In silence, Richard met a version of himself he'd been avoiding for years. *It wasn't that he had lost his moral compass; it was that he'd stopped checking it.*

What made this retreat different from a vacation or sabbatical was its structure. The discipline of silence was not passive. It forced attention inward, then held it there. When Richard became uncomfortable, there was no conversation, no caffeine, no distraction to dull it. The friction was the teaching. Each time he sat with a sensation, whether grief or pride or regret, something shifted. And beneath all the executive armour—the metrics, the strategy decks, the polished responses—he found a very old and simple longing: to live in integrity, not just perform it.

On the seventh day, a memory surfaced. Years earlier, he'd made a decision to quietly shelve a company programme that provided pro bono tech services to non-profits. It had been poorly resourced and difficult to scale, but it had meant something to the younger version of himself who co-founded the company. At the time, he'd told himself it was a necessary trade-off. But in the silence, he saw what had really driven that decision: the desire to look efficient to investors. "It wasn't a criminal choice," he later reflected. "But it was a betrayal. Not of the company—but of what I said it stood for." That realisation didn't come with shame. It came with clarity. *What Richard encountered in silence was not judgment—it was invitation. To repair, to reimagine, to re-lead.*

When the retreat ended, Richard didn't return with a five-point plan or a visionary slogan. What he brought back was subtler: a slower way of making decisions, and a commitment to clarity over consensus. He reinstated the shelved initiative—but this time, restructured it as a self-managed unit, decoupled from profitability metrics. He reworked the senior leadership team's annual retreat to include structured silent reflection. And perhaps most significantly, he rewrote his own job description, explicitly naming values stewardship as part of his remit.

The shift was not universally applauded. Some board members expressed concern that the company might be "going soft." But the real metrics told a different story. Staff retention improved. Internal conflicts dropped. Employee surveys began reflecting something rare in tech cultures: psychological safety. Richard also made a quiet but telling change—he stopped referring to the company as a "market leader," and started calling it a "systems contributor." "It wasn't about shrinking the company's ambition," he said. "It was about aligning it with what the world actually needs."

What's striking about Richard's story isn't just the personal transformation—it's the strategic yield of introspection. In a sector that prizes disruption, the most radical move he made was to pause. Not out of burnout, but out of responsibility. He saw that the velocity of his leadership had outpaced the depth of his discernment. And instead of masking it, he named it. *This, too, was leadership—but of a different calibre: one that understands that silence isn't absence; it's calibration.*

Corporate culture often lionises decisiveness and punishes hesitation. But Richard's experience challenges that bias. What if the capacity to pause—to deliberately withdraw and reflect—isn't antithetical to leadership, but foundational to it? What if the moral clarity required to navigate complex, high-stakes environments can't be accessed at speed? The silent retreat didn't change Richard's title, nor his IQ. What it changed was his relationship to influence. He no longer saw leadership as performance, but as stewardship. Not a role to inhabit, but a trust to honour.

There's a broader implication here for organisational life. As burnout surges and purpose becomes commodified, leaders are increasingly facing the same crisis that brought Richard to retreat: a quiet erosion of alignment. Metrics multiply, but meaning thins. And yet, very few corporate environments make space for the kind of deep pause required to recover integrity. The idea that a CEO might sit in silence for ten days, not for strategy but for self-inquiry, still reads as indulgent in many boardrooms. But what if it's not indulgence at all? What if it's insurance—against moral drift, performative leadership, and cultures of fear disguised as excellence?

There is also a human story beneath the leadership veneer. Richard didn't just return a better CEO. He returned a different man. Less reactive. More congruent. He spoke of finally being able to look his teenage children in the eye without the gnawing suspicion that he was modelling the very kind of hollow ambition he warned them against. He began hosting small circles for leaders interested in integrating contemplative practice into their work—not as a side project, but as core capacity-building. "We don't need more genius in business," he said at one gathering. "We need more groundedness."

That language—groundedness, alignment, congruence—is rarely found in the pages of management textbooks. But perhaps it should be. The story of Richard's silent awakening is not one of personal epiphany alone. It's an argument, gently made but forcefully felt, for a new kind of leadership literacy—one that understands silence not as retreat from responsibility, but as its deepest expression. And in a time when so many systems are built on noise, distraction, and performativity, perhaps it is those who dare to pause—fully, honestly, quietly—who are best equipped to lead what comes next.

Conclusion
The Sensitive Path as Mastery

For much of history, sensitivity has been misread as weakness, as if an attunement to nuance somehow undermined strength. It has been conflated with emotional excess, hesitation, or impracticality—qualities quietly devalued in boardrooms, overlooked in leadership training, and sidelined in cultural narratives that prize speed over depth, reaction over reflection. Yet this misunderstanding is becoming increasingly untenable. The challenges we face today—ecological, relational, institutional—demand precisely the perceptive intelligence, ethical discernment, and regenerative insight that sensitive individuals cultivate naturally. We are not witnessing the twilight of sensitive leadership; we are recognising that it was leadership all along.

The capacity to perceive deeply, to sense misalignment, to feel the subtle toll of unsustainable systems—these are not liabilities. They are diagnostic tools in a disoriented world. What was once dismissed as hypersensitivity might now be reframed as hyper-relevance. It is no coincidence that some of the most transformative voices in organisational change, social innovation, and trauma-informed practice come from those who once felt "too much." Their sensitivity became a laboratory for observation, teaching them to detect patterns behind surface noise, to pause when others rush forward blindly, to listen where others overlook. Sensitivity is not the opposite of resilience; it is its foundation, provided it is respected rather than forced to conform to desensitised norms.

This is why the retreat cycle is essential—not an indulgence, but a structural necessity for sustainable sensitivity. Sensitive individuals do not burn out because they are weak; they burn out because they navigate systems that punish natural pacing, exploit emotional labour, and offer no vocabulary for the rhythms that sustain them. Retreat reveals a more biologically, emotionally, and ethically sane cadence—a life that allows for exhalation, not endless inhalation. When sensitive minds reclaim retreat—not as escape but as recalibration—they reclaim agency. They are no longer trapped in a binary of full engagement or total withdrawal; they move like a tide: advancing, receding, and advancing again, with intention, grace, and self-respect.

Mastery, in this context, does not mean perfection. It means attunement. It means recognising the signals of a nervous system under strain—not as failure, but as a request for honour. It means designing lives, careers, and relationships that accommodate both presence and withdrawal, allowing wisdom to guide engagement. Mastery is not conquering sensitivity; it is fluency in its language and guardianship of its dignity. One need not override instinct to participate fully in the world; one must structure participation around it.

The sensitive path is not an anomaly in leadership—it is a model for its next iteration. Imagine institutions designed not for those who endure exhaustion, but for those who notice it early and respond wisely. Imagine social norms that allow retreat without guilt, silence without suspicion, and emotional acuity without dismissal. What might excellence look like if it were defined not by constant visibility but by calibrated presence, where showing up includes knowing when not to?

Across sectors, the limitations of extraction-based models are becoming stark. Healthcare workers abandon overburdened systems; teachers leave classrooms where care is unsustainable; leaders privately question whether innovation has outpaced integrity. These are not isolated crises; they are invitations. Invitations to redefine health as rhythm rather than output, creativity as spaciousness rather than productivity, maturity as discernment rather than detachment. And above all, they invite us to see the sensitive mind not as a problem, but as a culture-making force crucial to the sustainability of our next chapter.

There is also a profoundly personal dimension to this reframing. Many readers may find themselves at a threshold, recognising that long-standing strategies—pushing through, pleasing, shrinking needs—no longer suffice. The old coping mechanisms are failing not due to inadequacy, but because evolution is underway. Sensitivity becomes unsustainable only when it lacks structure. This book offers not a cure but a scaffold: practices, permissions, and rhythms that make sustainable sensitivity possible.

Here, mastery meets practice. The retreat cycle is lifelong choreography, not a one-time reset. Missteps and regressions will occur, but each return to stillness is a reminder: value is not measured by what is given away, clarity grows in quiet, and leadership depends not on endurance but on the courage to honour what is needed before breaking.

When protected and structured, sensitivity becomes a form of leadership that is less about assertion than stewardship. It moves with depth rather than noise, cultivates resonance rather than applause, and meets a world desperately in need of attuned, responsive guidance. Leaders who hear what goes unspoken, and systems that allow the attuned to remain whole, create spaces where human flourishing is possible.

Let this chapter rest as a gentle hand, reminding that sensitivity is not an inconvenience but a gift to be mastered. That power does not require hardening. That rest is not antithetical to effort, but its essential companion. And that the cycles of retreat and re-emergence explored throughout these pages are not mere practices—they are pathways to the kind of leadership the future demands: discerning, regenerative, and unapologetically alive.

Sensitivity as Leadership

Leadership, as traditionally defined, has long been anchored in performance optics: decisiveness, assertiveness, and an ability to override emotion for the sake of expedience. The cultural script has rarely included sensitivity as a trait of influence—much less one of mastery. But this premise is crumbling under the weight of global complexity. In an era where relational intelligence, ethical discernment, and regenerative resilience are non-negotiable, *sensitivity is no longer a liability to be managed—it is a strategic imperative.* Those who feel deeply, process intricately, and perceive the unspoken are not outliers. They are the architects of a different kind of leadership.

To understand why, one must first unlearn the myth that sensitivity is synonymous with weakness. Sensory and emotional attunement, when structurally supported, grants a leader enhanced access to nuance, relational feedback, and systemic ripple effects. This is not about introversion versus extroversion, nor softness versus strength. It is about *precision of perception*. Consider the sensitive leader not as fragile, but as finely calibrated. When such individuals are given the bandwidth to honour their inner rhythms—through practices like retreat, reflection, and recovery—they develop a unique kind of executive function: one that includes pattern detection, long-range thinking, and empathetic clarity. *They do not just respond to problems—they anticipate them.* Not by analytic logic alone, but by reading the emotional and ecological cues that precede dysfunction.

Neuroscience is beginning to affirm what many have intuited for years. Highly sensitive individuals—those with heightened responsiveness in the sensory processing sensitivity trait—exhibit greater activation in brain regions related to empathy, awareness, and emotional regulation. This translates into leadership that is less impulsive and more integrative. In organisations, such individuals often notice micro-tensions before they escalate, identify cultural undercurrents overlooked by more transactional minds, and sustain vision in contexts where others burn out. Yet, despite this capacity, many sensitive leaders remain hidden or self-doubting, having been told—implicitly or explicitly—that their wiring makes them ill-suited for high-stakes environments.

This misunderstanding stems largely from misalignment, not incapacity. When sensitive minds are placed in environments that demand constant output, relentless engagement, and suppress emotional reflection, they falter—not because they are less capable, but because the system itself is hostile to their pacing and process. But when environments are structured to honour cycles of deep work and deep rest, discernment and action, solitude and collaboration, *sensitive leaders don't just keep up—they outperform.* They become culture-bearers, not merely culture-followers. And their style of leadership—more ecosystemic than egoic—offers an essential counterweight to extractive paradigms.

Let us look beyond theory. In the field of restorative justice, sensitive facilitators are often the ones who can sit with long silences, track emotional shifts in a room, and navigate high-stakes dialogue with calibrated empathy. In healthcare, clinicians with sensitive temperaments tend to excel at patient-centred care models, often detecting subtle diagnostic cues missed by more detached approaches. In design and innovation, it is often the intuitive thinker—the one who pauses, who questions, who listens—that catalyses breakthroughs not through speed, but through depth. These are not outliers. These are glimpses of an emerging template for leadership: one that replaces reactivity with resonance, command with clarity, and imposition with inclusion.

Yet sensitivity, when unsupported, can distort inward. Without structure, it collapses into anxiety or burnout. Without community, it calcifies into self-doubt or withdrawal. This is why regenerative frameworks matter. The sensitive leader requires *rituals of return*—not only retreat in the literal sense, but the internal practices of nervous system regulation, emotional processing, and meaning-making. Leadership for the sensitive mind cannot be extracted from wellbeing; it must be designed in symbiosis with it. The notion that leadership is about pushing through fatigue is an artefact of industrial-age paradigms. *What we require now are leaders who know when to pause before a system collapses—not after.*

This regenerative lens also reveals that sensitivity is not merely reactive—it is generative. The sensitive leader is not just someone who absorbs others' emotions; they are often the ones who create emotional atmospheres in which others can thrive. They stabilise teams not by dominating dynamics, but by attuning to needs, offering clarity without coercion, and modelling humility as a strength rather than a posture. This is a radical departure from command-and-control models, yet it is precisely what makes teams resilient in uncertain times. A calm nervous system is contagious. So is principled restraint. So is the capacity to listen without fixing. These are not soft skills. They are *structural competencies* for 21st-century leadership.

Of course, sensitivity alone does not guarantee ethical clarity or visionary insight. It must be integrated with skill, honed through experience, and supported by systems that do not punish difference. But when cultivated with rigour, the sensitive mind becomes an agile instrument—able to tune into context, calibrate response, and adapt without fragmentation. It is precisely this fluidity, not rigidity, that the future demands. The leader who can retreat without disappearing, who can feel without collapsing, who can speak with care without appeasement—this is not the exception. This is the evolution.

Culturally, we are already seeing this shift. From trauma-informed leadership models to the rise of conscious capitalism, from climate adaptation to social repair, the qualities most in demand are those previously considered "too soft" for leadership. Emotional literacy. Systemic perspective. Presence. The ability to hold paradox. These are the competencies that emerge naturally in many sensitive individuals—so long as they are not overtaxed by environments that drain their capacity before it can be cultivated.

It is time to challenge the default assumptions baked into institutional design. What would leadership development look like if it were built around sensory awareness rather than sensory suppression? What if recovery time were not treated as indulgent, but as a pillar of responsibility? What if retreats were not seen as escapes from productivity, but as vital interludes that sharpen it? The sensitive leader does not need fixing. The context in which they lead needs reforming. And in doing so, they may become not just effective executives or empathetic mentors—but architects of entirely new relational cultures.

This reframing also serves a deeper purpose: it allows sensitive individuals to stop apologising for their natural disposition. Leadership is not a monolith. It is a mosaic of styles, temperaments, and timings. When sensitive minds are taught to override their needs in pursuit of someone else's blueprint, everyone loses. But when they are taught to *trust their perception, pace their energy, and lead from a place of rooted clarity*, they model an entirely different ethos: one in which strength is not defined by domination, but by discernment; not by certainty, but by responsiveness; not by charisma, but by coherence.

Let us not underestimate the power of the leader who sees what others miss—not because it is louder, but because it is more subtle. Let us not overlook the wisdom of the one who pauses before they speak, not out of insecurity, but because they are listening to more than words. And let us remember that mastery is not always loud. Sometimes it looks like knowing when to step back so that others can breathe. Sometimes it sounds like silence in a noisy room. Sometimes it feels like attunement so precise that it shifts the whole field. This is not sensitivity as indulgence. This is sensitivity as infrastructure. As strategy. As leadership.

Mastering the Retreat Cycle

Modern productivity culture frames fatigue as a failure of will. Burnout is treated as an anomaly, a lapse in discipline, or a deviation from optimal workflow. Yet, when viewed through the lens of ecology, rhythm, and human physiology, exhaustion is not a breakdown; it is a signal. It is not the enemy of resilience, but its tutor. *True resilience is not the ability to endure unbroken, but the capacity to renew deliberately.* Mastering the retreat cycle demands we replace heroic narratives of endurance with intelligent rituals of withdrawal and return.

The idea of retreat carries cultural weight. For many, it conjures images of monks or mystics, far removed from deadlines and demands. But retreat is not a luxury reserved for spiritual elites. It is an adaptive strategy—a regenerative arc encoded in the biology of rest, the psychology of pacing, and the wisdom traditions that span centuries. The modern sensitive mind, often pathologised for its overwhelm, is not weak. It is highly attuned. And for such minds, *cyclical restoration is not optional—it is essential to sustainable contribution.*

What distinguishes mastery from mere participation in a retreat cycle is intentionality. Anyone can collapse from exhaustion and call it a retreat. What matters is recognising early signs, structuring exits before crisis, and designing re-entry as skilfully as withdrawal. The first shift, then, is epistemological: to see retreat not as escape but as an advanced form of engagement—one that includes the wisdom to pause before productivity turns corrosive.

From a neurobiological perspective, periodic rest enhances—not impairs—higher-order cognition. When the default mode network of the brain is active, typically during rest or daydreaming, it engages in memory consolidation, pattern detection, and scenario simulation. These are not passive functions; they underpin creativity, decision-making, and long-range vision. In overstimulated systems, this network becomes drowned out by constant task engagement. Regular withdrawal from stimulation is therefore *not a retreat from relevance; it is the condition for relevance.*

The structured retreat also resets our relationship to time. In capitalist societies, time is flattened into a single mode: productive, linear, monetisable. The retreat cycle reintroduces pluralities of time—deep time, seasonal time, sacred time, bodily time. This multiplicity invites nuanced perception. We are not machines running at steady output. We are organisms moving through ebbs and flows, capable of immense clarity *precisely because we stop to gather it.*

In cultures that have preserved seasonal intelligence—whether in agriculture, indigenous practice, or ritual—the wisdom of retreat is non-negotiable. Soil must lie fallow to remain fertile. Fields are rotated to preserve balance. Human systems, too, require rotation of effort and repose. Yet in institutional life, these rhythms are ignored. Leaders ascend without pause. Caregivers serve until collapse. Students sprint without seasonal reflection. The result is not just burnout—it is epistemic fatigue, the erosion of clear seeing and moral imagination. Mastery of the retreat cycle corrects this at its root.

Practically, this mastery involves pre-emptive design. Retreat must be built into systems, not squeezed into absence. For an academic, it may mean blocked periods of reading and long walks not tethered to output. For a therapist, it may mean silent mornings or scheduled sabbaticals. For a policymaker, it may require cycles of field immersion alternating with solitude. These are not indulgences. They are boundary technologies—structures that protect depth of insight against the erosion of immediacy.

Critically, mastering the retreat cycle also involves *reskilling our sense of internal thresholds.* Many high-performing individuals lack the literacy to detect when they are nearing internal depletion. They override early signals—emotional flatness, shortness of breath, difficulty focusing—in the service of deadlines. In contrast, those who excel at cyclical mastery develop intimate familiarity with their own inflection points. They know what "yellow light" states feel like before burnout goes red. They track not just outputs but *sensation, desire, aversion, and intuition.* These softer data points are not frivolous—they are *predictive analytics of the nervous system.*

Cultural conditioning often complicates this process. Many individuals, especially those from marginalised groups, have been socialised to override their own rhythms in order to be seen as reliable. To assert the need for pause may feel transgressive, even disloyal. Thus, mastery of retreat cycles requires not only somatic awareness but also *a re-authoring of internal narratives.* We must learn to say, "My value is not dependent on unbroken visibility." We must normalise language like, "I'll be offline to re-ground," or, "I need to let ideas steep before I respond." In retreat mastery, communication becomes *a boundary that signals integrity, not avoidance.*

There is also a spiritual dimension to this practice. Retreat is not merely restorative; it is revelatory. Extended periods of quiet can surface truths we have long displaced. Grief, desire, fear, vision—they surface not to derail us, but to remind us what lies beneath the surface performance of functioning. The sensitive mind, when given space, often brings forward uncensored intelligence. But this demands we stay present through the discomfort of unmasking. Mastery here involves tolerating discomfort not as a failure of progress, but as a portal into precision.

The arc of retreat and return also mirrors rites of passage. Anthropologist Arnold van Gennep observed three phases in traditional transitions: separation, liminality, and reintegration. Structured retreats—when engaged with consciousness—move through these exact phases. The withdrawal (separation), the unstructured quiet (liminality), and the deliberate re-entry into one's roles (reintegration) mark not just a rest cycle but a *psychological and even ontological renewal.* Those who master this arc are not simply better rested; they are more discerning, more agile, and more ethically grounded.

Consider the case of a design executive who institutes a quarterly mini-retreat for herself. These are not vacations, but deliberate pauses from screens, strategy sessions, and stakeholder meetings. She leaves with no agenda, no deliverables. In one such retreat, she realises that her team's velocity masks conceptual drift—they are producing more, but solving less. She returns and reorients the workflow to prioritise friction-rich debate over speed. The result is fewer outputs but greater impact. This is *retreat as recalibration*, not withdrawal.

Contrast this with the more familiar model of annual burnout followed by reactive absence. Here, the retreat is framed as a rescue, not a ritual. Re-entry is jagged. Insight is accidental. The lesson is clear: *retreat must be rhythm, not emergency.*

To institutionalise this at a cultural level requires collective permission. We must shift organisational cultures from visibility-based trust to rhythm-based trust. Instead of asking, "Are you always available?" we must ask, "Are you sustainably present?" Instead of rewarding stamina, we should value discernment—the capacity to know when to surge and when to step back. This shift is not soft; it is *strategically necessary* in systems increasingly saturated by complexity and speed.

Mastering the retreat cycle is ultimately about claiming agency over our time, attention, and creative force. It is not a personal indulgence but a public responsibility. The leader who knows how to pause avoids downstream chaos. The caregiver who schedules restoration avoids resentment. The thinker who disappears into quiet returns with clarity that cuts through noise. *Resilience, properly understood, is not armour—it is rhythm.* It is the art of knowing when to act, when to rest, and how to return with more than we left with.

What emerges from this mastery is not just survival, but evolution. Our work sharpens. Our relationships clarify. Our ideas deepen. Not in spite of stepping back—but *because* we step back wisely, regularly, and with reverence for what quiet restores.

A Lifelong Practice — Leaves the reader with a clear, empowered vision of sustainable sensitivity as a lifelong, evolving art

Sensitivity, when misunderstood, is often pathologised—mistaken for weakness, fragility, or indulgence. Yet in its mature form, sensitivity is one of the most sophisticated adaptive capacities a person can develop. It is not merely the capacity to feel deeply; it is the ability to register nuance, perceive complexity, and remain responsive to internal and external cues that others might overlook. But for this gift to become sustainable, it must be deliberately cultivated. *Sensitivity is not simply an inborn trait—it is a discipline, a rhythm, and ultimately, a lifelong practice.*

At the heart of this practice is the recognition that sensitivity does not stabilise into equilibrium by default. It operates in waves—ebbs and flows of stimulation and restoration, presence and withdrawal, expression and inwardness. Attempting to override this rhythm in favour of linear productivity or constant accessibility is the surest path to burnout. Instead, those who live well with sensitivity come to treat their nervous systems as ecosystems: not machines to optimise, but habitats to nourish. Just as a forest requires periods of dormancy, composting, and seasonal change, so too does the sensitive psyche.

One of the key developmental tasks of sensitive individuals is to build a resilient structure around their needs without becoming rigid. This structure is not a fortress, but a framework—a series of adaptive practices that make it possible to remain available to life without being overwhelmed by it. These practices include intentional retreat, relational boundaries, restorative rituals, and environments that support rather than erode sensory integrity. Importantly, these are not emergency measures to be enacted during periods of crisis; they are routine acts of maintenance that prevent crisis from occurring in the first place.

Resilience, in this paradigm, is not the capacity to "push through" or "toughen up." It is the ability to anticipate when one's inner reserves are dwindling and respond before collapse. It is the insight to recognise the cost of overexposure and the self-respect to withdraw without explanation. It is the subtle wisdom of honouring one's own thresholds without needing validation. This is not the heroism of the dramatic comeback. It is the quiet, ongoing practice of stewardship.

Sensitive individuals who mature into this form of leadership often become deeply effective in their fields. Not despite their sensitivity—but because of the calibration it fosters. They are often the ones who make outstanding therapists, educators, designers, and systems thinkers. Their acuity enables them to connect patterns, spot misalignments, and create inclusive, empathetic structures. But without a sustainable relationship to their own nervous systems, this same acuity becomes a liability—leading to hypervigilance, reactivity, or collapse.

A sustainable practice of sensitivity, then, must include a spiritual or philosophical core—not necessarily in the religious sense, but in the sense of orientation. Sensitive individuals must know not only how to retreat, but why. They must have a north star that reframes rest not as absence, but as a generative presence. For some, this may be found in nature; for others, in meditation, creative solitude, or contemplative study. What matters is not the form, but the fidelity to that inner compass.

Many sensitive individuals fall into a trap early in life: they attempt to function as if they were less sensitive than they are. They mimic the energy of peers, ignore their exhaustion, apologise for their limits. But over time, this dissonance becomes intolerable. True mastery begins at the moment one stops pretending. From there, a new kind of self-trust becomes possible—the kind that allows one to say no without guilt, to disappoint others without collapse, and to live at a humane pace regardless of external expectations.

The lifelong practice of sensitivity is not about escaping the world. It is about engaging it with discernment. It requires the individual to build a life that is not merely reactive to overstimulation, but proactively nourishing. This may mean reducing social obligations, creating quieter work environments, or choosing slower mornings. It may also mean curating relationships that respect—not just tolerate—retreat. Over time, these choices accumulate into a lifestyle that aligns with one's deeper nervous system architecture.

The most empowered sensitive people are not those who have avoided hardship. They are those who have turned self-awareness into scaffolding. They do not wait for others to accommodate them; they take responsibility for crafting conditions that support their flourishing. They do not treat self-care as an indulgence, but as an ethical imperative. And they do not apologise for their needs—they model them clearly, giving others permission to do the same.

This maturity is often invisible to those who have never wrestled with high sensitivity. It does not arrive through epiphany, but through repetition. The sensitive individual may cycle through burnout and recovery many times before recognising the pattern. But once this pattern is seen, it can be worked with consciously. And with enough practice, it becomes second nature—not because the person has hardened, but because they have learned how to move with, rather than against, their own design.

To live with sensitivity as a lifelong practice is not to seek an endpoint. It is to develop rhythm literacy—the capacity to anticipate one's cycles, to design for them, and to honour them without apology. It is to understand that retreat is not a retreat from life, but a return to it. And it is to embrace the idea that the most generative contributions often come not from constant visibility, but from depth, pacing, and presence.

This is the art of sustainable sensitivity. It does not promise ease, but it offers clarity. It does not guarantee immunity to overload, but it provides tools to recover more quickly. And most importantly, it replaces the shame of sensitivity with strategy, self-trust, and long-term vitality. It is a path not only of self-care, but of cultural contribution. For in a world increasingly defined by noise, speed, and extraction, sensitivity—properly understood—is not a weakness to manage, but a form of mastery to be cultivated.

About the Author

Miriam Everhart is a researcher and writer whose work sits at the intersection of neuroscience, contemplative practice, and lived experience. Holding a PhD in psychological science with a focus on emotion regulation and sensory processing, she brings both empirical rigor and a compassionate voice to The Art of Retreat. A long-time advocate for sensitive souls, Miriam combines her research on nervous system regulation with personal rituals of retreat—walking the talk she writes about. Her writing has appeared in reputed mindfulness and psychology journals, and she guides workshops for introverts, artists, and caretakers finding strength through renewal. With The Art of Retreat, she offers an original, evidence-informed path to reclaim vitality and inner clarity in a world made for extroverts.

www.ingramcontent.com/pod-product-compliance
Lightning Source LLC
Chambersburg PA
CBHW031340230926
51848CB00002B/318
* 9 7 8 9 3 7 1 7 7 2 1 1 2 *